Michael Haringer

Life of the Venerable Servant of God

Michael Haringer

Life of the Venerable Servant of God

ISBN/EAN: 9783337801052

Printed in Europe, USA, Canada, Australia, Japan

Cover: Foto ©Lupo / pixelio.de

More available books at **www.hansebooks.com**

VEN. P. CLEMENS MARIA HOFBAUER

Insignis Propagator Cong. SS. Red.

LIFE

OF THE VENERABLE SERVANT OF GOD

CLEMENT MARIA HOFBAUER

VICAR GENERAL OF THE CONGREGATION
OF THE MOST HOLY REDEEMER

BY

FATHER R. P. MICHAEL HARINGER,
CONSULTOR GENERAL OF THE CONGREGATION

TRANSLATED INTO ENGLISH

BY

Lady HERBERT.

FR. PUSTET & CO.
NEW YORK AND CINCINNATI.
1883.

PREFACE.

IN the year 1864, when Cardinal Rauscher, Archbishop of Vienna, initiated the ordinary process on the life and virtues of that great servant of God, Clement Maria Hofbauer, I, to call public attention to the character of this truly apostolic man, wrote a short notice of his history which was then published. But as this little biography touched only on the principal events of his life, I felt that it gave a very imperfect picture. Many feared that, 44 years having elapsed since F. Clement's death, and so many of his cotemporaries and witnesses of his virtues having died, very little new matter would be gathered in the episcopal enquiry which had been set on foot. But, contrary to all expectation, such a number of excellent witnesses were found and such stupendous acts in his life discovered, that there was no difficulty whatever in finding abundant material for a complete biography. And although from the birth of Father Clement to the beginning of the cause for his beatification 113 years had elapsed, still, in his native country, a woman was found who, having known him and his mother and sister, could give us many little anecdotes of his childhood. And as many other witnesses were found to tell of his great works in Warsaw and in Germany, so a still greater number could testify to his last years in Vienna.

The sworn depositions of these witnesses, which may be found in the *"Summary"*, drawn up by the Congregation of Rites and especially on his *"Virtues"*, were the principal sources from which I have drawn the materials of this life. I have also made use of various original M. S. and letters written by F. Clement to different friends; as also of certain notes, written down at the time and carefully preserved by his disciples. I have also had the advantage, not only of talking with all the witnesses examined in Vienna, but also with many other private persons who were his friends and penitents: hence this book contains many things which naturally were not included in the cause of his beatification.

If, therefore, anything has been added to the original history, the reader may feel convinced that it has only been stated on the best authority. I have omitted references, so as not to increase the number of notes.

I have on most occasions quoted the actual words of the witnesses: and though this may have interfered a little with the purity of the style, I think it is more than compensated by the increased interest which the narrative presents. Father Clement was chosen by God to transplant and consolidate, north of the Alps, the work begun by St. Alphonsus; that is, the Congregation of S. S. Redeemer. He began his Apostolic Ministry two years before the death of our Holy Founder. And whilst St. Alphonsus by his writings, combated the false doctrines of the revolution, and died in 1787, before the breaking-out of the reign of anarchy and terror in France, so it fell upon F. Clement to struggle and suffer in the very midst of the storm which that fearful revolution had raised. He witnessed the fall of Royalty in France; the fearful excesses of the Reign of Terror; the birth of the Empire and its fall; the ruin of Poland; and the overthrow of Religion in Germany and elsewhere. But in the midst of all these terrible events, Father Clement was firm as a rock; and amidst the storms and darkness around him, he was as a luminous light-house pointing out the only path of safety. The Church, in the office for the Feast of St. Alphonsus, alluding to the light which he brought to the century in which he lived, applies to him this passage in Ecclesiasticus: *"He shone in his days as the morning star in the midst of a cloud and as the moon at the full. And as a sun when it shineth, so did he shine in the Temple of God"* (50th chap. 6. and 7. verses) which words, it appears to me are equally applicable to F. Clement, for he too shone in the Church as the morning star and as the sun in the fulness of its light. He had to maintain a brave front in the saddest times, although miscalled times of progress and liberty: and to hold up the lamp of faith and purity amidst the errors and darkness of the age.

Like St. Alphonsus, F. Clement was indefatigable in preaching the faith, in combating error, and in defending the rights and liberties of the Church: for which cause he had to suffer the hardest trials. Nor, finally, am I afraid to point out his likeness to St. Alphonsus in character: in his devotion to the mysteries of the Incarnation and the Passion of our Lord Jesus Christ, in his love towards the august Sacrament of the altar: in his tender devotion towards Mary immaculate: and in his burning zeal for the glory of God and the salvation of souls.

And as Father Clement only died in 1820, his life is recent enough to touch almost our own days: and unhappily the events recorded in his time have their counterpart now: so that I hope that his example may be no small encouragement and guide to us, who have to go through the like trials and difficulties.

The Author.

Rome, Feast of the Purification 1880.

PREFACE OF ENGLISH TRANSLATOR.

IN giving to the English public a translation of Father Michael Haringer's beautiful life of the venerable Clement Hofbauer, I feel bound to mention that I have made some omissions in the fourth and last book which contains a detailed account of his miracles and the cause of his beatification and also a chapter entirely devoted to his German disciples, which I thought would not be interesting to ordinary English readers. I have been reminded, however, that I was bound to give some account of one, Father Frederick de Held, as he was the founder of the English Province and was a person well known to English Catholics.

He was born in Brunn near Sta. Maria of Enzersdorf on the 17th of July 1799 and describes his first acquaintance with Father Clement in the following words: "I was 18, and studying philosophy at the University of Vienna, when, by the kindness of F. Springer, I had the good fortune of becoming intimately acquainted with that great servant of

God, F. C. Hofbauer. At the very first sight of him, he inspired me with such confidence that I chose him at once as my confessor and constantly went to visit him in the evening." Frederick was one of the first to enter the noviciate after F. Clement's death and on the 2nd of August 1821, made his religious profession. On the 21st of August 1823 he was ordained Priest and began his apostolic labours in Stiria. From thence he was sent to Mantern where he was theological lecturer for some years. In 1832 he went to Naples to the General chapter called together for the election of the Father General: and the following year was sent to Belgium to preside at the foundation of the houses of Tournay and Liege. In 1839, he went to Rome for the Canonization of St. Alphonsus: and in consequence of a Pontifical Decree creating new Provinces, he was appointed Belgian Provincial with residence at Liege. At that time the American Colleges were incorporated in the Belgian Province and so, to ascertain the state and the needs of the American Houses, F. de Held in 1845 started for those distant regions. The Congregation under his guidance became so numerous in America that it was found necessary to form a fresh Province there. Father de Held having accomplished this great work, turned his steps towards England, which he had previously visited in 1838, being then a guest at Prior Park. The first idea of the Redemptorists' settling in England was when they were banished from Portugal and touched at an English Port in 1833. Then Dr. Baines invited them to make a foundation in this country: but it was delayed till Father de Held's arrival. His first idea was to settle in Scotland; but that having failed, he made the first foundation at Falmouth on the 17th of June 1843, when a church was opened under the title of "Our Lady of Victories." Other foundations followed whilst Father de Held was in America: one being at Hanley Castle, with a *Succursale* House at Red Marley. But when Father de Held returned to England in 1848 negotiations had been already set on foot for purchasing a house in London as being in every way more central and suitable for the Congregation. The idea of this foundation was eagerly supported by several gentlemen, among whom were Mr. Herbert of Clytha, Mr. Philp, Mr. Scott Murray, Monsignor George Talbot and others, who all came forward generously to assist in the expenses. Cardinal Wiseman warmly approved of the proposed foundation and finally Lord Teignmouth's house at Clapham was bought which had been the head-quarters of the Clapham Evangelicals and of the Bible Society; and it was first occupied by the Redemptorists on the 31st of July 1848, the first mass being said on St. Alphonsus' Feast. Previous to that, the Congregation had accepted various small missions or Chaplaincies: such as a station at Upton on Severn (from Hanley) in 1846: the Chaplaincy at Llanherne, accepted until July 1850; and the Chaplaincy at Rotherwas to Septbr. 1849. These Chaplaincies were served by the Redemptorist Fathers who had been temporarily expelled from Vienna by the revolution. There was also a station at Great Marlow, near Mr. Scott Murray's, which continued till the 25th of March 1851. But at a meeting of the Superiors of the Congregation at Bischenberg in Alsace in 1850, it was decreeed that all these smaller missions in England should be abandoned.

The next important foundation was at *Bishop-Eton*, near Liverpool, a house bought from Dr. Brown on the 19th of March 1851, and which was first occupied on the 10th of

June of that same year. A beautiful church was built there and dedicated to "The Annunciation". This has become the house of the noviciate. A foundation in Ireland was the next thing contemplated by Father de Held: but it does not appear that he remained in this country long enough to make the desired foundation himself. His biographer states that in 1855 he assisted at the General Chapter in Rome: after which he passed several years in the Redemptorist house at Aix la Chapelle, from which he was expelled by the May laws of 1873. He then returned to England and having passed some time in his old home at Clapham, he returned to the Continent, and died at the advanced age of 82, on the 21st of April 1881 at Vals in Dutch Limburg, where the Fathers of the Rhenish Province had taken refuge after their expulsion from Prussia.

The work he had inaugurated, however, was carried out the following year and on the 25th of Novbr. 1853, the house at Limerick was opened and dedicated to St. Alphonsus. One thing should be mentioned in connection with this house at Limerick and that is, *the confraternity of the Holy Family* which is attached to it. It meets every week and as it numbers 4,300 men, one half have to meet on Monday evening and the other on Tuesday. Each night the large church is crowded to excess, some sections being placed in the sanctuary for want of room in the body of the church. This great work was begun during the Provincialate of the Bishop of Southwark in the year 1868 and it has gone on increasing ever since. At first, as I have before mentioned, the houses in this country belonged to the Belgian Province: but in 1854, the Anglo-Dutch Province was provisionally erected; and in the following year, 1855, in the month of

November, it was definitively separated from the Belgian Province. Father Swinkels (who afterwards was the Superior of the Redemptorist House at Surinam in Dutch Guiana, South America, and at the same time Vicar Apostolic of that district was the first Provincial of the Anglo-Dutch Province. But in 1859, the Revd. Robert Coffin, Rector of Clapham, was nominated by the Superior General, Vice-Provincial of the English part of the Anglo-Dutch Province, which then consisted of the three Houses of Clapham, Limerick and Bishop-Eton.

Father Coffin continued to be Vice-Provincial till 1865, when the English Province was separated from the Dutch and he was nominated Provincial of the newly erected independent English Province. This was on the 24th of May 1865. He continued to hold that office till he was appointed Bishop of Southwark.

The houses founded during his term of office were:

Perth—dedicated to Our Lady of Perpetual Succour—opened on the 19th of March 1869, the previous work of the Congregation in Scotland having been begun at Dundee from 1867 to 1868;

Teignmouth—dedicated to St. Joseph, founded on the 3rd of November 1875;

Dundalk—also dedicated to St. Joseph—founded on the 8th of September 1876;
and lastly,

Singleton, New South Wales, opened on the Feast of the Patronage of St. Joseph 1882 by Father Edmund Vaughan.

But in addition to the great extension of the work of the Congregation under Father Coffin's wise and prudent administration, he consolidated it by two important measures.

The first was the establishment of a noviciate which had not before existed in this country and which was fixed by the Father General at Bishop-Eton. It was opened on the 18th of May 1860, being the Feast of St. Venantius. It was the first day likewise of the Novena of the Holy Ghost, which is made every year in the Congregation in preparation for the Feast of Pentecost. Mass was said in the noviciate oratory by the very Revd. the Father Provincial (Bishop Coffin). There were at first but four novices: but after the mass, the Veni Creator was sung and the Redemptorist noviciate was declared to be opened in England.

The second important work which Father Coffin established was a separate house of studies for the students of the Congregation. This was begun at Bishop-Eton in 1871: but in 1875 the students were transferred to Teignmouth to a house rented from the Bishop of Plymouth, where they remained until the present new house was finished in 1880. Teignmouth is now the House of studies, while Bishop-Eton remains the noviciate of the Congregation.

But not content with embracing great Britain in his charity, Father Coffin could not turn a deaf ear to the cry for help which came from the Australian Colonies, and in the spring of last year, yielded to the intreaties of the Bishop of Maitland and sent four Fathers and two lay-brothers under the care of Father Edmund Vaughan, as Superior, to found a fresh house at Singleton in that distant country.

The English Province at the present moment including N. S. Wales numbers 122 subjects, including professed Fathers, professed students, choir novices, professed lay-brothers and novice lay-brothers.

It seems perfectly incredible that such a small number

of men should have done so gigantic a work as may be seen by the following Tabular Statement.

In Great Britain and Ireland from 1848 to 1883.

Missions given	1,373
Renewals of Missions	236
Clergy Retreats	354
Retreats to Colleges and Communities	1,151
Retreats to the Confraternities of the Holy Family	372
Converts made at home and on the Missions	16,838

This does not include the Missions and Retreats already given in Australia, where the Fathers are overwhelmed with work, and Missions and Retreats are asked for in every Parish of each Diocese!

"*Messis multa — operarii vero pauci.*"

May we not hope that by a study of the Life of the great servant of God of whose biography I have now given an English version, many fresh vocations may be called forth, and that his prayers and sacrifices may thus bear fruit even to the uttermost ends of the earth.

MARY ELISABETH HERBERT.

Herbert House
Belgrave Square.
Febr. 9. 1883.

CONTENTS.

	PAGE.
Preface of Author	III
Preface of English Translator	VI

FIRST BOOK.
FROM THE BIRTH OF CLEMENT IN 1751 TO HIS ENTRANCE INTO THE CONGREGATION OF THE MOST HOLY REDEEMER IN 1784.

CHAPTER I.
The Birth and Infancy of F. Clement. From 1751 to 1767 ... 1

CHAPTER II.
Clement is taught a Baker's Trade which he exercises in the Monastery of Bruck. From 1767 to 1776. 4

CHAPTER III.
He practices the Trade of Baker in Vienna. He goes on a Pilgrimage to Rome. The Condition of the Austrian Empire and the Journey of Pius VI. to Vienna. From 1778 to 1782 8

CHAPTER IV.
Clement returns to Rome and goes to the Hermitage at Tivoli. From 1782 to 1783. 11

CHAPTER V.
Clement returns to Vienna to resume his Studies. He contracts an intimate Friendship with Thaddeus Hübl. From 1783 to 1784 . 14

CHAPTER VI.
He goes back to Rome: joins the Redemptorist Congregation and is ordained Priest. From 1784 to 1785 17

BOOK THE SECOND.
FROM FATHER CLEMENT'S DEPARTURE FOR WARSAW IN 1786 TO HIS RETURN TO VIENNA IN 1808.

CHAPTER I.   PAGE.
Father Clement's Journey to Warsaw. From 1786 to 1787 23

CHAPTER II.
Beginning of the Foundation in Warsaw. The State of Poland. The first Disciples of Father Clement 26

CHAPTER III.
His apostolic Works in Warsaw. He founds an Orphanage. His profuse Charity towards the Poor 35

CHAPTER IV.
Other Apostolic Labours in Poland. F. Clement's Account of the lamentable State of Religion in that Country 41

CHAPTER V.
His indefatigable Zeal for the Diffusion of good Books, and especially of the works of St. Alphonsus 47

CHAPTER VI.
The Redemptorists in Stralsund and in other Stations of Poland. From 1795 to 1807 51

CHAPTER VII.
The incessant Anxiety of Father Clement to propagate the Congregation in Germany. His Pilgrimage to Prague. 1795 55

CHAPTER VIII.
His Anxiety for higher Education 61

CHAPTER IX.
The State of the Church in Germany at the End of the 18th Century and the Beginning of the 19th. Who were Dalberg and Wessenberg 64

CHAPTER X.
F. Clement founds a House in the Diocese of Constance. His Journey to Rome and Return to Warsaw. From 1802 to 1804 74

CHAPTER XI.
New Labours of Father Clement in Germany. A fresh Journey to Mount Thabor. He founds a House at Triberg, which, however, was speedily suppressed. From 1804 to 1805 80

Contents.

CHAPTER XII.
Clement takes Refuge with his Brethren at Babenhausen. The Virtues he there exercised. From 1805 to 1806 85

CHAPTER XIII.
Persecutions endured by the Redemptorists at Babenhausen. Father Clement returns to Warsaw. 1806 93

CHAPTER XIV.
The Redemptorists are driven from Babenhausen and take Refuge in Switzerland. A short Notice of Father Clement's first Disciples. From 1806 to 1807 99

CHAPTER XV.
The Redemptorists in Coire. Their Troubles and Persecutions. Driven from thence, they take Refuge in the Valais. 1807 104

CHAPTER XVI.
Father Clement an Example of all religious and domestic Virtues to his Brethren 116

CHAPTER XVII.
Great Anxiety as regarded the House at Warsaw. The Death of Father Thaddeus Hübl. From 1806 to 1807 124

CHAPTER XVIII.
Who Father Thaddeus was: and how he was esteemed and revered by all. His solemn Funeral 128

CHAPTER XIX.
The Congregation is destroyed in Warsaw and the Fathers barbarously driven away. 1808. 134

CHAPTER XX.
Father Clement with his Brethren detained at the Fortress of Cüstrin. His Journey to Vienna 147

THIRD BOOK.
FROM THE ARRIVAL OF FATHER CLEMENT IN VIENNA IN 1808 TILL HIS PRECIOUS DEATH IN 1820.

CHAPTER I.
His Arrival in Vienna. His Residence near the Italian Church, in which he exercises his Zeal and greatly promotes the Worship of the Blessed Sacrament. From 1808 to 1813 154

CHAPTER II.

F. Clement is made Confessor and Director of the Ursulines. Deplorable State of the Church in Vienna. Who was Archbishop Hohenwarth. The daily Occupations of Father Clement. 160

CHAPTER III.

Father Clement by his Faith and Zeal, inflamed the Viennese with a like Ardour. 168

CHAPTER IV.

The Devotion of F. Clement for the Mysteries of our Redemption. His Zeal for the worthy Celebration of the Divine Offices 178

CHAPTER V.

F. Clement's Devotion to our Lady, to the Saints and to the Souls in Purgatory 186

CHAPTER VI.

Father Clement as a Preacher. His Way of announcing the Word of God. 192

CHAPTER VII.

The principal Subjects of Father Clement's Preaching. His Maxims and Spirit 198

CHAPTER VIII.

Father Clement is powerfully helped in his Apostolate by Frederick Zacchary Werner. Who this celebrated Orator was. 206

CHAPTER IX.

Father Clement in the Tribunal of Penance. His Anxiety for the Salvation of Souls 212

CHAPTER X.

With what Charity and Prudence he treated his Penitents 218

CHAPTER XI.

Father Clement as Director of the Ursuline Nuns 221

CHAPTER XII.

Father Clement's Love and Zeal for the Sick 231

CHAPTER XIII.

His paternal Sollicitude for the Poor 237

CHAPTER XIV.
His Efforts for the Christian Education of Youth 241

CHAPTER XV.
Father Clement converts many Jews and Protestants 245

CHAPTER XVI.
The Meetings and Evening Conferences in Father Clement's House 255

CHAPTER XVII.
His Anxiety for the Welfare of the Universal Church, and especially at the Time of the Congress in Vienna 259

CHAPTER XVIII.
His Zeal for the Purity of the Faith. His Judgment on Sailer and Bolzano 265

CHAPTER XIX.
Father Clement deserves well of Catholic Literature 267

CHAPTER XX.
The Vicissitudes of the Congregation in Switzerland. Father Clement sends Missionaries into Wallachia. Who was Father Libotzky . . 270

CHAPTER XXI.
The Anxiety felt by Father Clement for the Reestablishment of the Congregation in Poland. A further Notice of the Life and Death of Father Podgorski 277

CHAPTER XXII.
A new Persecution is started at Vienna against Father Clement. Francis I. shows himself to be favourable to his Cause 281

CHAPTER XXIII.
The extraordinary Graces and Miracles granted to Father Clement in his Life-time 289

CHAPTER XXIV.
Father Clement begins to be seriously ill, but still continues his Apostolic Labours. 1820 298

CHAPTER XXV.
The precious Death of Father Clement. 1820 301

CHAPTER XXVI. PAGE.
The solemn Funeral of Father Clement 307

CHAPTER XXVII.
Father Clement's personal Appearance and Character 313

FOURTH BOOK.

CHAPTER I.
On the Foundation of the Congregation in Vienna. 1820 317

CHAPTER II.
The Veneration shown to F. Clement's Tomb in Sta. Maria di Enzersdorf. Solemn Translation of his Relics to Vienna in 1862 . . . 322

CHAPTER III.
His Apparition after Death. His Miracles 326

CHAPTER IV.
The Fulfilment of Father Clement's Prophecy on the Spread of the Redemptorist Congregation 329

CHAPTER V.
Conclusion 337
Appendix 341

THE FIRST BOOK.

FROM THE BIRTH OF CLEMENT IN 1751, TO HIS ENTRANCE INTO THE CONGREGATION OF THE HOLY REDEEMER IN 1784.

CHAPTER I.

THE BIRTH AND INFANCY OF CLEMENT.

[From 1751 to 1767.]

CLEMENT Maria Hofbauer, whom God designed to combat the pretended intellectual progress which was just then becoming the fashion of the age and to revive the dying piety of the faithful, was born on the 26th of December 1751, at Passwitz, a considerable town in Moravia in the neighbourhood of Znaim on the borders of the Austrian Empire. According to the pious custom of that believing people, he was carried to the Parish Church (which was dedicated to the Assumption of the Blessed Virgin) on the very day of his birth and received in holy Baptism the name of John, which was afterwards changed to that of Clement. A Premonstratensian Father of the Monastery of Bruck, called Adolfo Dujardin, performed the Baptismal Ceremony; and his Godfather was Michael Jahn, the father of the man who became afterwards so famous for his writings. — Clement's own father, who was born at Budwitz, in Moravia, was called

Peter Paul Dworżak; but, according to custom, he changed it to Hofbauer when he was transferred to a German county. He was a thoroughly pious, upright and excellent man — a butcher by trade — but preferring to that the cultivation of his fields and the care of cattle. The maiden name of Clement's mother was Maria Steer. Heaven blessed this pious couple with 12 children, only five of whom, however, lived to grow up, i. e. 4 boys and 1 girl, of whom Clement was the youngest. To his mother belonged the task of sowing the seeds of piety and virtue in the soul of this privileged child: and when, in 1758, his father died, in the prime of life (being only 47 years of age) all the care of the family devolved upon her. Clement was then only a little more than six years old. —

Even when she carried him in her womb, this holy mother had dedicated him in spirit to the service of God. After his father's death she led him to the foot of the Crucifix and said to him: "From henceforth this must be thy father. Be careful to walk in the path most pleasing to Him" — which words made a profound impression on the child, who, young as he was, never forgot them. In the very last years of his life, he spoke of the blessing which had been vouchsafed to him in the piety of his parents and especially dwelt on the tender veneration he entertained for his mother, who had kindled in his heart that flame of divine love which was afterwards to become in him a consuming fire. —

From his earliest years she accustomed him to prayer and to other little exercises of piety and virtue, and the child corresponded so entirely to the mother's wishes and became such an example of filial docility and obedience, that already he was marked out as an instrument chosen by God for the fulfilment of his designs.

His fervour before the Blessed Sacrament and his zeal in honouring our Lady and the Saints were remarkable from his earliest years. He used to delight in fasting on Saturdays and on all the Eves of the Blessed Virgin's Feasts in order to testify his love and devotion to her. His mother while secretly admiring her boy's piety, nevertheless insisted that in all things he should act according to her will, to accustom him to conquer himself and his own inclinations, in which consists the highest virtue. Therefore, without express permission from his mother, the child did not dare fast. And as she knew how willingly and joyfully he was prepared to make such sacrifices, she made use of this disposition to incite him to still greater virtue, so that she only granted his request when he had behaved unusually well. Nor did she ever praise him for such little acts of self-denial or speak of them to others in his presence, as many less wise mothers do: but treated them with discreet and grave reserve. The food or other little delicacies which Clement denied himself on those days, he obtained permission to distribute among a certain number of poor children, whom it was his delight to supply in this way: and the money which his mother gave him from time to time to spend as he liked, was instantly distributed among the poor, or saved up to have certain masses said for his intention.

He was always ready to pray: and the Rosary which in most children's hands is more a plaything than anything else, was said by him with an affection and devotion far beyond his age. Often he would induce his brothers and sisters to join him: and whilst the rest were playing at some game, Clement would steal away to pray before the Blessed Sacrament. A little story told of him when he was only 8 years old, will give a fair idea of the state of his mind. He went one day with his mother to call on some relations and one of them being asked "what they did in the day?" replied: "O! kill time!" The boy had heard the question and asked for an explanation of the answer, which, when his mother had given it to him, he exclaimed with astonishment: "But if they have nothing to do, why do they not pray?"

What holy wisdom in the soul of the child do not these words reveal! —

No one can be surprised that he was loved and appreciated by every body. In the day-school he attended he was as great a favourite with the masters as with the boys: and the former were constantly quoting him as an example to the rest. In the same way, the priests of the place, whose masses he constantly served and one of whom taught him the rudiments of Latin, were daily more and more edified at his devotion, obedience and innocence. In fact, he gave abundant promise in those early years of the eminent virtues which afterwards made him the apostle of his country.

CHAPTER II.

Clement is taught a baker's trade, which he exercises in the monastery of Bruck.

[From 1767 to 1776.]

THIS beloved Benjamin of his mother's house remained at home till he was 16, when a change came over the fortunes of the family. His sister Barbara married, his mother gave her up her own house: and his three brothers who had followed their father's trade left Passwitz. Charles after having served in the army and made a campaign against the Turks, established himself in S. Andrea, near Temesvar. Herman settled at Znaim: and Laurence in the neighbourhood of Nikolsburg.

But Clement, whose only dream was to devote himself to the service of God in the ecclesiastical state, which was also his mother's wish, refused all proposals to join them. Only, as he had not the means to follow his studies he resolved to learn a trade so as to earn money for this purpose and chose that of a baker. — In the month of March 1767 he accordingly left his loving mother and went to the old Town of Znaim to learn his business. And here it happened as it had at home — that he won the hearts of every body and especially of his master, Francesco Dobsch and his wife. Their little boy, a child of 5 years old, took the most violent fancy for him and insisted on accompanying him when he went out to carry the bread. But as the little fellow could, naturally, only take short steps and thus hindered Clement in his work, he implored his mistress to keep him at home. The good mother, however, who was not slow in finding out the great advantage it was to her boy to be as much as possible with Clement, implored him to have patience and to continue to take the child with him. Clement, not wishing to vex his mistress by a refusal, but, on the other hand, anxious not to displease their customers by want of punctuality in delivering the bread, bethought himself of the expedient of carrying the little fellow on one arm, while, with the other he bore the basket of bread. When the people saw him pass in that way, with the child on his shoulder, they cried out: "O! here is St. Christopher!" Clement had never read that story of the Saint and so, fancying that they were talking of some one else, turned round to look. But amused at his simplicity, the people then cried out: "But you are yourself St. Christopher!" On returning home, he asked his master what they meant. On hearing the Legend and how St. Christopher carried the Infant Jesus on his shoulder, he exclaimed: "O! would that I were indeed St. Christopher, that I might bear in my hands my Lord and my God!" — This, in fact, was his aspiration day and night: and often when his work was done would he watch till dawn, praying that God would open a way for him to serve at His Altar. But our Lord did not allow such a desire to remain long unfulfilled and brought about the accomplishment of his wishes in a most unexpected manner.

Clement had been working for 3 years with this master, when he was sent for to act as baker in the monastery of Bruck, where he found the opportunity of exercising not only his trade but charity to his neighbour and that in an heroic degree. The year 1771, was memorable for a fearful famine which reduced the people of Bohemia to the greatest misery, so that from all parts of the country the people came to beg for bread at the doors of the monastery. The monks did all they could: but Clement, not thinking of his own labour or fatigue, quadrupled the usual quantity of bread made and besides, fasted himself continually, so as to increase the portions given at the gate. The famine was followed by fever, as is so often the case, which decimated the unhappy population and still further touched Clement's loving heart. So that after having laboured all day, he would watch half the night to appease the wrath of God and implore His mercy before the altar.

The Abbot Gregory Lambeck, a gentle and benevolent old man, having watched Clement's conduct and being greatly struck with his eminent virtues, became warmly attached to him and removed him from his post as baker to serve as his personal attendant. And soon finding out his intense desire to become a Priest, gave him leave to spend all his free hours in studying Latin and other things in the Grammar School attached to the monastery. Clement joyfully availed himself of this unexpected permission, and from 1772 to 1775 passed through all the four classes of this college, although his other duties prevented his studying as he would have wished. To show the spirit which animated him we will mention one of his speeches about this time to a cousin and fellow-countryman of his, John Jahn, who was a Religious in the monastery. Perceiving in him an inordinate love of study, especially of abstruse sciences, he one day said to him gently: "Learning is a great thing—but sanctity is a greater. You must pray more, otherwise you will some day get into trouble." — A warning unheeded at the time, but the truth of which was made but too apparent later, when Jahn by his clever but rationalistic writings, found himself in disgrace with the Holy See which forbid the circulation of his works.

About the year 1775, Clement left the monastery, either because of the death of the good Abbot who had been as a father to him, or because he did not feel himself called to join the Premonstratensian Order. He then found himself in one of those critical positions in which a man can only throw himself unreservedly into the Arms of Providence. His own great anxiety was to continue his studies. But there were two difficulties—the one, the want of means—the other, that at 25 years of age, he could hardly go into a public school. He had also a great dread of the irreligious spirit which at that moment invaded most of the colleges. On the other hand, the great love he had for prayer and the hidden life suggested to him that it might be the will of God that he should serve Him as a hermit. For this purpose, he retired to Mühlfrauen, a little country place not far from his old home, to serve the beautiful church which had been built there by his old friend and patron, Abbot Lambeck. This church is dedicated to our Lord bound to the column; and being the site of many miracles was very much frequented by pilgrims and devout persons. Clement with the help of his brother Herman, built himself a little cell in the neighbouring wood, where he lived in perpetual union with God: thus gaining in this retreat treasures of grace which he was afterwards to dispense to others. The pilgrims who visited him in his hermitage provided him with what was absolutely necessary for his sustenance: and he repaid them by holy instructions and opportune admonitions: and sometimes accompanied them to the church bearing a heavy cross, while he gave lighter ones to the pilgrims, so that they might bear them in the spirit of penitence. —

One year alone was allowed him of this holy quietude. Then the irreligious government of Joseph the 2nd abolished all hermitages under the pretence that they were not suited to the days of advanced civilisation: and thus Clement was turned out of his humble cell, which is shown to this day. He felt the blow heavily: but Divine Providence thus guided his steps. The hermit was to be changed into the apostle who should combat the very evils which had driven him from his solitude. And it was on this occasion that he went to Budwitz, his father's native city, where he learned the Sclav language, which from its affinity to the Polish, became most useful to him when employed in his future missions. —

CHAPTER III.

HE PRACTISES THE TRADE OF BAKER IN VIENNA. HE GOES ON A PILGRIMAGE TO ROME. THE CONDITION OF THE AUSTRIAN EMPIRE AND THE JOURNEY OF PIUS VI, TO VIENNA.

[From 1778 to 1782.]

CLEMENT did not stay long at Budwitz, for in 1778 we find him in Vienna, where he was plying his old trade of baker in a house called "The iron Pear", behind the Ursuline Monastery. There he matured a plan which he had long entertained of making a pilgrimage to Rome to pray on the Tombs of the Princes of the Apostles. There was a young man working in the same bakehouse, named Peter Kunzmann, a native of the Diocese of Erbipoli, with whom Clement contracted a close friendship and they encouraged one another in the practice of every virtue. Clement having confided the idea of his Roman Pilgrimage to his friend, Peter joyfully acceded to it, following thereby the impulse of his heart. But their joint savings not sufficing for so long a journey, they made up their minds to sell all their best clothes, which being ornamented, according to the custom of their country, with old silver buttons, had a certain market value. Then they started, travelling all the way on foot, praying out loud or singing hymns and spiritual songs and that even in populous towns, not minding the ridicule of the passers-by. Having at last arrived in the holy city, they spent their whole time in visiting the sanctuaries and frequenting the Sacraments: after which they returned to Vienna, greatly strengthened in faith and with their hearts filled with holy emotions and generous resolves.

In the year 1782, Vienna was honoured by a visit from the Holy Father Pius VI himself, who, as a Father anxious for the welfare of his children, had determined to communicate directly with the Emperor Joseph; and therefore, leaving Rome on the 27th of Febr., arrived in Vienna on the 22nd of March.

This Emperor, Joseph the 2nd, who had succeeded his mother Maria Teresa, had determined to inaugurate certain changes in the Government of the Church. These notions, which afterwards, unfortunately, obtained powerful supporters in the persons of the Jansenists, Gallicans, and other similar schismatics, found a strong exponent in Joseph, who determined to put them in practice in his own dominions. The theory which gave the right to the civil power to interfere in the spiritual as well as the temporal interests of its subjects, suited his despotic temperament. Consequently no sooner had he ascended the throne, than he set himself to work to reform the Church according to his own ideas. The faithful were no longer to hold direct communications with Rome. The imperial "*placet*" was necessary to all pontifical Bulls, or Rescripts before they could be promulgated: the education of the Clergy was to be taken away from the supervision of the Bishops: the Diocesan Seminaries were to be closed, and the ecclesiastical students were to be placed in seminaries under the direction of the Government. The

laws regarding matrimony were to be settled by the State.
and the Bishops were to be compelled to grant dispensations,
which, before, had always been referred to the Holy See; to
which not even reserved cases of conscience could be brought
save through the medium of the Imperial Ambassador. All
institutions of Christian education, convents and monasteries, especially those of the contemplative orders, were declared useless and either suppressed altogether or reduced
to half their numbers. And to such lengths did this "*Josephism*" go, that it was proposed to appoint a Government
Committee to regulate the forms of Divine worship, the vestments of the Priests and the ringing of the bells!! — Pius VI
had not ceased to remonstrate, but hitherto in vain. He
hoped, therefore, that his august presence in Vienna might
induce the Emperor to retrace his steps before it was too
late. The people received him with intense joy and enthusiasm: but not so the perverse King. Before he was halfway
on his journey, he had sent to tell the Pope that nothing
should induce him to alter his system. And the result was,
that this visit only heaped further humiliations on the head
of the afflicted Pontiff: and the infamous Libel called "*What
is the Pope?*" by the well-known Eybel, was circulated through
the Town in order to discredit his mission in every way.
After a month of fruitless negotiations, the Pope returned
to Rome by Bavaria and the Tyrol, where the Faith and
Love of the people consoled as far as possible his paternal
heart. —

It did not please our Lord that the Emperor's proposals
should thus be stifled in the birth: but He permitted that
they should become the punishment of a people too forget-
ful of His love. Yet, His infinite goodness was even then
preparing an instrument to remedy the evil. As the Holy
Father passed through the streets of Vienna blessing the
multitude, his benediction lit upon our saintlike though
humble Clement whom God had destined for this special

work. What the Pope, surrounded with all the splendour of the supreme Pontificate could not effect, this humble workman was to carry out, at least in a great measure. The joy which he had experienced in seeing the Pope within the walls of Vienna was saddened by the failure of his mission: and when he sought for consolation before the Blessed Sacrament, even then he was pained at seeing the altars despoiled by the orders of the State, and the Church enslaved in a manner unprecedented in that Catholic country. —

CHAPTER IV.

CLEMENT RETURNS TO ROME AND GOES TO THE HERMITAGE AT TIVOLI.

[From 1782 to 1783.]

THE sad events of the times roused, once more, in Clement's heart, the longing for the quiet of his hermit's life; and speaking of it to his friend Kunzmann, he proposed to him a second Roman pilgrimage. Kunzmann entertained the proposal willingly enough: but when their master heard of it, he did everything in his power to dissuade him and even proposed to give him his own daughter in marriage. But this notion only made Clement hurry his departure the more, so averse was he to any idea of marriage! In the autumn, therefore, of 1782, the two friends started again for Rome, on foot as before, praying and singing and suffering every kind of hardship. When they were obliged to sleep in the open air, Clement would draw a circle on the soil and recommend himself and his friend to the care of their Guardian Angels and the Holy Apostles in the centre of the circle where they rested. When they had fully satisfied their piety in Rome, they walked on to Tivoli, where they hoped to find the much-wished-for hermitage. On the 25th of December of the preceding year, a Benedictine, Father Barnabas Chiaramonti (who afterwards, was elected Pope in a conclave held at Venice under the name of Pius VII) had been promoted to the Bishopric of Tivoli. To him our pious pilgrims presented themselves and craved permission to found a hermitage in his diocese. This holy and learned Prelate examined them carefully in order to prove their spirit and set before them the duties and the difficulties attending such a life; but finding them constant in their intention he blessed them and gave them the hermit's habit. On this occasion our venerable servant of God took the name of "Clement" and Kunzmann that of "Emanuel".*

In the midst of an olive grove stood a small church which they were appointed to look after and alongside was the little dwelling assigned to them with a small orchard. —

In this little church, which was called "*La Madonna di Quintiliolo*" there was a Byzantine picture of our Lady over the High Altar which was held in great veneration by the people. They had recourse to her to obtain a good harvest: and every year from the 7th of May till the Feast of the Assumption this picture was exposed in the Cathedral of Tivoli and daily devotions performed in her honour. The church is called *Quintiliolo*, because it is built on the ruins of the old Villa of Quintilio Varo, the unfortunate Captain of the Emperor Augustus.** Even to this day people admire the magnificent ruins which serve as a shelter to the shepherds and their flocks in a storm.

* Clement of Klinkowstroem deposed as follows: "He took this name in order to have St. Clement of Ancira as his patron, this Saint having suffered a martyrdom of 38 years, thereby proving gloriously the constancy of his faith and his courage in bearing adversity. Having had F. Hofbauer as my Godfather, I took the same name and have in consequence always kept a picture of the Saint and martyr which F. Hofbauer gave me." —

** Varo was defeated with all his army in the German forests; which made Augustus exclaim:
"*Vare! Vare! redde mihi legiones meas!*"

This spot is not only venerable from its antiquity but is also one of the finest positions in the neighbourhood of Tivoli. Towards the East there is a beautiful view of the Town, of the Temple of Sybil, of the grand waterfall of Ariene and in the distance, of the mountains which form a background to this magnificent picture. On the other side, the Roman Campagna stretches out its vast plain to the Mediterranean and the eye rests on the eternal city, the cupola of St. Peter's standing out impressively against the clear sky.

This was the spot assigned to Clement and his companion where they spent a year of austerity, yet of complete peace and happiness. The crops which they planted and cultivated in their little orchard were almost their only sustenance: but what was wanting in corporal comforts was made up in spiritual ones. The beauties of nature led them to contemplate the wonders and infinite goodness of the Creator: and when they turned their eyes from the ruins of Pagan Rome to the marvels of Christianity, their hearts were filled with the tenderest gratitude towards that God who had deigned to allow them to be born in the Catholic Church. But such a rest was not long allowed to Clement, who was to endure all the trials which our Lord permits to fall upon such generous souls as He destines to do great works for His glory and for the good of others. So happy did he find himself in this solitude, so far from any disturbance from without, and so near to God, that in later years when the multiplicity of his cares and obligations prevented his giving as much time to prayer as he wished, he would look back longingly to this hermitage and exclaim to those around him: "O! if you did but know the delicious position of Tivoli! There one feels one's soul quite separated from the world and entirely united with God!" He would have gladly continued to spend his days there: but our Lord did not intend him for a contemplative but for an active life of labour in His Vineyard. Therefore, after the solemn procession of the 15th of August, when the picture of our Lady was taken back to Quintiliolo, Clement was again compelled to quit his beloved solitude and to return to Vienna: where in 1783 he resumed his studies. — His Divine Master began his ministry after 40 days' prayer and fasting in the desert: and His faithful servant was prepared for his apostolate by the solitude of Tivoli and the intimate communications he had there held with God. —

CHAPTER V.

Clement returns to Vienna to resume his studies. He contracts an intimate friendship with Taddeo Hübl.

[From 1783 to 1784.]

A grave difficulty arose on his return to Vienna as to where he should find the means to go on with his studies. He trusted mainly in Divine Providence which did not fail him: but in the meanwhile, he did not give up his baker's trade, which at least procured him the necessaries of life.

Dividing his day between his work and his studies, he did not, in consequence, neglect spiritual things. Every Sunday he went to the Metropolitan Church of St. Stephen to serve mass. There were three sisters named Maul, who lived in the neighbourhood and frequented this church, who were very much struck and edified at the extraordinary recollection and piety of this new Server. It happened one Sunday that a violent downpour of rain came on just after the service was over and obliged them to take refuge in the vestibule of the church. Clement was coming out at the same moment and seeing their distress, offered to run and get them a carriage to go home. The Ladies gratefully assented: and Clement, without minding the torrents of rain, went and got one. The sisters insisted on his sharing it with them and

Clement accepted their offer. This seemingly simple, everyday incident was the turning-point in his life. For these Ladies entered into conversation with him and being more and more charmed with his replies, asked him why he did not go on with his studies? and if he did not wish to become a Priest? Poor Clement answered, somewhat sadly, "that this had been his ardent desire from his infancy, but that he had been obliged to give it up for want of means."

"If there be no other impediment", exclaimed the eldest sister, "be of good heart, for we will see about the means and supply all your wants."

And they were as good as their word and from henceforth they undertook all necessary expenses, not only for himself but for a friend of his, of whom we will say a few words.

One day Clement was coming out of the church, when he saw a little notice on the door of a lad who offered his services as a copyist. "This must be some poor and humble student", he said to himself and immediately determined to find him out. He was a certain Thaddeus Hübl, of Cermna, in the Diocese of Königgrätz, the son of a forrester of Prince Lichtenstein's, poor in this world's goods, it was true, but good, pious, and full of talent. Clement soon conceived the warmest affection for him and introduced him to his kind patronesses, who, finding he had the same desire as Clement, extended likewise their generosity towards him. This youth became the intimate friend and companion of Clement during the rest of his life and an eminent member of the new congregation about to be established in Poland. Our Lord abundantly blessed these pious sisters for their charity; and they had the joy before their deaths, of seeing Clement's reputation everywhere established and of hearing him preach in the Ursuline Church.

Through this unexpected and providential generosity, Clement was, at last, enabled to give up his trade and devote himself entirely to his studies. He related one day, how hard he had worked at that time: "I spent the whole day and often the night in studying and not to be overcome by sleep, I used to walk up and down, holding a candle in one hand and my book in the other, so as to save time." But he did not, therefore, neglect prayer or spiritual exercises. On Feast Days and Sundays especially he would devote himself to his religious duties, serving one mass after the other in the Church of St. Saviour's and always with the same fervour of spirit. At this time, likewise, he was thrown into intimate relations with F. Albert Diesbach, one of the members of the suppressed Society of Jesus, whose ardent zeal and great ability was then employed in combating the Josephism of the day and reviving the religious faith of the people. Curiously enough, it was through him that Clement became first acquainted with the ascetic works of St. Alphonsus Liguori, with which he was at once greatly impressed and delighted.

Although Clement was so keen in his studies, yet at the end of the scholastic year 1784 he found himself compelled to give up the Vienna University, in consequence of the conduct of the new Professors, who endeavoured in every way to sow the seeds of Protestantism and infidelity in the hearts of their pupils. One day, a certain Professor having held some outrageous language of this sort, Clement could stand it no longer; and rising bravely from his seat, interrupted the speaker, saying: "Sir, what you are teaching us is not in conformity with the doctrines of the Catholic Church," and then leaving his place, he walked out of the schools. It is fair to add that this public reproof had a good effect and made such an impression on the mind of the Professor that, on reflection, he felt that his pupil was in the right and renounced ever after his heretical teaching. Many years after, this old Professor met Clement in the street and having asked him "whether he were not his old pupil Hofbauer?" On his reply in the affirmative, he thanked him warmly for his timely correction, which, though at the moment it had filled him with anger and shame, had saved his soul and opened his eyes to his error. —

This being the wretched state of things in Vienna, Clement felt he must seek elsewhere for the completion of his studies: and thus Providence led him by strange and unexpected ways to the place where he was to find his true vocation.

CHAPTER VI.

He goes back to Rome: joins the Redemptorist Congregation and is ordained Priest.

[From 1784 to 1785.]

AFTER long and earnest prayer to God that He might show him the path He wished him to follow, Clement received an internal assurance that he was to return to Rome, where he would attain the object of all his wishes and prepare himself in the best way for the Priesthood.

When once our Lord had thus spoken to him, all obstacles seemed easily overcome: and so great were his Faith and confidence in God, that, in answer to all objections, he only replied simply: "Our Lord will smooth away every difficulty."

He first told his plan to his friend Thaddeus and asked him to accompany him. Thaddeus was very ill and in Hospital, so that he was greatly astonished at the invitation. "And how is it possible for me, ill as I am, and without a farthing, to undertake such a journey?" Clement replied: "As to your health, God will restore it, and as to the money, I undertake to collect it". — And so it turned out: Thaddeus suddenly and unexpectedly recovered and Clement received from his old benefactors enough for the journey. They went on foot and were visibly protected by God in the midst of many dangers. On one occasion a huge black dog flew at Thaddeus who was very much frightened. Clement simply said: "Let us say the Psalm my mother taught me: '*Qui habitat in adjutorio altissimi*', and then we shall be free from all dangers." —

When they got to Rome they took a lodging near the Basilica of Sta. Maria Maggiore and determined to go there on the ringing of the first bell in the morning. At dawn of day however, the first sound came from another little church near and they hastened in there to pour out their hearts before God in thankfulness for their safety and in earnest prayer for guidance as to their future path. In the church, was a religious Community absorbed in meditation. Their great recollection and the expression of happiness and peace in their faces struck Clement at once and filled him with love and veneration towards them. Coming out of the church, he asked a child to what order those Religious belonged? The child replied: "They are Redemptorists: and some day you will be one of them!" — These words astonished Clement, who felt as if our Lord had spoken by the mouth of a child to make known His Divine will. Without any further hesitation therefore, he knocked at the door of the monastery and asked the Superior the object of his Congregation. Great was his delight when he found out that it was a Congregation of Priests lately founded by Monsignor Liguori for whose works he had such a veneration: and that the main object of the Institution was to give missions and to bring back to God the most abandoned souls, and those who were most in need of spiritual aid. The Superior further informed him that they were consecrated to God by three simple vows of poverty, chastity and obedience; and that they bound themselves by a vow of perseverance to remain in that holy estate until death. But Clement's amazement was at its height, when, at the end of their conversation, the Superior spontaneously offered to admit him into the Congregation— he, a perfect stranger, a foreigner, without any money and

33 years of age! He saw in this unexpected solution of his
doubts, however, the hand of God and accepted the offer
with the deepest gratitude and humility. —

But God who does not often permit His servants to enjoy
unmixed consolation in this world, subjected Clement to a
sharp trial. His friend Thaddeus did not at all approve of
the step Clement had taken; he declared that he had acted
with far too great precipitation in taking so important a step
and that it was especially cruel to abandon him after he had
induced him to undertake so arduous a pilgrimage. Clement
seeing his friend in such a state of annoyance, had recourse
to prayer and spent the whole of the following night imploring our Lord to grant to his friend also the grace of a
vocation to the Religious state. And his prayers were immediately answered: for the next morning as he came out of
Sta. Maria Maggiore, Thaddeus met him and said: "Do you
know what has happened? I am going to stay with you and
I also am to enter the Congregation." —

Clement's heart was so full of gratitude and joy that he
went back into the Basilica to pour it out in thanksgiving: and he declared that all his life long the remembrance
of this great grace would abide with him. One day, many
years after, he happened to be speaking of his youth and
saying how much it had cost him then to keep the Fasts of
the Church, perhaps owing to the hard work he had in his
trade: "but", he added, "from the moment I entered the Congregation, I fasted not only with facility but with joy, in
gratitude to God for the sudden vocation He vouchsafed to
give both to me and to my dear friend." —

The Superior of the Redemptorists, made no difficulty
about receiving Thaddeus into the Congregation. But as he
was a Foreigner, poor, ignorant of the language and 23
years old, which is above the age when ordinary candidates
are received, it required the special hand of God in the
matter for the Superior to make so extraordinary an excep-

tion to the ordinary rule. But these two youths thus unexpectedly received into the little house of St. Giuliano, were destined to be, more than all the rest, the columns and ornaments of the growing Congregation.

At that time, its holy Founder, St. Alphonso Liguori was still alive; and when he heard of the entrance of the two Germans into the Congregation he was filled with joy. And while the Neapolitan Fathers laughed at the idea proposed by them to found a house some day beyond the Alps, Alphonsus highly approved of it and said in a spirit of prophecy: "*God will not fail to promote His Glory by their means. Their mission, however, will be different from ours. In the midst of the Lutherans and Calvinists among whom they will be placed, the catechism will be more necessary than preaching. These good Priests will do a great work: but they will have need of greater light.*"

His Fatherly Benediction and the fruit of his prayers speedily reached Rome and strengthened the vocation of his first German sons.

Clement and Thaddeus began their noviciate in the House of St. Giuliano on the Esquiline, which was then the residence of the Superior and of the Procurator General. This House was behind the Church of St. Eusebio. (It was destroyed in 1873 in order to make way for the "*Piazza Vittorio Emmanuele*".) On the 24th of Oct., being the Feast of the Archangel Raphael, they both received the habit at the hands of F. Landi, who, being one of the earliest and most faithful Companions of the holy Founder, knew better than any one else how to infuse his spirit into the souls of his two novices. Under the direction of this master Clement was initiated into the duties of the Religious life. Hardly any details have been preserved of his doings during the noviciate: but as he was so soon chosen to transplant the Congregation beyond the Alps, we can judge of the eminent virtue which made his Superior at once consider him worthy of so important a post. One little fact is mentioned of him showing how averse he was to any thing which savoured of luxury or self-indulgence. Not knowing the custom in Italy of changing one's linen whenever a long walk had overheated one, he looked upon it as too fastidious a proceeding on the part of his fellow-novices, and one day addressed the master of novices as follows: "Revd. Father! I, with one change of linen, which, in fact, I had on my back, made a journey of 400 leagues and was none the worse. And now, for a little walk of a league or two, must one make such a fuss?" — From that day, the novices dreaded the excess of his zeal for mortification in which, as in every thing else, he was a model and an example to them all.

He was of a strong constitution and used to the substantial and somewhat heavy food of the north: hence, he suffered not a little from the very light meals of the Romans. Afterwards he related smiling that so terribly did he suffer, the first few months, from positive hunger and thirst, that it was all he could do to refrain from eating the bunches of grapes which hung outside his window! —

In consequence of their age and still more owing to their extraordinary fervour, the noviciate of the two friends was considerably shortened, so that on the Feast of St. Joseph (19th of March, 1785), they made their Religious Profession in the hands of F. Francesco di Paola, who was then Superior General of the Congregation. This great favour was quickly followed by another, which had been the earnest wish of Clement's heart for so many years. For they were sent directly after their profession to the College at Frosinone and on the 29th of March were ordained Priests at Alatri, the Bishop of Veroli being ill. — Alatri being only 5 kilometres from Frosinone they were able to return home at midday. The Rector, wishing to prove the virtue of the new Priests, ordered Clement to serve, and Thaddeus to read at table, while he made no difference whatever in the quality or quantity of the food, but behaved as if it had been an ordinary day. But so far from this being a mortification to Clement, it only added to his joy: as he had bound himself to the Priesthood not to increase his honour and dignity, but to be able to do more for the glory of God and the good of souls. The young Priests continued studying so diligently and practised all religious virtues with such fervour, that F. Altarelli, a noted Neapolitan Missionary, who was then their companion, declared that they were a subject of edification and admiration to the whole Community.

THE SECOND BOOK.
FROM F. CLEMENT'S DEPARTURE FOR WARSAW IN 1786 TO HIS RETURN TO VIENNA IN 1808.

CHAPTER I.
F. CLEMENT'S JOURNEY TO WARSAW.
[From 1786 to 1787.]

FATHER Clement and his companion had not long been ordained Priests when they renewed their petition to the Superior General for leave to try and transplant a branch of the Congregation to the north of the Alps. Leave was gladly granted, for it was the object for which they had been originally admitted. Accompanied by the prayers and good wishes of all their brethren, they started accordingly towards the end of the year 1785 and decided to begin first by Vienna, passing thro' the Tyrol. But if ever there were a bad moment to begin a religious foundation in Vienna it was then! By one stroke of the pen a thousand monasteries had been suppressed, including the most famous of the ancient Abbeys. They found it, therefore, impossible to attempt to start their work in Austria at that moment and accordingly wrote to the Father General, explaining this sad state of things and placing themselves at his disposal to preach the Gospel elsewhere. The F. General went to the

S. Congregation of the Propagation of the Faith, who joyfully accepted the offer of their services for Stralsund in Pomerania which then belonged to Sweden. This was a mission full of difficulties, the Government being so hostile to the Church and there being very few Catholics in that city. But F. Clement never was deterred by difficulties and especially when the will of God had been made known to him by the mouth of his Superiors.* Of this stay at Vienna we have very few details. We only know that they could not exercise their sacred ministry; but that the edifying life of F. Clement and the loving, charitable temperament of F. Thaddeus, made a most favourable impression on the Viennese and ensured to them friends and benefactors for the future foundation there.

Sent by the Holy See and provided with the necessary faculties by their Superiors** our two Missioners left Vienna for Warsaw in October 1786, which was the residence of the Superior of the Missions in the North, who was the Apostolic Nunzio at the Polish Court.***

An unexpected consolation was granted to Clement by our Lord soon after leaving Vienna. While sailing down the Danube, they found on their vessel a poorly dressed Hermit: Clement drew near him and discovered that it was his old companion in the hermitage of Tivoli, Emanuel Kunz-

---

* In the Archbishop's register Office in Vienna very interesting documents have lately been found, among the rest an account which F. Clement had written of his first arrival in Vienna and of the beginnings of the House at S. Bennone.

** It was not till 1798 that Clement was appointed by the Superior General, F. Blasucci, Vicar General of the transalpine provinces.

*** This was Monsignor Ferdinand M. Saluzzo, Duke of Corrigliano. Pius VI. had named him Archbishop of Carthagena, and after his return from Warsaw in 1793, he was made Delegate of Urbino, where he suffered very much from the French invasion. In 1801, Pius VI. created him Cardinal: but because he refused to assist at Napoleon's 2nd marriage, he was imprisoned in various cities of France. He died in Rome on the 3rd of Nov. 1816 and was buried in the Church of St. Anastasia.

mann, who was then on a pilgrimage to visit the Tombs of the three Kings of the Magi at Cologne. Great was their mutual joy at this unexpected meeting and finding that Clement was already a Priest, Emanuel implored his blessing. Clement perceiving in this a sign of Providential guidance, proposed to his friend to join the Congregation and follow them to Poland. Emanuel joyfully accepted the invitation and was the first novice north of the Alps.

As a man of experience and solid virtue, he rendered most invaluable services to our two Priests to whom he acted as laybrother. To prove how favourable was the impression produced by our three travellers, we will mention the following anecdote. On their way towards Znaim, which journey they performed on foot, they were joined by the Schoolmaster of Retz, who was driving on the same road. The weather and the roads were horrible; and when the good man saw these poor Priests on foot, he stopped and courteously invited them to come into his carriage and to lodge with him for the night, offering also to be their guide to Znaim the next morning. The weather being so bad, F. Clement gratefully accepted his offer. And his conversation and manner made such a favourable impression both on him and his family, that they felt convinced they had harboured a Saint and accordingly preserved as a relic everything that he had used on that occasion. The bed on which he slept was never used from that year 1786 to 1823; and only on that occasion by Father Udalric Petrak as an exceptional favour, because he had been Clement's disciple. They were delighted with a letter which Clement wrote to them from Znaim 12th of Oct. 1786 to thank them for their kindness, to assure them that he would always remember them in the Holy Sacrifice and to implore their prayers, so that he and his companions should faithfully fulfil the duties of their state. This letter to which Clement had added a little memento from the Holy House at Loreto and a picture of the Ven. F. Gennaro M. Sarnelli* was preserved by the family as a precious treasure. And so it happened that in the year 1864 when documents were sought for on all sides for the cause of F. Clement's Beatification, this letter was found carefully preserved by the descendants of that pious family, who likewise affirmed that a blessing from Heaven had fallen on their house from the hour of Clement's arrival.

From Znaim, Clement made a little detour to see his native country, to pay a visit to his sister Barbara, to pray over the tomb of his mother, who had died the year before to his great sorrow, and to offer the Holy Sacrifice for both his parents. Then he resumed his apostolic journey with his companions, which was the more fatiguing because it was done on foot and in the depth of a very severe winter, the snow being deep in many places. Finally, in February 1787, protected by their Angel Guardians, they arrived safely at Warsaw, the Polish Capital, which was to be the scene of their first labours.

CHAPTER II.

BEGINNING OF THE FOUNDATION IN WARSAW. THE STATE OF POLAND. THE FIRST DISCIPLES OF FATHER CLEMENT.

NO sooner had our Missioners arrived at Warsaw than they went to present their respects to, and receive instructions from the Nunzio. Monsg. Saluzzo being a Neapolitan, received the sons of St. Alphonsus Liguori with joy: and wishing to make more intimate acquaintance with them, he ordered them to remain in Warsaw till the end of the spring when their journey would be more easily accomplished.

* This was a celebrated Neapolitan Missionary and one of the first Companions of St. Alphonsus. He died in the odour of sanctity in the year 1744.

Very soon, the thousands of Germans who inhabited Warsaw made up their minds that they would do their utmost to keep them in that city. For the need of German Priests was urgent: as, since the suppression of the Jesuits, their National Church of St. Bennone was so deserted that not a single German Ecclesiastic could be found either to say mass or instruct the children, even in the rudiments of Catholic Doctrine.

They intended F. Clement, therefore, to remain with them altogether. He replied that he could not go from the orders of his Superior General. — Then they petitioned the Nunzio, the Bishop, and the Primate: and at last obtained leave for them to remain in Warsaw till the answer from the Superior General could be received. In the mean time, our two Fathers began to preach and administer the Sacraments in the German Church before mentioned of St. Bennone. King Stanislas having heard of their arrival, desired to see them and they were presented to him by the Nunzio. The Missioners made the most favourable impression upon the King and he was delighted with Clement's clear explanation of the object of the Redemptorist Congregation. At the end of the audience, the King expressed the strongest desire that they should remain in Warsaw and promised that his Government should protect them against all adversaries, and would provide for all their wants. He also promised them 5000 florins a year from his private purse: while the Germans undertook to make them an annual payment of 1500 florins. But our Lord, who wished to prove the virtue of His servants, allowed these fine promises to remain a dead letter: for in 1793 on the 23rd of May, we find F. Clement writing: "Our house is kept going by a miracle: for what we receive is so little that it scarcely suffices to pay for the candles, oil and wine of the Church. The King has not found himself in a position to fulfil his promises." And again, in 1800, he says: "The Confraternity of St. Bennone, who administer the revenues of the Church, have not paid us anything for six years, for the houses belonging to the Church are heavily mortgaged." —

In the mean time, the answer had come from Propaganda and from the Father General, giving leave for them to remain in Warsaw: so that the two Fathers were speedily put in possession of the Church of St. Bennone with the little house adjoining and could begin their work. Privations, fatigues and difficulties were not wanting, however in this new and humble foundation. Their whole fortune consisted in three Thalers; the little house had scarcely any furniture, and in fact, one table and two chairs, which they turned into beds, was all it contained! The walls were so damp besides that the water poured down them. The good laybrother Emanuel knew nothing of cooking, so that F. Clement had to help him. And very often he went straight from the kitchen into the Pulpit there to dispense the food of the Word of God. The very few necessary kitchen utensils had been borrowed: all except the spoons, which Clement had himself made out of wood. We must not fancy, however, that such utter poverty discouraged the good Fathers. On the contrary, they rejoiced in it for the love of God: feeling sure that as they were labouring for Him, He would not allow them to want the absolute necessaries of life ..

What distressed them far more than their own wants, was the miserable state in which they found religion in Poland. The spirit of infidelity, always hostile to the Church, had there made frightful progress. The license under the name of liberty which the Protestants had obtained from Catherine the 2nd of Russia, had annihilated that which had been Poland's greatest strength — namely, the salutary influence which Catholicism had exercised on the public life of the State. Jansenist and Gallican doctrines had likewise crept into Poland, alienating men's minds from the Holy See, and depriving them of the frequent reception of the Sacraments, that inexhaustible source of grace and virtue. Throughout Poland also, Freemasonry had been established: and inscribed on its books were the names of some of the oldest nobility, ministers of state and Priests. German Philosophy without God was glorified into pure Science: the works of Voltaire, Rousseau and other French writers of the same stamp were eagerly read: while good books of any sort were almost impossible to obtain; nor was there any library or bookseller who cared to provide volumes for which there was no sale. With the decay of Faith there was an equal decay in morals. The bad examples given by the nobility had been copied by the commercial classes. Sensual pleasures and religious indifference characterised the whole population of Warsaw. Father Clement's writing on the 23nd of May 1793, thus expressed himself: "Scandalous vices have nowhere come to such a pitch as in this city. From (even) the Priesthood down to the poorest beggar, all are corrupt and I see no hope of amendment. I fear lest God should '*remove their candlestick out of its place*'. Let us pray that they may repent before it be too late!" Prophetic words which were but too abundantly fulfilled in the destruction of the Kingdom of Poland the following year. —

Equally sad, in a political sense, was the condition of the nobility. With refined cunning Catherine had managed to create a Russian party among the Polish magnates, which sowed disunion in their camp. The King himself was without character or energy and more anxious to flatter Catherine's caprices than to be mindful of the welfare of his subjects. Add to this, the discontent produced in the country by the cession of territory to the neighbouring states; as the predominant feeling in the mind of every Pole is hatred of foreigners and especially of those in whose favour the cession had been made. Above all, the secret societies fanned the flame, so that the disunion soon had still more serious consequences.

We can easily imagine, then, the difficulties of Clement's position. As an Apostle and a Religious, he was a special thorn in the eyes of the atheists; as a foreigner he was an object of scandal to the false patriots; and so much so, that for a long time not a single Pole would come near them: so that the poor "*Bennonites*" (as the Redemptorists were called, from the name of their church) were declared more than once to be Lutherans! —

They remained, therefore, in this great city* as in the midst of a hostile camp. The calumnies and persecutions of every sort which rained upon them at this time, grieved Clement less for himself than for his companions, some of whom were not yet inured to such sufferings. He wrote in May of that year, that, several times, he was on the point of leaving Warsaw and returning to Italy: but was deterred by the Nunzio, who always implored him to persevere and to bear his trials courageously. Clement was, at last, persuaded that it was God's will that he should go on striving to cultivate this wild and neglected Vineyard. And this intimate conviction strengthened his faith in God — for, as his friend F. Frederick Rinn asserted, it was enough to say to him: "*This is God's will*" for Clement to brave every obstacle and face enemies however numerous. Notwithstanding all these difficulties, however, our missioners' work among their neighbours began to tell and to bring forth abundant fruit: so much so that Clement himself wrote "that in desiring them to remain, the Nunzio had followed a Divine inspiration". —

The extreme poverty in which the work was begun did

---

* Warsaw contained at that time 124,000 inhabitants, among whom were 28,000 Jews. In 1798 it was made the seat of a Bishop, as before, it had been under the Archbishop of Gnesna, Primate of Poland, who governed it by means of an Archdeacon invested with the dignity of Vicar General.

not last, as God raised up friends and benefactors to come to their assistance and so unlimited was Clement's confidence in God, that, on one occasion, being in grievous straits, he threw himself down before the Tabernacle and knocking at the door, implored the help of Our Lord. At the very same moment, a gentleman came and presented him with a large sum of money. Having thus proved the faith of His Servant, God not only provided him with what was needful for his Congregation, but with sufficient means to relieve the poor and to repair the poor little ruined house in which they had lodged for 14. years. To this work, many contributed — some giving even their manual labour — so that before long a spacious building was erected enough not only to accomodate the growing Community, but also to carry on other works which Clement was about to start.

To enlarge the Church, which, at first, would only hold about a 1000 persons, he built, in 1801, a large side Chapel to which you ascended by twelve steps: so that by degrees the Services could be better performed. The original Church of St. Bennone, placed on a little hill at the end of what was called the "New City", was built in the 17th Century by Ladislaus IV. and his wife Cecilia Renata. There were three Altars: over the principal one was a statue of St. Bennone, Bishop of Misnia and Apostle of the Slavs: but as it had been injured by time, F. Clement replaced it by a fine picture of the Saint. Below was a little picture of the Blessed Virgin, under the title of "Mary Help of Christians". One of the other Altars was dedicated to St. Joseph, whom Clement had chosen as Patron of the House and whom he looked upon as his advocate on every occasion. Upon this Altar, according to the Feasts of the day, he exposed other pictures, such as that of Our Holy Redeemer, of St. Michael, St. Raphael, etc. The third altar was dedicated to our Lord and there a Statue representing Jesus bound to the column was a very favourite object of devotion to the people.

In the new Side Chapel which he had built, Clement placed a very fine picture of Jesus of Nazareth and another of the Mother of Dolours, which had been sent him from Vienna.

Such was the Church in which, for so many years, Clement exercised the sacred functions of the ministry. But alas! it has now been converted into a workshop and no trace remains of the former Sanctuary: while instead of the voices of prayer and praise no sound is now heard within its walls save the reverberation of hammers and the noise of machinery.

As neither F. Clement nor F. Thaddeus were well versed in the Polish language, they called in two or three Polish Priests to their aid. The German Priests were only six in number: but so zealous and so edifying was their conduct, that the Nunzio could not find words strong enough to express his admiration of their merit. The King and the Senate were equally delighted: and in consequence the new Congregation was formally acknowledged, in 1793, as a Religious Corporation. —

Among this little body, F. Clement was the first Rector and F. Iestersheim, a native of Silesia, was Minister; and being an excellent musician, he had also the charge of the Choir. Later on, Clement named F. Thaddeus as Rector; and after his death, F. Iestersheim. This Father was most highly esteemed by Clement, who proposed him, in 1808, as his Successor in the post of Vicar General. —

The two laybrothers, Emanuel Kunzmann and Matthew Widhalm, were also men of rare virtue. The latter had known Clement in Vienna and had come on purpose to join the Congregation at Warsaw: but when he arrived at St. Bennone he was seized with such trepidation, that he almost made up his mind to retrace his steps then and there, without even seeing F. Clement. By a special internal warning, Clement became aware of this and hastened to meet him and lead him into the house. This was enough to remove all hesitation from Matthew's mind: and he at once asked to be admitted into the Congregation. He was always an exemplary laybrother, followed the missioners to Bucharest, was greatly beloved by his superior (who called him the "*Holy Father*"), and finally closed a life full of merit in the Redemptorist House in Vienna, in 1826.

The first Pole who was admitted into the Congregation was John Dukla Podgorski whom Clement speaks of as a youth of singular piety, extraordinary talent and equal innocence. Later on (1799) he praises his ardour for religious perfection and his zeal in preaching and hearing confessions. He made his vows in 1794, and in 1797 was ordained priest. But before that, Clement had made him preach constantly, and from his great readiness of speech and extraordinary talent, his sermons produced extraordinary fruit. When the Congregation was suppressed in Poland, F. Podgorski was transferred to Vienna, where his distinguished qualities attracted the notice of the Nunzio, who proposed him as Bishop of Bucharest. And he would have been compelled to accept it if he had not, by earnest entreaties, induced the Nunzio to desist from his proposal.

In the same letter (of the 22nd of July 1799) Clement praises also his subdeacon, Michael Sadowski.

Another Pole, Charles Blumenau[*], made his religious profession in 1796. And several other Poles followed his example. So that Clement was able to dispense with the services of the secular priests and appoint his own religious Sons to all the necessary offices.

In 1799, the Community of St. Bennone amounted to 25 persons of whom 9 were priests: two deacons, 2 subdeacons, 3 clerical students, 2 novices, and 7 laybrothers. The number of priests was not greater, because

---

[*] He was born in Warsaw and his real name was Kwiatzowski, which, translated into German, was Blumenau or Blumenauer.

some had been sent to Mietau, and three had died in 1796, besides, one deacon. Their deaths were a heavy blow to Clement, for they were all men eminent for learning and piety. Writing to his Superior General at that time he says: "These faithful servants have doubtless received their reward: but we are consumed with grief. Such, however, is evidently God's Will".

In 1795, a French novice joined the Redemptorists who was destined to succeed Clement as Vicar General and render most important services to the Congregation. Joseph Passerat was born on the 30th of April, 1792, at Joinville in Champagne and made his first studies in the seminary of Chalons sur Marne. He was going in for Theology when the Revolution of 1790 broke out. He was first thrown into prison and then taken out solely to serve in the Republican Army, where from his great height, he was appointed drum-major and quarter-master. This forced service was the more painful to him from the fact that he was compelled to witness all the excesses of the revolutionary army. As soon as he could, therefore, he deserted and fled over the frontier, arriving in Germany and continuing his studies at Treves, Münster and Würzburg. In this last city he heard of Clement and his Congregation; and by a sudden inspiration felt that his vocation lay with the Redemptorists and hastened to Warsaw, where he was admitted, in 1795, professed the next year and, in 1797, was ordained priest. He became one of Clement's best subjects and most devoted friends and we shall constantly find him referred to in this biography. The other three Frenchmen became also zealous and admirable Religious: but all died in the prime of life, very few years after their reception into the Congregation. We have only here mentioned one or two of Clement's most eminent companions in Warsaw. But in speaking of the whole community on the 31st of December 1796, he writes: "They make equal progress in virtue as in science;

and it is permitted to hope that through the grace of God, they will do great works both for the glory of God and the good of souls: and be an honour besides to the Congregation".

Nor is it to be wondered at that such were Clement's first disciples; as it was his extraordinary zeal that animated, his fire that inflamed, and his example that encouraged them in every good work.

CHAPTER III.

HIS APOSTOLIC WORKS IN WARSAW. HE FOUNDS AN ORPHANAGE. HIS PROFUSE CHARITY TOWARDS THE POOR.

WE have mentioned that St. Bennone was the National Church of the Germans and that Clement had undertaken to provide for their spiritual wants. But he did not intend to confine his labours to them. His charity embraced all needs: and whenever there was a want or a misery, there he hastened to bring relief. He made himself "all things to all men" that he might win them to Christ, while his magnificent charities gained the hearts of the most obdurate sinners. The wonderful thing was how he contrived to do so much in so short a time and with such small means.

In the year 1794, he was an eye-witness of the burning of one of the suburbs by the Russian general, Suwarow, whose barbarous troops massacred upwards 20 thousand persons, men, women and children. The house of St. Bennone was just in front of this suburb and near the Vistula: and so the poor Religious had to watch these horrors without being able to alleviate them and with the additional dread of being themselves included in the universal ruin. The shells rained upon Warsaw: but luckily, though St. Bennone was three times struck, none of the shells burst. F. Clement lifted up his heart to God in this emergency, imploring Him to spare the city and promising to make a pilgrimage to the shrine of St. John Nepomucen in Prague if his prayer were granted. Our Lord hearkened to the pleadings of His faithful servant. Warsaw remained intact; and F. Clement kept his vow the following year.

But the burning of the suburb and the miseries of the siege had left hundreds of orphan children dying of hunger in the streets. This sight so moved Clement's heart that he resolved at once to open a home for these poor little abandoned creatures trusting in the Providence of God to find means for their support; and thus to provide for the wants both of their souls and bodies. It was a beautiful sight to see him receiving these poor children, washing them himself and doing for them all the little services that a mother would have done. And when their ever increasing numbers made their maintenance a matter of enormous difficulty, he did not hesitate to turn beggar, from house to house, in order to obtain additional funds. One day he went into an inn where he found several men gambling. He pleaded for his orphans; some of the players looked up and in answer, insolently spit in his face. The servant of God, without appearing offended at this insult, quietly took out his handkerchief and wiped his face and then said: "That was for me — now do me the favour to give me something else for my poor children". Such self-command and deep humility confounded the miscreant, who hastened to make amends by giving him a large sum, while he published everywhere the heroic gentleness of F. Clement, who ended by converting him entirely and becoming his confessor.

If he were anxious about their temporal welfare, still more was he about the spiritual condition of his adopted children. He gathered them round him continually and spent hours in telling them Bible stories and in impressing upon them the holy fear and love of God. At other times he would lead them into the church, and making them kneel before the image of Our Lady would teach them to say this little ejaculatory prayer: "O! Mary, my Mother, if thou wilt pray for me, I shall be saved".

When they were old enough to be taught a trade he opened workshops and got masters to teach them: but those who showed a talent for study and a vocation for religious life he placed among the younger students of the Congregation, so that their future was provided for in all ways. Nor did his charity confine itself to the boys. The orphan girls were equally provided for under the care of Sisters, to whom he gave a simple rule and who looked after the Christian education of these poor little ones.

In fact, towards the poor of every kind and sort his ingenious charity knew no bounds. He relieved those who came to the door with food and clothing: but he visited himself the sick and destitute in their own homes, especially those who had seen better days: and many people gave him large sums to distribute in this manner, for he one day wrote: "If all the money which was given to me in Warsaw to spend among the poor were put into a sack, it would come to so large a sum that no man would be able to carry it!"

Very often, however, the Father Minister, whose business it was to look after the temporalities, was in despair at his extraordinary liberality and would venture to remonstrate at the amount of his expenditure, which often exceeded their means. But his holy Superior would laughingly say: "*Date et dabitur*", these two words are twin sisters. "Be not anxious for the morrow. God will provide". He was specially desirous to increase this holy confidence in God in the minds of his priests and used to say: "Nothing will be wanting to a priest who does his duty: and if there were but one loaf in all the world, God would give him half of it."

In proportion as his charities increased, so did he win the confidence and affection of the people. The confessionals became crowded with penitents, and the sermons, which were preached both in German and Polish, were eagerly listened to.

Father Clement writing in August 1800 says: "The Feast of our Holy Redeemer was kept this year with unusual solemnity and a mission of eight days followed, closed by the Papal Benediction. On this occasion, the Benediction was given by F. Hübl, who preached for the first time in Polish. The people were so moved that several times their sobs compelled the preacher to stop and the crowd was such that the church would not hold half of them."

Six years only after the opening of the house, the Nunzio writing to the Father-General said:

"I can assure your Reverence, for your consolation, that among all existing Religious orders, your Congregation have distinguished themselves beyond all others, not only for their zeal tempered with prudence; but for the extraordinary amount of conversions which have attended their labours."

The increase in the number of the communicants was another proof of the success of their work. They amounted to 48,000 in 1799—1800. And the year before the dispersion of the Congregation, (in 1807) the number amounted to 104,000 and would have been even more numerous, wrote the Superior General, "had the church been larger and the number of priests greater."

From all parts of the city and from the neighbouring country places people were continually coming to St. Bennone for spiritual help; so that it may be said to have served as a perpetual mission. We will here give the order of the day in that church, which kept the Fathers at work from 5 in the morning till 8 at night, save for the dinner-hour and subsequent short recreation.

At 5 in the morning after the general meditation, a certain number of the Fathers repaired to the confessional, while one of the younger ones gave catechism to the servant class. Then followed a High Mass, during which time the people sang devout hymns in Polish. After mass a sermon was preached in the same language, generally by F. Blumenauer, whose preaching produced extraordinary fruits, the people hanging, as it were, upon his words. He used to take as his text the Gospel of the preceding Sunday: and as he preached almost every day, a complete course of instruction was thus given on dogmatic and moral doctrines. After a second High Mass in which the hymns were generally sung in Latin by the Sisters of St. Joseph, Father Clement himself would go into the pulpit and preach in German, his attractive, winning manner gaining the hearts of his hearers in a most extraordinary manner. He chose the epistles as his text and explained them with such clearness and precision as to dissipate every doubt. Sometimes, in order to rouse the attention of the audience, he would turn to one or others of the students who were present and ask them a question: but as he had always previously suggested an answer, there was no fear of their failing or being ashamed to reply. This likewise doubled the attention of the students: and he would reward them by promising them a remembrance in his mass. Whilst F. Clement was preaching to the Germans F. Thaddeus said mass in a side Chapel for the Poles. The last solemn mass, unless a Bishop or some other Prelate were present, was always sung by F. Clement. And as many eminent singers both professional and amateur, offered their services, the music every day was excellent.

At $1/_23$. the Services were renewed by a second sermon in German, followed by vespers (sung) and by exposition of the Blessed Sacrament. Then the Germans having gone out to make room for the Poles, Father Podgorski preached in their language on eternal truths, and that with such vigour as to fill his audience with a horror of vice and an admiration of all Christian virtues. Then followed the Via Crucis or way of the Cross, which was said in German on Festivals and in Polish on other days, ending with the Benediction of the Most Holy Sacrament. The day closed with a public examination of conscience and a recitation, with the people, of the acts of Faith, Hope, Charity and Contrition. But to strengthen their faith and piety still further, F. Clement started several Confraternities. One of them, which was specially for the young and included both boys and girls, was placed under the Patronage of St. Joseph. Clement drew up certain simple rules suited to their state and position; and was rewarded by witnessing an extraordinary increase in consequence of piety and good conduct among its members. These Confraternities gladly joined in all the processions on solemn feasts, such as the Assumption, the Patronage of St. Joseph, the Feast of our Holy Redeemer, etc. On Corpus Christi or the Sunday after, the Procession went outside the church. Fifty children dressed in white and bearing torches followed, and on such days there was a General Communion of all the Members of the Confraternities. F. Clement multiplied himself on such occasions, preaching, singing High Mass, giving Holy Communion, regulating the processions and finally giving Benediction of the Blessed Sacrament. But it was specially on the Feast of Corpus Christi that St. Bennone was in all its glory. F. Clement himself superintended the lighting of the church and the disposal of the flowers, and he had enlisted the services and enthusiasm of all the ladies in Warsaw, so that they gladly contributed towards the expenses. A troop of children dressed as angels, spread flowers before the B. Sacrament, while twelve priests incensed it and other children dressed as Cherubims marched on each side of the magnificent Baldachino (a present of the ladies which had cost upwards of six thousand Francs in gold) under which was borne the King of Glory. All the fathers dressed in beautiful chasubles, as in Rome, immediately preceded the Blessed Sacrament: and before the Procession, F. Clement in German and F. Blumenauer in Polish made a little allocution to the people on the glories of the Festival.

It would be difficult to describe the joy of F. Clement at thus seeing his most earnest wishes fulfilled. This church once so deserted now so overcrowded! he, beginning with one only companion, now surrounded with fervent priests and Religious of his own order! and the inhabitants of Warsaw, once so tepid and indifferent, now so zealous and filled with such holy enthusiasm!! O! how good is God towards those whose heart is in the right place! And how wonderfully were the humble aspirations of the poor Vienna baker, the poor Tivoli hermit, answered by the Divine Clemency of Him who moulds all human agencies according to His will!

CHAPTER IV.

OTHER APOSTOLIC LABOURS IN POLAND. F. CLEMENT'S ACCOUNT OF THE LAMENTABLE STATE OF RELIGION IN THAT COUNTRY.

A good number of Frenchmen had come to Warsaw in consequence of the war and the Revolution and these were as sheep without a shepherd till F. Clement undertook their care and sent them a preacher in their own language whom Providence, as we have seen, had sent to the Congregation as if on purpose for this work.

The Prussian Protestants were his next care. They were attracted by the beautiful music at St. Bennone and also by Clement's preaching. Many came to him afterwards for a solution of their doubts and difficulties and were received into the Church. At last their numbers increased so much that the house was not large enough to hold them and F. Clement had to hire a large room outside for their instruction.

Even the Jews were moved to enquiring into the Doctrines of the Catholic Church and for this work F. Lenoir was appointed, as he was an excellent Hebrew Scholar and well versed in the Talmud. Many, in consequence, petitioned for the grace of Baptism and were received into the true Fold.

In 1796, the Redemptorist Fathers untertook the great church of the "Holy Cross in the Fields", which was much frequented by the people in the neighbourhood. The Prussian Government wished to give it up to the Protestants: so that the Archbishop hastened to make it over to the new Congregation with its revenues. As it was not far from St. Bennone the Fathers could live in community and only go there to say mass and administer the sacraments. Every year they likewise gave a great public retreat to the people in the Church of St. Andrew, at which a very large number of the faithful assisted.

After the suppression of the Jesuits in Poland, missions had ceased altogether. This was a great anxiety to F. Clement who had them much at heart; so that after many fervent prayers and great exertions, he obtained leave from the Prussian Government in 1801 to give them again under the name of *"Public Instructions"*, as the word *"Mission"* or *"Retreat"* sounded terrible in anti-Catholic ears. The result was that in that same year, three missions were given by the Fathers, one in Warsaw; one (in October) in the Provinces; and another in November at a place about 15 leagues from Warsaw. F. Clement wrote on the 19th of Decbr. 1801, speaking "of the extraordinary fruit of these missions, which exceeded all expectation". We will give an account of one of them.

Father Thaddeus, five other missioners and one laybrother started one day for the parish where they had been sent by order of the Bishop and under the authority of the senator, Count Lasocki. The Parish Priest, however, did not conceal his aversion to their proceedings: but the missioners, trusting in the intercession of the Blessed Virgin, went calmly on, not doubting that her power would destroy the machinations of the enemy of souls. And so it happened; for after the first sermon, the Parish Priest hastened to the Missioners' House, threw himself at their feet and burst into tears. Then he confessed his previous hostility and implored their pardon, which the Fathers gave instantly, sending him home happy and consoled. From that moment all hearts were changed and the mission produced extraordinary fruits. The devil endeavoured, however, in a variety of ways to hinder the good done. On one occasion as the missioner was preparing the people for a General Communion, an extraordinary cry was heard, as of a child being strangled. Every one turned round to see where the child was, but there was not one in the church. After about half an hour, quiet was restored and the solemn act was reverently and devoutly concluded. Another time, the cry arose: "A woman with child has been crushed in the crowd!" and this being disproved, a fresh cry arose: "That the Church was in flames". And a dense smoke seemed to issue from the beams. But when the roof was examined, there was not a trace either of fire or smoke. By a merciful interposition of Providence, no one was hurt, in spite of the panic and the great crowd; and every one being reassured, the General Communion was made with extraordinary devotion. At 3 o'clock of that same day, which was the Sunday after the 13th of November, when they were keeping the Feast of St. Stanislas Kotska, the Congregation were consoled by a wonderful sight. The altar of St. Joseph seemed suddenly enveloped in a cloud and a vision of Our Lady appeared in the midst, bright with light and of heavenly sweetness. Not only the poor people, but Count Lasocki and the priests all witnessed this consoling apparition; and nothing broke the intense and silent admiration of the witnesses, save sighs and whispered invocations of the name of Mary.

After about an hour, the beautiful vision disappeared, leaving an ineffable feeling of consolation in the hearts of the people. This mission lasted a whole month, and upwards of 11,000 persons received Holy Communion. Until the suppression of the Congregation, these missions were continued. And so extraordinary was the effect they produced, that a Polish Canon, seventy years after the expulsion of the Redemptorists, attested that the good results of them were still visible in all the localities where they had been given and of which the tradition had been religiously preserved in spite of the many subsequent revolutions.

It may be easily imagined, however, that every one did not approve of Father Clement's proceedings and thought his zeal imprudent and excessive. The Superior General considered it right to make some observations to him on this subject which Clement answered as follows, (1799 to 1800): "Our works in this city have been singularly blessed by God. The Government not permitting formal missions in the city, we have undertaken in our church what may be called a perpetual mission ..... If your Reverence could see with your own eyes the miserable state of religion in this depraved city, you would not wonder at the frequency of our sermons, but rather wish us to preach more. Nor must you fancy that we thereby weary our Congregation. It would be so in other countries: but here, the anxiety to hear the Word of God is ever increasing, in proportion as men realise more vividly the difficulty of saving their souls in the midst of such perils. The Bishops have their hands tied and do not dare act without the permission of the Political Council, which is composed of the scum of the earth, of men without any faith whatever, who remain quiet spectators of the gravest scandals and even favour and encourage them, provided only the taxes be paid and no fresh revolution breaks out. Only the other day, a religious threw off his habit and married, without even saying a syllable to his superior: two others soon followed his example; while a fourth has given the unheard-of scandal of becoming a Jew. All the laws of religion and morality are violated with impunity and the corruption is universal .... But if the poor pastor cannot keep the wolf from his fold, at least his dogs can bark to give warning of the danger. This we are doing, with the help of God, and the numbers who crowd the church are incredible and increase daily. The greater proportion are of course, of the lower orders, but the nobles are now beginning to come likewise".

In another letter of the 1st of Oct. 1801 he writes again: "The fame of our instructions, preachings and catechisms has spread even to Moscow, and throughout Russia, even to Siberia. The fruits of this are incalculable. Not only the people of the town, but from all parts of the country and even from distant provinces, persons come for five, six or eight days, hear the word of God, receive the sacraments, and go back to their homes strengthened and comforted by God's grace" ... Again he writes: "With the exception of the Missioners of St. Vincent of Paul, and certain Franciscans, named "*Recollects*", the other priests in Warsaw only preach once a week and that in a way the people cannot understand. Certain Jansenists from France crept in some years ago and brought with them a species of rigorism, deterring the people from coming to the sacraments ... And this is the more unfortunate, because they have the largest parishes in the city. But after having assisted at our Missions two or three times, I am thankful to say they are beginning to give up their system and adopt ours."

In the same strain, Monsg. Litta,[*] first Nunzio at Warsaw,

---

[*] Lorenzo, Marquis Litta of Milano, was born on the 23rd of Feb. 1756. He was created Archbishop of Thebes by Pius VI: and in 1793 sent as Nunzio to Warsaw. In the midst of the fearful political struggles in that unhappy Country Litta showed extraordinary prudence and courage. With Kosciusko, he pleaded the cause of the innocent Bishop of Chelma who had been condemned to death and would have saved the Bishops of Liefland and

and then at St. Petersburgh, writes to the Superior General (18th of January 1800): "On my return to St. Petersburg, I passed by Warsaw, where I stayed more than a month. I found the House of the Redemptorists even more flourishing than before, with a constant increase of good works, a wonderful success in preaching and in the administration of the Sacraments and an extraordinary influx of people. Father Clement is the most apostolic man I have ever met, full of zeal for the glory of God and of charity for the salvation of souls. He works miracles by the grace of God. To give you an idea of his labours, I must tell you that the church is thronged day after day from five in the morning till late at night: and from morning till night, he is always hearing confessions, or preaching, or saying mass, or giving instructions, ending always with Benediction. They preach four times a day at St. Bennone — twice in Polish and twice in German — and each time the church is filled up to the very doors. I am not exaggerating! It is an extraordinary sight and the great blessing is, that it seems entirely to have transformed the habits of the people. Perhaps your Reverence may think what they do is more than enough? But you would not think so if you saw the enormous needs of this poor country, where no one else, seems to think of labouring in our Lord's Vineyard. I should not dare advise those good and holy Fathers to leave off one single work,

Wilna, if he had had notice in time of their sad fate. The Polish Kingdom being destroyed, he was sent as Ambassador to Moscow to assist at the Coronation of Paul I. Then he was created Nuncio at St. Petersburg where he provided for the wants of the Catholics there who formed 6 dioceses of the Latin rite and 3 of the United Greek. He was in Venice at the time of the Conclave in March 1800: and was made Cardinal by Pius VII. the next year. Driven from Rome, he was imprisoned in various towns of France, till he returned in triumph to Rome with the Pope, in May 1814. He was then first made Prefect of the Propaganda and afterwards Cardinal Vicar. He died in 1820 during a Pastoral Visitation in the Sabina. Six weeks before, Father Clement had passed to a better life, having always kept up a correspondence with him, of which unhappily, no trace can be found.

seeing that each brings forth such wonderful fruit: I should fear to oppose myself to the will of God and spoil His work. If you could only obtain in Germany a Seminary such as F. Hofbauer so earnestly desires, there is no doubt that the good done in the North would be even greater". Such an opinion from such an authority could not fail to carry weight.

CHAPTER V.

His indefatiguable Zeal for the diffusion of good books, and especially of the works of St. Alphonsus.

AMONG its other miseries, Poland, at the time of which we are writing, was inundated with bad books. Every impious or immoral publication in France or Germany was, either in the original or in translations, disseminated throughout the country: and unfortunately to console themselves for the ruin of their country, the Poles took pleasure in these readings which corrupted their morals while it destroyed their faith.

But Clement, as usual, had a remedy for the evil. First, he preached vigorously against the pernicious maxims and principles of the works in question, exposing their sophisms, and putting his hearers on their guard against them. Next, he determined to provide good substitutes for these bad books, and founded a Congregation called "Mariana", whose members were employed mainly in distributing innocent and yet amusing publications.* Then to revive the spirit of Christian piety among his flock, he wisely determined to place

* The venerable superior of the Salesians in Kaminiek, Maria Cecilia di Cholomiewska, was driven by the Russian Police from her Convent and had to take refuge in Lemberg. She wrote an account of this work of F. Clement's in Warsaw, which was incorporated among the papers employed in the cause of his beatification. She was born in 1786 and was therefore 93 years old, but her memory was still fresh. She died in 1881.

in their hands the works of St. Alphonsus. A good many of these works had already been translated into German.

In 1757, a Jesuit Father had translated his "*Visits to the Blessed Sacrament,*" and two years later his "*Practice of the Love of Jesus Christ*". Another Jesuit, F. Ignatius Neubauer, translated "*The Truth of Faith*" and says in his preface: "That Bishop Liguori was one of those learned writers whom God had specially raised up to defend the faith." Father Hyper, a Benedictine of Wessobrun in the Diocese of Augsburgh, had likewise translated from his work on "Nuns", all that was most useful for pious Christians: while a secular priest of the same diocese, Peter Obladen, had reproduced in German a quantity of extracts from the Bishop's works on the Priesthood. Father Clement employed one of his Religious, F. Thaddeus Hübl, to make a fresh translation of his "*Visit to the Blessed Sacrament*", and "*Love of Souls*" which he distributed gratuitously; while, for the Poles, he employed F. Podgorski, in a like manner: and a Parish priest, Dominic Waluszewicz, at the same time translated St. Alphonsus' Sermons for the benefit of the Clergy. Great was Clement's joy when the Prince Bishop of Plok, Michael Poniatowski, (brother of King Stanislas and Primate of Gnesen), wrote a pastoral, strongly recommending the moral theology of St. Alphonsus; which gave double weight to the exhortations of the humble Redemptorist.

There was another person who greatly assisted F. Clement in propagating the works of his Founder, and that was Father Joseph Albert Diesbach, of the suppressed Society of Jesus and Clement's intimate friend, of whom we will now say a few words. Diesbach was the son of a noble family in Berne, of a Calvinist Sect and was born on the 15th of Febr. 1732. At 15. he entered the service of the King of Sardinia and soon obtained the rank of captain in a Swiss Regiment, of which his uncle, the Count of Diesbach, was the Commanding Officer.

Certain Catholic books having fallen into his hands, he discovered the errors of Calvinism which he soon after abjured in the Jesuit College of Turin. Very soon after, he was summoned to the Court of King Charles Emanuel, to instruct his son Victor Amedeus II. in the art of war. About that time he married: but on the death of his young wife, he made up his mind to join the Society of Jesus which he entered in 1759 and soon distinguished himself by his zeal and great ability in preaching. It was his business to instruct Princess Elisabeth of Würtemberg in the Catholic Faith, who afterwards became the wife of the Emperor Francis; and also to warn Princess Charlotte, daughter of Victor Emanuel, against the errors of Protestantism, as she was betrothed to the King of Saxony. Among his published letters, there is an important one addressed to Leopold, when he was called from Tuscany to fill the Austrian throne, which the death of Joseph the 2nd had left vacant. In this letter he shows the enormous harm arising to the Church from secret societies and false philosophies and the miserable state to which the Empire was reduced by the absurd pretensions of his predecessor, Joseph II. Then he shows the way in which the evil may be remedied and ends with these frank words: "When this present life shall have disappeared like a flash of lightening before you and me; when the irresistible flight of time shall have brought us face to face with eternity; when, in the sight of God, we shall witness with stupefaction a new order of things, such as our dim but Divine Faith has darkly shown us here, these great and eternal Truths will exist for ever and will shine in the brightness of the only True Light. Then, shall we clearly see the perishable nature of all the goods of this world and the supreme majesty of God: the ineffable and eternal rewards of the good and the never ending torments of the wicked. Then we shall understand that there is nothing to be desired by a man save this: to be a living and faithful member of the Church of Jesus Christ, the sole depository of Divine Authority and the only power which can bind or loose human souls for all eternity. Therefore, the only true wisdom, O! King Leopold, consists in this: to honor this truth and to hold it in the highest esteem far above all earthly considerations. After all, what will it profit a man if he should gain the whole world and lose his own soul?"

Clement, writing of his friend Diesbach, says: "That in Switzerland he had converted innumerable souls, Waldensians, Calvinists, Zwinglians and others. And that he was universally called "The Apostle of the Alps". He was intimately acquainted with the venerable Alphonsus Liguori and held him in the highest veneration. After the suppression of the Society, he continued his missionary labourers as long as his corporal strength remained. He was as much distinguished for his learning as for his eminent virtue. Often, in my presence, I have heard him declare, that, after the suppression of the Jesuits, God had raised up Alphonsus, that he might he as an invincible wall against the enemies of the Church, to defend the purity of doctrine and the rights of the Holy See." — F. Tannoia also writes of Diesbach: "That he had contributed more than any one to make the theology of St. Alphonsus well known in Switzerland, France and Germany. He especially prized his ascetic works, considering them as filled with the spirit of God.

He distributed them in every direction, had them translated into several languages and recommended them every where as promoting true Christian piety among the People."

Diesbach had the glory of suffering martyrdom for our Lord's sake; for being employed at Court as Tutor to the Emperor Leopold's sons, certain evil disposed persons, dreading his authority, determined to get rid of him. They consequently hired certain ruffians, who waylaid and beat him so severely that he died a few days after in the ordour of Sanctity, i. e. on the 24th of Decbr. 1798. He was buried in the Cemetery of Maria-Enzersdorf and Father Clement on his return to Vienna hastened to visit his tomb and earnestly wished himself to be buried by his side, as appears in the process of his cause. Another Jesuit F. Louis Virginio, Rector of the Italian Church in Vienna, was equally anxious to promote the study of the works of St. Alphonsus. Virginio was for many years Clement's constant correspondent and the medium for his receiving communications from Rome and Naples.

CHAPTER VI.

THE REDEMPTORISTS IN COURLAND AND IN OTHER STATIONS OF POLAND.

[From 1795 to 1807.]

WE may remember that Father Clement had been destined for Courland by the S. Congregation of Propaganda, when he was stopped at Warsaw by the orders of the Nunzio and the King. The Bishop of Livonia most earnestly desired the advent of the Redemptorists; but F. Clement was unable to send any the first few years owing to the small number of his Religious. He wrote on the 29th of Decbr. 1794: "For more than five years the Bishop goes on imploring me to send some Fathers to Mietau in Courland. After the suppression of the Jesuits, who had a large establishment there, there was only one Catholic church left and one solitary priest, in the midst of that vast protestant and schismatic population: and yet the Catholics are very numerous! There would, therefore, be a vast field for work: but I fear to advance further north. The Parish Priest, who is also Vicar General, seems well-disposed towards us. and has set aside 50 Hungarian sequins for the expenses of the journey. But I have only two very young Fathers, whom I should send very unwillingly a hundred miles away from me! I would rather establish a novitiate in Germany and when France becomes quieter, I should like to establish a House there, where I have many friends who are very anxious to see the Redemptorists settled in France."

A little later, however, he received a letter from Goldberger, the zealous parish Priest of Mietau, imploring him to reconsider his decision, and not to let him die without having this consolation, while offering to procure the necessary passports from St. Petersburg for his Fathers.

This letter touched F. Clement very much, and he submitted it to the Father General. He adds: "I leave the decision in your Reverence's hands. It cannot be denied that there is a vast field for work for the glory of God and the good of souls. In the single town of Mietau, there are 7000 Catholics, and 42 Catholic parishes in the province. The faithful have scarcely any means of obtaining the Sacraments; and the priest has to travel 15 or 20 miles to administer the sick and dying. Since the suppression of the Jesuits there is no Catholic school. The only thing which makes me hesitate is, that I must send experienced Fathers from here and I have no one to replace them. The Primate of Poland, who lately died in the most holy dispositions, had already signed a Letter of recommendation to the Duke of Courland: and the Nunzio has given us, in writing, all the faculties and privileges which can be assigned to missionaries in Protestant Countries. The people of this Country are besides well disposed to accept the Truth. That good Parish Priest, who for 40 years, has laboured singlehanded in this Vineyard, says that the heretics are so ripe for conversion that in one day more than a hundred abjured their errors. I, therefore, implore your Reverence to tell me without delay what you think will be best before God. *And I will try with all my might to carry out whatever proposal you may devise for the promotion of God's glory, the propagation of Holy Church, and the welfare of so many precious souls.*"

On the 1st of April 1795 Clement received the answer from the Father General approving of the proposed new Mission and desiring him to send the Fathers without delay. Clement was delighted: "for", he exclaimed, "the will of God in this matter is clear as the noonday sun and it would be a great sin to resist any longer."

His only despair was, the immense difficulty of finding fresh subjects for the missions. In Poland, Catholic studies had so terribly declined that no one would choose the ecclesiastical state. The young men were ruined in the atheist Colleges and the clergy were looked down upon by the majority of the students.

Hence Clement's great anxiety to establish a noviciate in Germany, where there was a better chance of vocations. As to the Fathers to be sent to Mietau, Clement writes: "I am sending Father John Rudolph whose solid virtue and prudence I have known for 7 years, and with him, F. Joseph Wichert, whom the Nunzio ordained priest, and the Polish Cleric Kaminski." On the 15th of Septbr. 1795 he writes from Prague: "I have very consoling letters from F. Rudolph. He found the people in a state of gross ignorance even of the elementary truths necessary to salvation: but the Fathers have won their confidence and affection already: and even from distant provinces, protestants hasten to bring them their sick that they may lay their hands upon them and recommend them to our Lord.

In the same way they bring their children to them for instruction. The Catholic school opened by them has already done immense good. Four of the children have already become Catholic and many adults have been instructed and received into the Church. They have also baptised a Pagan woman from Great Tartary .... altogether the mission is already bearing fruit." His only anxiety, later on, was to send more labourers into this new vineyard, for the three missioners were overwhelmed with the daily increasing work. Then came a fresh difficulty. In July 1799 he writes: "For more than a year we have no news from our dear Fathers at Mietau. The Russian Government has absolutely forbidden all correspondence from without; so that we can get no news either directly or indirectly."

Nevertheless F. Clement at the beginning of this century, accepted two other missions, one in Lutkowa, the other in Radzumin. About one of these he writes in June 1803:

"For more than a year, the Protestant President of the Warsaw Government has not left a stone unturned to induce me to accept the house which he has enlarged and endowed for our missioners. But I did not dare accept it, fearing to injure St. Bennone by taking away workmen who are indispensable to that congregation. Not being able to persuade me, he had recourse to the Archbishop, to force me to yield. He sent for me and I exposed very frankly to his Grace the reasons for my refusal. I thought I had won the battle; when all of a sudden, from the Aulic Chamber, came an intimation to the Archbishop to force me to accept this new mission immediately: and that by reason of the supreme authority existing in the Kingdom of Prussia over all clergy whether secular or regular. And this order was to be obeyed within three months!! Consequently, very much against my will, I was compelled to send three Fathers and one laybrother to this mission, where they have been ever since January and where their labours have been crowned with singular success. Before our arrival, those poor people had not seen a priest for eight months. They are so ignorant that they do not know the most elementary doctrines of our holy Faith: but they are Catholics at heart, detesting Lutherans and Jews as they would the plague. I have given them F. Adalbert Schröter as Superior. So the poor House of St. Bennone has lost three priests and one laybrother and we are reduced to 15 Religious with a few clerical students and laybrothers."

CHAPTER VII.

THE INCESSANT ANXIETY OF F. CLEMENT TO PROPAGATE THE CONGREGATION IN GERMANY. HIS PILGRIMAGE TO PRAGUE. 1795.

DIVINE Providence had led F. Clement into Poland to help, in the first instance, the neglected German Catholics there. But not only in Warsaw but in all the large Polish cities, multitudes of Germans were collected, in whose hands was, in reality, all the commerce and trade of the country: but they, having no priests who could speak to them in their own language, by degrees gave up their religion, ceased to frequent the Sacraments and thousands of them, in consequence, perished miserably.

To meet this great need, F. Clement set his heart on opening a House in Germany for the training of German novices.

The work in Warsaw was so heavy and overpowering that it was almost impossible to cultivate properly the spirit of the noviciate, for even the young students were obliged to take their part: and could not be educated in that quiet and recollection which the rule justly exacted.

We have seen how F. Clement, when his house was in such peril from the burning of the neighbouring suburb, promised a pilgrimage to Prague if they were spared. This vow he now determined to fulfil and accordingly started with F. Thaddeus on the 31st of August 1795. They arrived in Prague on the 14th of Sept. and for nine days satisfied their devotion over the Tomb of this glorious martyr*, towards whom F. Clement had a special veneration.

"When our pilgrimage is over", wrote Clement, "we shall go to Constance, where there is a question of founding a new House which is earnestly desired by the Nunzio. God who is wonderful in his works, has disposed all things in an

* St. John Nepomucen.

admirable manner. When, on the Saturday after the Feast of the Assumption, I was preparing to say mass, a letter was put into my hands which I did not open till after I had celebrated. This was from the Provost of the College at Lindau, on the Lake of Constance, who is most anxious that a House of our Congregation should be established there. Being at Prague, I am now half way and please God, shall accomplish the rest of the journey, so as to confer with him as to the best means to be adopted. I have never seen him nor does he know anything about us. He only heard once of our Institute from a lady who had been to confession to me at Warsaw before going to Lindau. The Nunzio sees clearly in all this the hand of God and so has given me letters not only for the Provost but for the Vicar General at Constance. I will write later about the progress of this affair."

After leaving Constance he returned by Znaim in Moravia, from whence he writes to his Superior General as follows. "Finding myself in Vienna, I was ordered by the Nunzio to visit the Bishop of St. Hyppolitus who offered us a House and said that he wished all his clergy to make the spiritual exercises in a house of our order in his Diocese: and being also Vicar General of the army he wished to found in the same house a Seminary for the preparation of good military Chaplains. But as long as the Emperor's decrees are in force, which compel the Religious orders to send all their students to the University, we cannot accept any foundation in the imperial dominions; for the education given to the students in these Universities is of the most pernicious character. We must, therefore, put off this affair to better times."

A little later, it appears he was blamed for being so willing to make new foundations by his superiors and he justifies himself as follows: "I have never sought for fresh Houses: but I did not like to refuse those offered me by persons hitherto unknown without submitting the proposal to the

Superior General and awaiting his decision. A House was offered me in Switzerland and in spite of my continual refusal, a deputation arrived at Warsaw hoping to obtain by a personal interview what letters had failed to do. When they left, I gave them hopes that some day their wishes may be realised. I say frankly that those who do not know the condition of the North cannot form an idea of the enormous necessity which exists for the opening of a noviciate to form good subjects for the existing Houses. Do you not think it is a clear sign of the Divine will that at the very time that convents and monasteries are being everywhere destroyed and suppressed we are continually receiving, even from Protestants, fresh offers for new foundations? If we refuse them all, perhaps they will cease to be offered to us. I do not think we should accept these offers at once: but only when we have enough trained subjects. But even if we were to seek for fresh houses, could we be blamed? We should be only showing as much zeal for saving souls as the enemies of religion have for ruining them."

The holy Superior made another journey to Germany and Switzerland, but the letters are unhappily lost in the continual wars and disturbances of the period. We only know that in July 1797 he was at Nicolsburg near Passwitz and said mass in the Church of the Scolopian Fathers, as appears in the catalogue of the celebrants. The Apostolic Nunzio, Monsg. Litta, wrote on the 11th of Jan. 1800, "that F. Clement's project of opening a House in Switzerland must be postponed on account of the invasion of the French army: but that there was a hope of a House in the German Empire on a property of Baron Beroldingen's, whose brother was in Vienna." This hope, however, was not realised.

It was a moment of revolution and general war, and Religious Houses fare badly under such circumstances. The worst effects of the revolution at that moment were felt in Switzerland.

The Catholic Cantons were overwhelened with French emigrants who lived mainly on charity. The Nunzio distributed all his money amongst them and whatever he could get from the sale of his furniture. The revolution went on, especially in the Protestant Cantons, until the French Army invaded Switzerland, destroyed its independence and made the Nunzio prisoner in Lucerne, finally conducting him beyond the frontier.

Austria was scarcely in a better condition. After an unhappy war, she was compelled on the 18th of April 1797, to sign the preliminaries of peace at Leoben; and on the 17th of October, at Campo Formio, to subscribe to the hard conditions imposed by General Bonaparte. Even this humiliation did not induce the Emperor to change a system of Government which was so disastrous for the Church. And if it did not come to an extreme, it was mainly owing to the Faith engrained in the hearts of the people.

F. Clement not having succeeded in founding a house for his novices outside the frontiers of Poland, resolved at least to bring some youths from Znaim and Tasswitz with the hope of forming them into subjects at Warsaw. There was a certain Brunner, who was afterwards at Vienna, who had been carried by Clement to Warsaw with two others for this purpose, but unfortunately he did not remember the date of his journey. Probably however it was in 1792, as a paper was found stating that F. Clement had been imprisoned in Cracow in the Dominican Convent for having taken these two Austrian boys without the consent of the Government. It seems that a Government Official carried off the boys, who could only see F. Clement in the tribune of the church.

Clement soon after escaped from Cracow and returned to Warsaw: but he had managed to keep three lads from Tasswitz. One was his nephew, Francis Hofbauer, the son of his brother Lawrence: the 2nd was also a nephew, being the son of his sister Barbara, and a boy named Knapp. But he was as last compelled by order of the Government to send home these boys also, keeping only little Francis, who became afterwards a zealous priest in the Congregation.

After the third division of Poland, Warsaw fell into the hands of the King of Prussia, and the Redemptorist Fathers had to swear allegiance to him on the 7th of July 1796. At first, it was hoped that the change would be of benefit to the Congregation, because being especially for the Germans and preaching mainly in that language, the Prussians frequented St. Bennone in preference to all other churches. But these benevolent sentiments did not last long. Very soon, the Prussians began a steady persecution of the religious orders, if not with fire and sword, at least with Laws and Decrees which were equally disastrous. Father Clement wrote on the 1st of October 1801 to F. Tannoia: "Pray earnestly for us and ask all the other Fathers in Italy to do so also and recommend our poor Congregation to the mercy of God, because we are in a state of fearful anxiety. The Government under which we now live is possessed with the spirit of unbelief and has begun to persecute the clergy in every possible manner. It is true that the Catholic Faith is not directly prohibited: but they have so organised matters that unless some help comes from God, it will be speedily extinguished. The first thing the Government has ordered is, that under no pretext shall any ecclesiastic dare refer any matter to the Pope unless through the medium of the minister. All the clergy, whether regular or secular, are forbidden to hold any communication with their Superiors if abroad. No religious Congregation can accept any novices without the *bene-placito* of the Government, and if not nobles, they must likewise obtain from the Commandant of their province, an exemption from the enforced military conscription. It is virtually a prohibition to receive novices, and the result is, that except the missioners of St. Vincent of Paul, all the other Religious Houses remain without novices and we have only two. Until now, we and they had leave to accept novices: but the conditions are such as to make the permission a dead letter. The following are the required conditions. The candidate must have completed his 24th year, must wear a secular habit during his noviciate, and then submit to an examination by Protestants, chosen by the Government, both before and after the year's noviciate. These examinations are simply attempts to detach young men from following their vocations. Even after this, they must present fresh petitions to the Government for leave to make their profession. It is only after having gone through all these vexatious conditions thas a man is permitted to take the religious habit and make his vows.

This new decree makes it, therefore, almost impossible for any one to follow the Evangelical Counsels. When it was brought to us, we answered in writing: "That without the authority of our Superiors we could not assent to its contents, as it was contrary to the practice of the Church whether Latin or Greek." I believe the Superiors of the other orders have given an answer in the same terms.

We are living now as sad spectators of the hard and cruel oppression of the Church of God. How happy are you, beloved brethren, who have a King who, being a good Catholic, knows how to defend his clergy! As for ourselves, to whom can we look for redress?

We sigh under an authority which is all powerful. The Government has formed what may be termed an Ecclesiastical Council: but among the Councillors there is not one single Catholic: as for the President, no one knows what he is. He is neither Lutheran, nor Calvinist, nor a follower of Zwinglin's, not even a Christian. Hence he is the bitterest enemy of Convents and of all Religious Order. This is the man who dares to give orders to Bishops and to all the Clergy, and who is to decide all ecclesiastical controversies!

How infamously the Church is treated may he seen by this fact: i. e. that the President of this ecclesiastical council, has likewise two other offices: one to watch over the Jews, and the other, the public prostitutes, and they are all three bracketed together!

Their behaviour towards the Priesthood is equally scandalous. The city is gorged with atheists who occupy all important offices: and it is only by the great mercy of God thas the lower classes are not entirely perverted, but persevere in well-doing and listen eagerly to the preaching of that Divine Word which we endeavour to make as practical as possible. I tell you all this hoping that the knowledge of our sad position will make your prayers for us to the throne of God more fervent and constant."

It is certainly wonderful how, under these sad circumstances, the House as St. Bennone could be maintained in so flourishing a condition. It was mainly thanks to the extraordinary prudence, moderation and patience of F. Hofbauer. But he foresaw the coming ruin of the Congregation in Poland, and therefore was more than ever bent on a new foundation in Germany or Switzerland; so as to be able to form students who should eventually take the place of those who were sinking under their apostolic labours; and have them ready to go to any place to which Providence might call them.

CHAPTER VIII.

HIS ANXIETY FOR HIGHER EDUCATION.

THE work in Warsaw which suffered most from the despotic ordinances of the Prussian Government, was the college which had produced such abundant fruits and which had been opened close to the church of St. Bennone. The Redemptorist Fathers are forbidden by their rule to undertake the scientific instruction of youth and consequently cannot found or direct any distinctly Educational Institute. Their holy founder made this provision with a view to confine the occupation of his Religious to the work of giving missions, so that they might not be distracted from this their main object: and all the more because there were so many other Religious orders who had devoted themselves to the education of youth. But after the suppression of the Society of Jesus, and other religious orders, Pius VI. considered it advisable to dispense the Redemptorists from this rule and gave leave to the Father General Francesco di Paolo, to establish colleges, when required, in the houses of his order.

If the needs of Italy justified this change, still more necessary was it in the north: so F. Clement began one in Warsaw and afterwards in Germany. His first object was to form good and learned members for the Congregation: but the public were equal gainers by the establishment of this college, every one having full right to choose the state of life he preferred; so that excellent Secular Priests and equally good laymen were sent out of it.* Besides secular learning, the students (as writes F. Tannoia) received admirable instruction in all the branches of Theology; they were likewise practised in preaching, and carefully initiated in the forms necessary for the administration of the Sacraments.

The care thus bestowed was so great that Monsg. Litta (the Polish Nuncio) wrote to F. Paola as follows: "The Bishops assert that the Redemptorist students are better instructed than any others and always pass first in examinations for ordination."

Pius VI. finding the extreme poverty to which this Seminary was reduced in 1791, assigned them 100 Scudi annually from the Propaganda and in giving it, made use of

---

* In 1877 the Bishop of Varmia told the Author "that from F. Clement's Seminary had come some of his best priests, who had done great works in his Diocese."

these words: "*We see that in these youths the zeal of their holy Founder has been infused*".

Almost all the students received by F. Clement were so poor that they could not defray the costs of their maintenance. But he never would give this fact a moment's consideration, being fully persuaded that if this work were in accordance with God's will, He would provide what was necessary for their support. During the first years, F. Clement taught theology himself; later on, he charged F. Passcrat with this duty. He chose the most learned and capable of the Fathers as Professors and sent to Rome for all the best books which could be found for their respective studies. To encourage the students in every possible way, he would show them the most paternal affection, assisting them in their studies and showing the keenest interest in their progress. To amuse them he would often tell them stories of his own youth and take them expeditions into the country; while to reward their diligence, he would invent a variety of prizes, suited to the taste of each. This College for some time did not give umbrage to the Government, who looked upon it with a favourable eye. But when the anti-Christian changes were made in the administration, all F. Clement's plans and objects were destroyed. In addition to what we have before mentioned regarding novices, all the students had to pass a Government examination; or if they failed to do so, were mulcted of a hundred Thalers. And what was worse than all, the books ordered by the Government for the use of the public schools were full of hostile passages against the Church and against Religion, while the Professors and the Government inspectors were frequently Apostate Priests, or men of scandalous lives. It was this especially which gave a death blow to F. Clement's College; and who can tell how great was his sorrow and mortification at the destruction of a work on which he had built his fondest hopes?

Nevertheless, his generous soul would not yield: if beaten in one battle, he would instantly begin again to fight in a fresh field.

Hence his proposal to found a Seminary for his young students at Rome; which was only not carried out owing to the fears of the Father General: fears which were but too soon justified by the Pope, Pius VII., being carried to France, as a prisoner, while the Roman States were incorporated into the French Empire. But what Italy could not supply, F. Clement found in Germany and this time with complete success. But in order that our readers may form a correct idea of this apostolic work, we will say a few words of the religious state of Germany at that period.

CHAPTER IX.

THE STATE OF THE CHURCH IN GERMANY AT THE END OF THE 18TH CENTURY AND THE BEGINNING OF THE 19TH. WHO WERE DALBERG AND WESSENBURG.

AT the close of the 18th century the Church in Germany was in a pitiable state. If a certain number of men still practiced their religion and lived as good Catholics, if a few priests were fervent and by word and deed endeavoured to lead their people in right ways, these were but a poor minority who could not influence the multitudes who had fallen away from the Faith.

The bad seed sown by the Jansenists and other heretics had borne abundant fruit, and the advent of Joseph 2nd to the throne fostered their poisonous machinations. If we would characterise the malady in men's souls we should say that 1st all idea of the Church of God had been dispelled in their minds, and 2^{ndy} a profound disgust for all exercises of Catholic piety had replaced their former fervour.

The State of the Church in Germany.

Hence the cry against the pretended usurpations of the pope, and hence also the contempt and ridicule shown towards the salutary devotion of the Sacred Heart. Even the priests, many of whom were members of secret societies, fought against the Church, desiring to see it united and subject to the state, an incubus which for a long while oppressed the true Church in Germany.

In the year 1786 when, in Italy, Ricci, Bishop of Pistoia, held the famous Jansenist synod condemned by Pius VI. in his Bull *Auctorem fidei*, the three principal ecclesiastical electors, namely, the Archbishops of Cologne, Mayence and Treves as also the Archbishop of Salzburg, endorsed the Schismatical Articles called of Ems, which all rested on the Doctrines of Febronius and were worthy of the most declared enemies of the Holy See.

The Prince Elector of Cologne at that time was the Archduke Maximilian of Austria, brother of the Emperor Joseph II: of Treves Clement Wenceslaus, Prince of Saxony, formerly a Marshall in the Austrian army: and of Mayence Baron Erthal. These three electors were at that time the only Archbishops in the German Empire, but subject to them were many other Bishops and Prelates. Now, what they agreeed upon in the Ems convention was as follows:

1. That Christ had given to the Apostles and to their successors, the Bishops, an unlimited power to lose and bind persons, whatever might be the circumstances of their case, *without reference to the Pope*.
2. All rights conceded to Religious Orders, unless recognised and approved of by the Emperor, were to be abolished: nor could the said religious be permitted to receive orders from or depend on foreign Superiors.
3. It must rest with the Bishops to give dispensations in all cases hitherto reserved for the Holy See, and this even in cases of solemn vows. And no such vows were to be

considered valid unless made by men after the age of 25 and by women after 40 years of age.
4. It was to be no longer permitted to ask at Rome for faculties colled *quinquennali*, and whatever dispensations were granted by Rome would be invalid unless granted by the Bishop also.
5. No Pontifical Bulls would be considered as obligatory unless first accepted by the respective Bishops.
6. Finally—the Oath sworn to the Pope by the Bishops was to be done away with: and if the Pope refused to confirm the nomination of any of the Bishops, they would find, in the ancient discipline of the Church, means to preserve their offices under the Emperor's protection alone.

These and other similar clauses were contained in the famous declaration of Ems, which was forwarded to Joseph II. together with a letter full of insults to the Holy See. But Archbishop Colloredo of Salzburg considering even this not sufficiently violent against the Pope, added 21 more articles of a similar nature and sent them to the Emperor. But even he was startled at their violence and did not approve of them.

It is not necessary to state with what energy the Pope rose against these schismatical proceedings. And when he found that they ceased to apply to the Holy See for the Faculty called *quinquennali*, and gave dispensations on their own private authority in reserved cases, Pius VI. ordered Pacca, his Nunzio at Cologne, to signify in all the Parishes subject to the three Bishop Electors, that any marriages contracted under such impediments without the dispensation of the Holy See, would be considered invalid. The Prince Electors were furious at this circular, which the Nunzio immediately put forth, and the Archbishop of Cologne remonstrated upon the subject with the brother of Joseph II. and with the Pope himself. But Pius VI. replied that the Nunzio had acted by his orders, and that the decisions of the three

Archbishops were contrary to the Councils and to the universal practice of the Church. On hearing this, the Archbishops of Treves and Mayence withdrew from the schismatical league and appealed to the Holy See again for the faculty *quinquennali*. But the Archbishops of Cologne and Salzburg so far from making any attempt at submission, carried their accusations against the Nunzio to the Diet of Ratisbon, and so provoked a *Memorandum* from the Holy See.

But the hand of God did not fail to fall heavily on the heads of these schismatics. The Emperor reaped the fruit of his usurpations in a revolt which deprived him of the Low Countries, and learnt too late that obedience to the Church is the foundation of the obedience due to the civil authority, and that if that be destroyed, together with the principle of submission to authority, there will be no fidelity from subjects to their Princes. Joseph II., overwhelmed with every kind of misfortune, thus closed his mortal career.

The Elector Princes were despoiled of all their possessions and Electoral Dignities by the French war: while their principalities were secularised and given to secular Princes. The principality of the Archbishop of Salzburg passed to the Grand Duke of Tuscany. And in the Concordat concluded in 1801 between the Holy See and France, the Archbishoprics of Mayence and Treves were declared to be simple Bishoprics and Suffragans of Mechlin, and were given to other Bishops. The Prince Elector of Mayence, "who only remembered his Episcopal dignity", as Cardinal Pacca states, "when it was a question of attacking the Pope", did not survive this heavy blow and died on the 25th of July 1802. The Archbishop of Cologne, who had retired to Vienna, died the year before. The Archbishop of Salzburg did not, either, survive his humiliation, and also died at Vienna in 1812, and the same year witnessed the decease of the Elector of Treves, who, possessing another Bishopric, that of Augsburg had retired there. The same miserable fate befell the Chapters who had cooperated in the schism of the Archbishops. They too were secularised and their properties confiscated, while to the Canons was assigned only a small annual pension. Many of these were a rock of offence and a real stumbling-block of scandal to the people. They had embraced the Ecclesiastical state, not because they were thereto called by God, but because they could thus live like spendthrifts. Nor is to be wondered at that such men preferred hunting, shooting, gambling and every other worldly sport to singing Office in Choir! Very often it happened that a single individual appropriated several canonries and pocketed the revenues of the prebends without performing the smallest service to the Church. F. Clement wrote to Cardinal Litta on the 20th of Febr. 1817 in these terms: "The aristocratic Clergy in Germany, who shamefully appropriate the wealth of the Church, are in such a terrible state and have become such objects of ridicule and contempt to the people, that if any one wishes to express the depravity of any youth, they say: "He is a Count Canon!"

The storm which burst on the schismatics, destroyed also many of the monasteries. And if some of these had deserved such a punishment, there were many who had maintained regular discipline and were a serious loss to the people.

It was in these sad times that F. Clement came to Germany. If he found the rod of Divine Vengeance already lifted to scourge the enemies of the Church, it was impossible not to perceive the reason of the chastisment. On the ruins of the Church in Germany, Charles Dalberg had raised his throne, with the assistance of the Baron of Wessenberg. Dalberg not only continued to govern on the lines of the schismatical Council of Ems, but would, if it had been possible, have detached the Church in Germany altogether from the Roman See and made it Protestant.

Cardinal Pacca,* with great reason, compares Dalberg with Fozio, both having the same object in view which was to rend the unity of the Church. Dalberg arrived at ecclesiastical dignities in this wise. The Elector of Mayence by infamous intrigues, induced Pope Pius VI. to permit the Chapter to nominate him as his Coadjutor with the right of succession, and the King of Prussia sent Marquis Luchesini to Rome to obtain the necessary Brief. He made the Pope believe that if he would confirm this nomination, the Archbishop would be once more closely bound to Rome: that it would put an end to the schism: would nullify the Ems declarations, and would be the means of maintaining intact the rights and dignity of the Holy See. The King's Messenger added: "That he was charged both by his Sovereign and the Archbishop to tender to the Pope the most solemn guarantees for the faithful performance of these promises." The Pope was deceived and believed in their assertions: so that in 1787, Dalberg, to the great joy of all the Sectarians and Jansenists, and to the sorrow of all good Catholics, was elected Coadjutor to the Archbishop of Mayence.

Too late did the Pope realise the perfidy of his betrayers and the value of their promises: while the Archbishop applied to the Diet of Ratisbon for the abolition of all Papal Nunzios throughout the Empire of Germany.

Dalberg himself, not content with this first dignity, found means speedily to accumulate others. He became administrator of the Bishopric of Worms, and Coadjutor of the Bishop of Constance, and this last Bishop having died on the 14th of Jan. 1800, he took quiet possession of the Diocese and appointed Baron Wessenberg his Vicar General, he being then but 26 years old! Then, he played his cards so adroitly at the Diet of Ratisbon, that in 1803 he obtained

---

* See "*Memorie storiche*" by Monsg. Pacca on his sojourn in Germany from the year 1786 to 1794. Rome 1882.

the dignity of principal Elector, of Archbishop of Ratisbon, of Metropolitan and Primate of all Germany and the Arch-Chancellorship of the Empire! He was also nominated Secular Prince of Ratisbon, Frankfort, Aschaffenburgh, and other places. In this way his jurisdiction was almost unlimited and it may be said that Dalberg reigned over the whole Church in Germany. Add to this that in the first ten years of this century the few remaining Catholic Bishops died, so much so that this epoch was termed "The epoch of Vacant Sees". Finally, to crown the misfortunes of the unhappy Catholics in Germany, in 1809, the Pope was imprisoned; and so there was no redress and no appeal to any authority which could have remedied such gigantic evils.

Dalberg having, as we have seen, appointed Baron von Wessenberg as his Vicar General at Constance it was inevitable that he and F. Hofbauer should speedily come into collision. We will therefore say a few words of the history of this man.* Ignatius Henry Wessenberg sucked in with his mother's milk the sentiments he afterwards manifested so painfully; for in his paternal home the French revolution had been warmly applauded and Joseph II. was revered for his anti-religious innovations. In spite, however, of these views his father sent him in 1790 to Augsburg, to a college kept by the Fathers of the then suppressed Company of Jesus. But as what he heard there was all in direct contradiction to his pet theories, Ignatius disliked the place extremely. In consequence of this, after having, with his younger brother Lewis, obtained two very comfortable prebendaries in the Chapters of the Cathedral at Basle and Constance, he went with Lewis to Dillingen to attend the University courses in that place. "This University", writes Dr. Beck, "was the first in Germany which accepted and

---

* This history is taken from the *Life of Wessenberg* (published in Friburg in 1862) written by his friend Dr. Beck, an Apostate Priest and Aulic Councillor of the Grand Duke of Baden.

carefully cultivated Kant's philosophy. In the rays of this bright light, true scientific progress was made, together with serious critical investigations, unchecked by hostile influences; the fruits of which, namely toleration and humanity, rendered it as famous in South Germany as it was suspected and attacked by the priest-ridden and jesuitical followers of the old system.

"Among the professors of this school, three were distinguished above the rest: Joseph Weber, who by his lucid and philosophic explanations of Kant's doctrines, knew how to captivate the minds of his hearers, Benedict Zimmer, who in his dogmatical lectures threw continually fresh light on Kant's principles; and Michael Sailer, a theologian of profound convictions, who, with the burning zeal which carried him away and the beautiful language of which he was the master knew how to move all hearts and gain them over to his cause. And as Sailer leaned to a certain ecclecticism, his lessons on religion and morals were much frequented and were all based on the principles of Kant.

"To such men", continues Dr. Beck, "with all the youthful enthusiasm of a soul who only sought after truth, Ignatius Wessenberg warmly attached himself, and if he always regarded them with grateful affection, still more was he drawn towards Sailer, who soon became to him even more than a master."*

* The partial praise bestowed on Sailer by this apostate and unbelieving priest, became his worst condemnation. Nothing speaks more strongly against Sailer's writings than the exaggerated eulogiums bestowed upon them by Anti-Catholics, Deists and other heretics, together with his friendship for Jakobi, Boos, Gossner and other schismatics, who all venerated him as a Father. Therefore, if Sailer at the University, taught Kant's philosophy instead of Catholic theology, and magnified toleration and humanity above all other virtues, no wonder that his doctrines were impugned by the Ex-Jesuits of Augsburg and that the Bishop of that city refused him leave to teach. In the same way, the close intimacy which he kept up all his life with Wessenberg, certainly did not redound to Sailer's honour.

After Sailer left Dillingen, Wessenberg went on to the University of Würzburg, where he followed the lectures of Francis Oberthür, who was equally imbued with the new ideas and who is the author of a book on the scope and object of Chapters in Cathedrals and on the Divine Office: which book was speedily prohibited by the S. Congregation of the Index. From Würzburg he passed to Vienna to assist at the lessons on ecclesiastical history of the Arch-Josephin-Professor Dannenmeier, whose name also may be found in the index.

His studies being thus completed, it appeared to Baron von Dalberg (who had just been elected Bishop of Constance) that he was the very man to carry out his views in that Diocese as Vicar General. But first he had him at Ratisbon, where Dalberg got complete hold over him, and then he sent him to Switzerland, to confer with the Cantons on ecclesiastical questions and especially on those which regarded the temporal property of the Church.

It was in the beginning of the year 1802 that he took upon himself the Government of the Diocese of Constance. Being only a simple cleric, and a thoroughly worldly man, a vain and self-sufffcient youth, in fact, who knew nothing of theology, never having studied dogma, or morals, or canon law, and on the contrary, being puffed up with pride in his new theories, and in his admiration for the principles of the French Revolution, and for the Josephin reforms, he chose to consider every thing wrong in the institutions and practice of the Diocese and thought himself called upon to reform every thing. What pleased him above all was the idea that he should enlighten and instruct the people in his own views. Hence he considered it to be the first duty of the Clergy not to offer the Divine Sacrifice or administer the Sacraments, but to teach. He sent back the seminarists, therefore, to the Elementary Schools, so that from the new masters he had placed there, they should learn what they were to teach the children. Without in any way respecting the Decrees of the Holy See, he rejected the Roman Ritual, and substituted another in German, which he ordered should be used througout the Diocese. The old rituals he objected to, as being, as he said, "full of superstitions", and to take away the forms of Benediction therein contained he called them "*Esorcismi*" and forbade the Clergy to make use of them without his permission. He tried to introduce the German language in the celebration of mass, and commanded that at every mass, not only the epistle and Gospel, but other parts should be read to the people in German. Hence such priests as dared to celebrate mass in the vulgar tongue, were sure of carrying favour with Wessenberg. In fact so bitter was he against the august ceremonies of the Church, that he ventured to stigmatise them as vestiges of Paganism and Judaism, leading to a Religion of mere show and pretence! All through mass, he insisted on the people's singing hymns in German which he drew up and printed himself, and in which he inserted rationalistic sentiments drawn from the works of protestant poets. In every pious work he pretended to detect abuses and superstitions; and so he abhorred confraternities, pilgrimages and devotions to the holy Rosary. He set aside all good Parish Priests and zealous missioners, saying they were not up to the necessities of the times, and he placed men of neither faith nor character in the most important missions. In the Canton of Lucerne, which then belonged to the Diocese of Constance, he suppressed the Franciscan Convent of Wertenstein to plant a Seminary in its place: but when recalled by the Holy See to some sense of duty, he finally founded one in Lucerne; but placed at the head of it the infamous Dereser, the author of the Breviary in the German tongues. In accordance with Febronius' principles, he determined to usurp altogether the powers of the Pope, pretending that they were due simply to the ignorance of the middle ages, and that with modern progress the Bishops should reclaim their rights and Princes forbid the interference of the Popes in their dominions.

Such was the man placed at the head of the Constance Diocese. But the unhappy spirit which moved him predominated unfortunately at that moment throughout Germany. The result of which was that when F. Clement arrived to found a house there of his order, he was nearly driven to despair at the state of things, and ardently desired to die and be with Christ, "Suffering too much at seeing the desolation of one of the most ancient and important Dioceses of Germany. The evil is the greater from the extent of the Bishopric of Constance, which contains more than three thousand parishes": so wrote F. Thaddeus from Warsaw to the Father General on the 12th of March 1806.

CHAPTER X.

F. CLEMENT FOUNDS A HOUSE IN THE DIOCESE OF CONSTANCE. HIS JOURNEY TO ROME AND RETURN TO WARSAW.

[From 1802 to 1804.]

THE call to found this new house in Constance came from Prince John Schwarzenberg, encouraged thereto by the Apostolic Nunzio at Vienna, who was the great friend of Father Clement. This Prince, having in the Grand Duchy of Baden near Schaffhausen, a property called Iestetten on which was on old Convent called *Mount Thabor*, formerly inhabited by the monks of St. Norbert under the title of *Perpetual Adoration*, offered it to F. Clement, inviting him to establish there a Redemptorist Congregation, and though he did not assign to him any permanent revenues for the maintenance of the community, yet so anxious was Father Clement to have a house on German soil, that he accepted it at once, trusting in Divine Providence for the future.

In order to judge of the state of the place and make the necessary arrangements, he left Warsaw on the 11th of Novbr. 1802 with F. Thaddeus, a cleric, Francis Hofbauer, and a Novice, John Sabelli and arrived at Iestetten, passing by Vienna and Altoetting. It was by a special direction of Divine Providence that F. Clement was enabled to visit the famous Sanctuary of Mary at Altoetting, for by his presence and his prayers he thus sanctified a spot which, after his death, was to be the scene of the apostolic labours of his brethren. Sabelli wrote an account of F. Clement's extreme devotion to this Sanctuary. It seemed as if he could not tear himself away from that altar or from the image of Mary which is there venerated.

Arrived at Constance, F. Clement was obliged to present himself to the Vicar General, Baron von Wessenberg, to obtain faculties for preaching and confessing in his Diocese: after which he proceeded to Mount Thabor. It was on the 30th of December 1802 that he and his three companions arrived at Iestetten. The miserable state of the house did not deter him, he being so anxious to have a *pied-à-terre* in Germany where he could labour for the good of souls. Without waiting a single day he began his Apostolic work. On the 3rd of January he preached three times and afterwards four times on each Festival: i. e. during mass, explaining the Epistle or Gospel; and then at 10 o'clock, at 3 and at 1/₂5. The people came in crowds to hear him, first from curiosity and then from real interest, and soon thronged his confessional.

But his extraordinary activity and the great influx of people to his church naturally excited the jealousy of the parochial clergy, who felt that his zeal was a tacit reproach to their own lukewarmness. The Parish of Iestetten was a dependency of the Abbey of Rheinau and the Abbot of that day Bernard III., Mayor of Schauenstein made a formal remonstrance to Wessenberg. For once, however, Wessenberg did not dare decide against Father Clement, whose extraordinary gifts had made such an impression that he replied to the Abbot as follows: "I do not doubt that so worthy an ecclesiastic will willingly come to an understanding with your Reverence regarding ecclesiastical functions. He will show you the faculties given to him by myself; and his zeal will, I feel sure, be a valuable assistance to your Reverence in the cure of souls. All I wish is, that all should be done in harmony. *Semper quod bonum est, sectamini in invicem, et in omnes*, 1. Thess. 5. 15. v." And in fact, F. Clement managed to soothe the susceptibilities of the parish priests, so that their relations were improved; whereas he speedily came to be at variance with the Vicar General especially in 1805.

F. Clement not being able to remain permanently in charge of this house, summoned his favourite F. Passerat, of whose holiness and zeal he had had full proof in Warsaw, so that in July 1803 he was appointed Rector.

Very soon after, he undertook a journey to France and for this reason. The Royal Family of France, being exiles at Mietau in Courland, had made acquaintance with the Redemptorists both there and in Warsaw, and especially with F. Passerat, who was their countryman.

Hence, the Duchesse d'Angoulême entertained the hope that even in France a House of the Congregation might be established. F. Clement accordingly, taking with him F. Passerat, went to Joinville in Champagne which was F. Passerat's own county, to see what could be done. And as in France the hatred to priests still existed, they travelled in secular clothes, so that the sacerdotal dignity should not be insulted.

But they found insuperable difficulties in their undertaking: the religious spirit of the country had not yet sufficiently recovered the shock of the Revolution of 1793, and so F. Clement gave up the plan for the time and returned to Mont Thabor. To prove the tried virtue of F. Passerat and his fidelity to his vocation, the following anecdote will not be out of place. One day, his mother came into his room and to his great surprise presented him with an official paper which she implored him, with tears, to make use of, if he had any filial love left. This was a dispensation from his vows, which, without his knowledge, his mother had obtained from the Papal Legate, Caprara. But Passerat had given himself entirely to God and was so content with his vocation that he flatly refused to receive the dispensation and declared to his mother that he was determined to persevere in the Congregation till the hour of his death. A most plainful scene followed, and a less strong vocation would certainly have yielded to such an assault.

But he, notwithstanding his strong love for his mother, who employed every argument she could think of to dissuade him from his resolve, remained firm and resisted even his mother's tears and reproaches, till she felt it was in vain for her to plead any longer.

As soon as Father Clement had put every thing in working order at Mt. Thabor, he left for Italy with F. Thaddeus, taking with him the three Clerics, Francis Hofbauer. John Sabelli and Casimir Langanki, which last had been lately summoned from Warsaw. F. Clement's object was to get them ordained, which could not be done elsewhere: not at Warsaw, partly on account of the Govt. Examination and also because the Bishops had severe orders not to ordain any who were not Prussian subjects: nor at Constance, as there was no Bishop. Dalberg remained in his secular property: and his Vicar General Wessenberg, had received nothing but minor orders and was not consecrated Priest even till the month of September 1812, at Fulda! so that F. Clement had no alternative but to take his young Clerics to Italy, where he obtained from the Pope leave to have them ordained by any Bishop he pleased of the Latin rite in communion with the Holy See.

F. Clement came to Rome by Milan and the St. Gothard, about the middle of September. He took rooms in the *Via cnique Lume* with a respectable family who lived close to the Church of St. Augustine, so that he became intimate with the Augustinians. His young Clerics had remained at Spello, near Foligno, where the Congregation had a house: only F. Thaddeus accompanied him to Rome. Father Clement had set his heart on visiting the Tomb of his venerable Founder, Alphonsus di Liguori, which was at a short distance from Naples and on saluting the Father General. "But Divine Providence", (he wrote on the 17th of September 1803), "has ordained it otherwise. I could not get through my business here as quickly as I had hoped. In December I must be back in Warsaw: winter is at hand; and if we return by the St. Gothard, I am afraid it will be already covered with snow. Then I have to go again into Switzerland to settle some things in the house at Mt. Thabor: after which I am obliged to go to Vienna and then to Warsaw. Every thing considered, I fear I must follow the prudent advice of Cardinal Litta and give up my Neapolitan visits. I hope that God may grant me the grace before I die to see the Tomb of our Venerable Founder and to confer with your Reverence on many things which concern the welfare of the Congregation. Here I have seen a good deal of F. Giattini, Procurator General and Postulator in the cause of our Venerable Father Alphonsus di Liguori. He has treated me with fraternal benevolence and charity and has done me many services for which I shall be always deeply grateful to him".

By a decree of the S. Congregation of Propaganda (dated 3rd of October 1803) the Holy Father Pius VII. having granted the wished-for privilege, Clement returned to Spello and took his three Clerics to Foligno, where they were ordained

Priests on the 28th of Oct., by Bishop Marc Antonio Moscardini. They said their first mass on the Feast of St. Raphael and in the afternoon of that day, under the protection of the great Archangel, they started for Loreto, where they celebrated their second masses in the Holy House: and then joyfully proceeded on foot towards Switzerland. At Lucerne they paid a visit to the Nunzio, Testaferrata, and arrived without accident at Mt. Thabor on the 15th of November.

The three young priests obtained the necessary faculties for hearing confessions and began to work zealously in saving souls. Among the novices was a priest named Joseph Hofbauer of the Diocese of Metz. He was 40 years of age and had 14 years of Priesthood: but having always refused to take the so-called *Constitutional* oath, he could not perform any Ecclesiastical function and had been for some years even in peril of his life. He was of enormous advantage to the Congregation from his exemplary life and regular observance and as master of the young Clerics he was admirable. At the end of August 1803, he took the Religious habit together with Norbert Spitznagel, a laybrother.

Father Clement, on his return from Rome found besides three other men who wished to be received into the Congregation, namely John Forster, Martin Schoellhorn and Michael Baumgartner. Other candidates asked the same favour and filled his heart with joy and hope. He accepted them all and then, with F. Thaddeus, started on his way to Vienna. From thence he wrote on the 3rd of December to announce his speedy departure for Warsaw. But having been delayed by unexpected business and the winter being very severe, he did not arrive at Warsaw till the 1st of Jan. 1804.

CHAPTER XI.

NEW LABOURS OF FATHER CLEMENT IN GERMANY. A FRESH JOURNEY TO MOUNT THABOR. HE FOUNDS A HOUSE AT TRIBERG, WHICH, HOWEVER, WAS SPEEDILY SUPPRESSED.

[From 1804 to 1805.]

GREAT was the joy of the faithful in Warsaw at F. Clement and F. Thaddeus' safe return: and both zealously resumed their apostolic labours which were so visibly blessed by God.

But half the new year had not passed before F. Clement found himself again compelled to go to Switzerland, where his house was on the point of being abandoned for want of the commonest necessaries of life. F. Clement resolved to start at once to see what could be done and at any rate to console his faithful sons by his presence; so that towards the end of August he set out with Lewis Czech, whose narrative of their journey we will here give to our readers.

"Father Clement", he writes, "sanctifies his journey by continual prayer and intercourse with God."

He was obliged to stop two days in Dresden on business with the Royal Family, and three days in Augsburg and Constance. On the 21st of September we arrived at Mt. Thabor. But how describe the misery of this place! A ruined castle with 4 or 5 rooms, only habitable as long as the props remain which prevent the walls from crumbling to their foundations. The Clerics sleep under the roof of the church: the students in a tower where there are neither doors nor windows: and at which they arrive by a rope ladder. All the rest of the house is equally miserable. But even this state of things does not discourage the servant of God. He shares all the hardships of his companions, comforts them by his example, and has arrived at making them forget their misery in the joy of having so holy a Superior.

He is incessantly occuped in hearing confessions, in preaching on Sundays and Festivals, and in writing Letters on the affairs of the Congregation. The little time that remains is spent by him in prayer and meditation.

Our Lord, however, has given him one little bit of consolation. A deputation came from Triberg, a little town in the Black Forest, under the dominion of Archduke Ferdinand, begging him to send some priests to found a house of the Congregation in that place. There exists a Sanctuary there, once much frequented, but now neglected for want of priests. But the well-being of the poor people had greatly suffered from this cause: so that they made up their minds to establish some fresh priests in this Sanctuary; and having heard of the fame of F. Clement and his Redemptorists, applied to him to come to their assistance. So good an opportunity of labouring for the glory of God and the salvation of souls, was not to be lost and F. Clement accepted their offer with great cordiality. Archduke Ferdinand offered to assign 320 francs annually to each of the three priests who were to be sent there: so that just before the Feast of Pentecost 1805, we started for Triberg.

The journey was made on foot and as it poured with rain all day we were soaked to the skin. Night came on and we were still 9 miles from Triberg: there was no inn, so F. Clement knocked at a peasant's house und craved his hospitality.

F. Clement got us some good soup: and for beds some hay which was spread in a barn. But there was no way of drying our clothes. Soaking wet we took them [off and equally soaking we put them on the next morning! but the example of our holy Superior stifled all complaints or discontent.

We were received at Triberg with open arms. A large number of the citizens accompanied us to the Sanctuary and from thence to the house, which was a spacious one, with two stories; in the second lived two old priests who were unable to officiate: but on the first and ground floors there was plenty of room for F. Clement and his little band. He instantly began to work. Pentecost being so near at hand, no sooner was the news of the arrival of the missioners made known, than thousands of peasants came pouring down from the woods and mountains so that the church could not contain one half of them. F. Clement himself preached and produced so extraordinary an effect, that the Sanctuary at once recovered its old prestige. Many who had made a vow to go on a pilgrimage to Einsiedeln, obtained a dispensation to visit, instead, the shrine of Mary at Triberg. The pilgrims came in shoals and from early morning till late at night, the confessionals were thronged. Generally F. Clement himself preached and fed them, not with idle words, but with the true bread of life, penetrating into their hearts and souls, and producing innumerable conversions. Without thinking of fatigue or taking the smallest care of his own strength, he followed the example of our Holy Redeemer and sacrificed himself body and soul for the salvation of these multitudes, hungering for the word of God".

Very soon F. Clement had an additional consolation. F. Passerat had taken two of his Clerics to Lucerne (Antony Egle and John Hartmann) to have them ordained priests. Testaferrata, the Apostolic Nunzio, was, however, then at Solothurn, where the Diet was being held. There F. Passerat brought his spiritual sons, who were ordained by the Nunzio on the 9th of June: when they immediately joined F. Clement at Triberg and said their first masses on the altar of the miraculous Madonna. At this important ceremony, according to the pious custom of Germany, an immense concourse of people assisted and the joy was universal.

Thus, in an incredibly short time, the servant of God won the confidence and affection of all: and a wide field was opened, as in Warsaw, for the conversion of innumerable souls. Archduke Ferdinand, delighted at the success of the Fathers and the revival of piety in the town and district, offered to increase their revenues. But the people themselves came forward and supplied them with provisions and wood in abundance.

"But the enemy of souls" (continues F. Czech) could not endure that through the medium of F. Clement and his priests so many souls should be snatched from his claws. In his infernal rage he roused a jealous fury in the minds of the old priests who had formerly served in this Sanctuary: and they represented to the Bishop's Curia at Constance that the Redemptorists were only ill-judged fanatics. How unjust such accusations were may be seen by the Archduke's letter to the Curia, inserted in an article published by Baron Andlaw in a periodical entitled: "*Leaves of political history*"— (of the year 1858 vol. 41). In this article it is stated: "That the old priests who had previously had charge of the Sanctuary, had given great scandal to the people by their immoral lives and were moreover suspected of heresy from the innovations introduced by them in ecclesiastical functions. But when that great servant of God, F. Hofbauer began to preach in the fulness of faith, recommending the frequent reception of the sacraments, devotion to our Lady and the recital of the Rosary, the people at once recognised them as faithful and true priests of the Church of God and felt that they could trust them implicitly. This irritated the innovators and especially the Vicar General, Baron von Wessenberg, who saw themselves thereby thwarted and hindered in their pretended reforms. In consequence, an active persecution was raised against the Fathers and the two new priests who had been ordained by the Apostolic Nunzio, were suspended from their ecclesiastical functions for that sole reason. Two other priests ordained in January 1805, were subjected to a rigorous examination in Friburg on the subject of confession and civil rights, and because they necessarily could not satisfy the demands of the hostile examiners, they too were suspended, to the intense grief of the people." Wessenberg then sent two secular priests to serve the Sanctuary. One was an inexperienced youth; the other an incapable and ignorant old man, who had given up the trade of bookbinding to become a priest. He had grown-up sons, and both utterly disgusted the people. The Government sent a severe reproof to Wessenberg for this change, which irritated him profoundly, tho' in the life-time and under the Government of the Archduke Ferdinand he was obliged to dissemble his resentment. But unhappily, in the following year, Friburg and the Black Forest were ceded to the Grand Duchy of Baden, and then Wessenberg having no longer any check, suspended the remaining Fathers. In vain did the poor inhabitants send deputations to Constance and Carlsruhe, the seat of Government, imploring the reinstatement of the Congregation. The Government being Protestant were only too glad to second Wessenberg's views and the Redemptorists were suppressed. Clement, therefore, sorrowfully was compelled to abandon this promising field of operations. He had already started a small college of 12 boys in Triberg and was instructing them in Latin and other things. But only one followed him, John Kaltenbach, who afterwards became a most zealous missioner.

Two illustrious Prelates have borne witness to the great work done by F. Clement during his short stay in Triberg. One is the Archbishop of Friburg, Herman of Vicari, who in a letter written on the 1st March 1865 to H. H. Pius IX, says: "The venerable F. Clement opened a flourishing house in this country (Triberg) and acquired by his great virtue

and his indefatigable labours so much veneration and esteem from all the good, that his name and his memory, even to this day, are held in highest honour."
The other, a Vicar Capitular, Lothair Kübel, Bishop of Leuca l. p. l. in a letter to Cardinal Patrizi of the 29th of August 1868, writes: "The memory of this holy Priest, so inflamed with zeal for the glory of God and so eminent for the sanctity of his life and conversation, is a benediction to the people even to this hour." While among the records of the Parish Priest of Triberg, we find the following:
"The Redemptorist Fathers came here on the 30th of May 1805. Their community consisted of five priests, their Superior being a certain F. Hofbauer, who by the holiness of his life was called by the people *"The Holy Father."*

CHAPTER XII.

CLEMENT TAKES REFUGE WITH HIS BRETHREN AT BABENHAUSEN.
THE VIRTUES HE THERE EXERCISED.

[From 1805 to 1806.]

ANTONY of Nigg, Vicar General of the Diocese of Augsburg, formerly a student of the German College at Rome and always a faithful son of the Church, was a great friend and admirer of F. Clement's, and by his advice, Clement applied to a Prince of the Empire, Anselm of Fugger in Babenhausen, to give an asylum to his persecuted Religious. The Prince gladly acceded to his request and Clement hastened to Augsburgh with F. Sabelli to obtain the consent of the Prince Bishop Clement Wenceslaus, who was Elector of Treves. Although he arrived on the 6th of October he could not succeed for a long time in obtaining what he sought: for the French army had entered the city, led by the Emperor Napoleon. Finally towards the end of the month he obtained faculties to found a house in this Diocese and therein to exercise his sacred ministry.

F. Sabelli records a grave danger which befell F. Clement between Augsburg and Babenhausen. He was stopped by a French soldier, who, putting the point of his sword to his breast, imperatively demanded his cloak. F. Clement without being the least disturbed or frightened, quickly unclasped it and gave it to him; and then went on with his journey quite contentedly and without showing the least vexation.

The first days of November 1805, Clement had already gathered round him in Babenhausen all the community from Mt. Thabor and from Triberg. The excellent Parish priest of Weinried, F. Wagner, with singular charity, housed them all in his own presbytery and generously maintained them. From want of beds, however, several of them slept upon straw placed in one of the rooms. Soon after, they hired a small house in Babenhausen: but that again was much too small to hold them: and here again the F. Rector Passerat, slept upon straw and most of his community had to do the same. Under such circumstances, F. Clement gratefully accepted the Parish priest's proposal to remain on for the present in his house: not because he was more comfortable there, but because he could preach and hear confessions at Weinried, which the Parish priest at Babenhausen would not permit. The moment these saintly avocations were fulfilled, he would hasten to Babenhausen, which was only a quarter of an hour from Weinried, minding neither rain, nor snow nor the bad roads, and there share in the community life and in the education of the students and console and edify all by his kindness and sympathy. One day, for instance, being the 23rd of January and his name-day, he took a walk of three hours to go and congratulate a good peasant woman who had done him a service and whose Feast it likewise was; and he seasoned his walk with such pleasant and holy talk that the students who accompanied him thought themselves only too fortunate to be able to profit by his conversation. As his Divine master did not come upon earth to be served but so serve others, to this holy Superior in his charity and humility, did not hesitate in like manner to serve his brethren. At that time they had a brother, Norbert, who was an abominable cook and especially when he tried to prepare any meagre dish. F. Clement determined to teach him himself, and during that Lent, after having cooked the dinner, he would sit down with the rest, not to eat (for that he did alone towards evening), but to listen to the spiritual reading.

The house they had taken at Babenhausen was not only much too small, but terribly damp and unhealthy. In consequence, they moved in February into a larger one: but there they suffered even more from the intense cold and the lack of fuel. But neither poverty nor suffering ever discouraged the servant of God or disturbed his habitual tranquillity: he being persuaded that apostolical labours are the more blessed by God and the more fruitful in the salvation of souls, in proportion as the travail and mortifications accompanying them are greater. Whilst some of the Fathers had to attend to the training and instruction of the clerics, the others devoted themselves to the sacred ministry. But F. Clement was the apostle of the district, especially in Weinried, where his unwearied zeal produced the most extraordinary change for the better in the habits of the people. Both there and in the neighbouring Parish of Kirchaslach, where he often went with F. Sabelli, the people flocked from all parts to hear him and marvellous were the conversions which resulted from his preaching and his confessional.

All this time, he was in a very suffering state of health, which we find out from a letter written by F. Thaddeus on the 12th of March 1806 to the Superior General Blasucci: "Our holy Father Vicar" he writes "has had, with his Fathers, to bear the whole brunt of the war in Germany: but he is indefatigable in his zeal for souls and though not able to give missions, he is instant in preaching and expounding the word of God and confessing with wonderful fruit. For seven months I have not received a line from him, as, owing to the war, the greater part of our correspondence is lost, and the letters I have received are written by his secretary and not by himself, for he is too ill to do so. May I intreat your Reverence to pray earnestly for him and to get the other Fathers in Italy to do the same, that his health may be restored; for I really do not know what we should do without him. We need him more than I can express."

The Parish priest of Weinried, Lewis Vicari, in the deposition made by him during the cause of his beatification writes: "All those who ever knew the venerable Father Clement here speak of him with the like affection and veneration, not only for his zeal in preaching and hearing confessions, but also for his devoted care of the sick and dying. His sermons were simple in style and intelligible to all, but wonderful in their effects. While reading the Gospel in the vulgar tongue before the sermon as is the custom in Germany, he would very often interrupt himself to explain this or that passage; and sometimes he would ask questions of his audience, promising to those who answered well that he would say mass for them. However short the notice might be, if he were going to preach in some fresh church, the people would come there in crowds and very often after the sermon would beg to make a general confession. He was quite untireable in the Confessional. Sometimes, while he was saying his office in church, some one would come in, looking for a confessor perhaps and he would at once go up to that person and ask if he or she wished to go to confession? And all invariably replied "Yes, Father", although some had not thought of it before. He was very skilful also in giving penances according to the characters and circumstances of each, in which he showed extraordinary prudence and discretion.* In fact his apostolic zeal so penetrated the hearts of the people, that in that parish and neighbourhood from that hour till now, persons began to lead and have continued to lead, the most perfect and pious lives, which they attribute entirely to this great servant of God and his teaching. Most edifying above all was his way of saying mass. He endeavoured by every means in his power to procure splendour and beauty in Divine Worship, and any spare moments found him invariably in church in adoration of the Blessed Sacrament. He would say office and sing hymns in honour of our Lady with his brethren with such fervour and devotion that people used to exclaim: "Hark at the angels singing!" He introduced in Weinried the recitation of the angelical Rosary (the habit of which is still in use), a devotion admirably calculated, to incite faith, adoration of God and veneration of the B. Virgin.** To revive the faith and love of the people, this great servant of God distributed gratuitously among them the works of St. Alphonsus. His faith in Divine Providence was so great that if any one asked him "how they lived?" he would always reply: *"By the Providence of God."* And never did it fail him. On one occasion, when he and his congregation were reduced to great straits, there suddenly arrived at the door a whole cart-load of provisions, and no one could find out who had sent them. F. Clement was always praying: in the house, out of the

---

* For instance, he would give, as a penance, to one person to cut her bread on the side she liked least: or, not to look out of window for so many days, no matter what persons or carriages passed, and the like.

** This "angelical" Rosary differs from what is found in the "Raccolta", and is in honour of the Blessed Trinity by the frequent repetition of "*Sanctus, Sanctus, Sanctus, Dominus Deus Sabaoth*", as well as of the Blessed Virgin. When the writings of Father Clement were sought for by order of the Holy See in 1868, the Parish Priest of Pless sent this Rosary to the Bishop's Curia at Augsburg, adding: "Blessed is the Parish which offers up this sublime Prayer to the Throne of the Most High. It was my edification and joy for more than $10^{1}/_{2}$ years."

house, in church, in the street, always did he seem to be conversing with God in his heart, and holding his rosary in his hand. One day when he was saying his office in winter behind the house, some one having asked him how he could bear such great cold, F. Clement answered quietly: "*The love of God warms everything*". Intent only on bringing back stray sheep into the fold, he never minded cold, or heat, or bad roads or any other hardship when it was a question of exercising his apostolate. Thus, one day, he carried on foot and for a long way a very heavy sum of money which had been given in restitution, his shoes all the time being filled with snow-water. Sometimes when he was sent for to sick people who lived at a great distance, the Fathers would try and dissuade him from going so far. But he would answer: "So much the better, for I shall then have time to say the Rosary more often for the sick person." In the same way, he showed heroic charity towards his enemies. Once having been abused and insulted by a youth who went to the length of breaking the windows of his house, the neighbours ran out to punish him. But F. Clement called out: "Don't hurt him! I am just going into church to say mass for him".

He continually admonished the people to pray more for great sinners and this never failed to produce its effect. With the simplest words he would bring back people into the right way and induce them to lead holy lives. One day, the wife of the blacksmith of the country, a woman of a certain age, and probably not far from having to appear in the presence of God, came to see him, when he spoke to her upon the duty of frequenting the sacraments more often. She answered:

"But, Father, what would people say if they saw the wife of the blacksmith receiving the Sacraments so frequently?" F. Clement sent her away without adding anything more: but soon after, when preaching on that very subject, he said: "You all know that the frequent reception of the Sacraments is a holy and necessary thing: but the wife of the blacksmith answers: "What would people say if I went so often?" O! my good lady! what would people say if the wife of the blacksmith were to go to hell?"

Another day, when he was preaching, he saw a young man langhing: "O! my boy!" he exclaimed, "this is not a place in which you should laugh. I fear you have never thought of your faults or of doing penance for them!" which simple words had such an effect on the youth, that from that moment he began to lead a thoroughly good and Christian life. On another occasion, finding a mountebank who, for a small sum of money, was singing improper songs, F. Clement stopped him and exhorted him to follow another trade if he wished to go to Heaven, as the bread he gained in that way was baked by the devil. Nor did he give him up till he had found him some other employment. There was a certain notorious atheist in the place whom no one could do anything with and who was a man of infamous character besides. F. Clement succeeded in converting him; and to every one's astonishment, this very man came to the Parish Church one Sunday and on his knees asked pardon of the congregation for the scandal he had given. The venerable old Parish Priest was so overjoyed at this conversion that he jumped about like a child.

We have mentioned the sum of money, by way of restitution, which F. Clement carried one day. The person to whom he brought it refused to accept it: but F. Clement insisted: "It would not be well for you to give back this sum to the man who had cheated you and who is now thoroughly penitent; for otherwise he might think less of the sin of theft."

The good people seeing that F. Clement's coat and cassock were all worn and threadbare, had some fresh cloth dyed and presented him with a new suit, which he accepted with great gratitude and was delighted with the gift. But every where the fame of his humility and charity was spread abroad. When, one day, I was speaking about collecting evidence for the cause of the beatification of this great servant of God, one answered me: "What? they talk of cannonising F. Clement! But he was a Saint already when he was living amongst us!" And another added: "I am but a rough soldier: but I would have given my life for F. Clement." When he came into the church, the people would all rise and bow profoundly, many sighing and saying they felt as if it were our Lord himself passing by. They would kiss the hem of his cassock when he was not looking and preserved every little thing he had used or touched as a precious relic. It was only to the thoroughly bad or to the hardened schismatics that he was an object of hatred and dread. In order to keep back any one from doing wrong, or encourage him in virtue, the people still have the habit of exclaiming: "*What would Father Clement say?*" Many attribute to him not only their own salvation but the material prosperity of the country, thinking that he had obtained that grace from God as a reward for their fidelity to his teaching. I gave one day a picture of the Saint to an old woman of 70, without saying whose it was. She had hardly taken it into her hand, than she exclaimed joyfully: "O! this is our dear and holy Father Clement", and covered it with kisses—so strong was the impression that even his features had made on the memory of a person who had not seen him for 50 years! One of my predecessors in the Parish of Weinried, a most excellent priest, told me solemnly that if it had not been for Father Clement, he should not have had a hope of being saved. And this was only one of the thousands of souls he had converted."

To this interesting account from the pen of the Priest Vicar, we will only add one or two more instances of the veneration in which his memory is held in that place.

In August 1867 we found ourselves for a few hours only

in Babenhausen and several people came to us who had known F. Clement personally. One of these, who, as a boy, had served his mass, said that he never could forget the devotion with which he offered the Holy Sacrifice. Another mentioned with what intense charity he would assist the sick in the Hospital, of which the Parish priest had given him the entire care. He sent every day one of his Fathers to say mass there: and instructed a certain number of youths to act as infirmarians, the Sisters of Charity having been exiled. In the presbytery we saw, not without emotion, that the little room which F. Clement had inhabited, had been always kept as a Sanctuary, and contained a large picture of him which was held in great veneration. And this is the more remarkable, as the house being very small, this room would be very useful. But no one has been allowed to occupy it since; and it is looked upon as a holy place.

In fact, we can only say, in conclusion, that F. Clement exercised the most wonderful and salutary influence over all with whom he came in contact, and the marvellous thing is, that he was only ten months in this place, where his memory is so tenderly cherished and revered!! while other excellent priests are forgotten who yet had passed their whole lives in the Parish and laboured with zeal and fidelity in the discharge of their duties.

CHAPTER XIII.

PERSECUTIONS ENDURED BY THE REDEMPTORISTS AT BABENHAUSEN. FATHER CLEMENT RETURNS TO WARSAW.

[1806.]

THE apostolate and the cross are twins and inseparable one from the other. As our Divine master said to His disciples: "The servant is not greater than his master. If they have persecuted me they will also persecute you." (St. John XV. Chap. 20. V.) If F. Clement had had to drink of the bitter cup of persecution in Triberg, what could he hope for in Babelhausen? It would have been strange indeed if the devil had allowed such spiritual triumphs in a place, without endeavouring to destroy them.

The enormous success of F. Clement and his disciples and the great veneration shown them by the people, gave umbrage to certain priests; partly because the zeal shown by the Redemptorists was a reproach to their own idleness; partly because, being imbued with the false and heretical ideas of the day, they hated all that was so essentially Catholic and Papal.

Even Prince Anselm of Fugger, who was so attached to the missioners that he had himself made a design for a new College and Church for them, and who had implored F. Sabelli to undertake the education of his sons, was deceived by these men into believing many things which were falsely adduced against them. However, when he saw how bitter and unjust was their persecution of F. Clement and his Fathers and how patiently they bore it, he did his best to protect them. But unfortunately in July 1806, he lost his rights as Prince of the Empire and then could no longer defend them.

F. Clement foresaw the coming storm and wrote in June 1806 to the Procurator General in Rome imploring the prayers of their Italian brethren. "It is impossible to foresee," he writes "into whose hands this country will fall". And again in a letter of the 21st of July, in which he warmly praises the Vicar General of Augsburg, Antony of Nigg, he adds: "We have so many enemies in this place that we need warm friends. We are living in the midst of terrible auxiety and need to take Heaven by storm that we may obtain help from God."

The vilest and most absurd lies were circulated against

F. Clement, which no one could believe who was not eaten up with prejudices. Amongst other things, they declared that on his going to visit the sick at Illerberg, he had broken open the tabernacle door to get at the sacred particles, because the Parish Priest had refused him the key. This calumny, which was even carried to the judge at Roggenburg, was emphatically denied by word of mouth and in writing by the Parish Priest himself. It was true that F. Clement had been to Illerberg and taken Holy Communion to some sick people there: but with the full consent of the Parish Priest, who had begged him, moreover, to spend the night in his house and to say mass in his church the next morning and in a parochial note dated the 20th of February 1806 this very priest writes: "F. John Clement Hofbauer, Vicar General of the Order of the Redemptorists, came here to-day. The object of his Congregation is to revive the Faith in these days of unbelief. He is trying to found colleges everywhere with the consent of the local authorities and the Princes, for the education of youth in our holy religion. Father Clement is a man of great eloquence and learning and besides most courteous and pleasing in manner, and full of holiness and zeal for religion. He speaks German beautifully and knows all the great people in Vienna even of the Imperial Court. We supped together and had a most interesting conversation on spiritual and scientific subjects".

In the same Parochial Diary we find on the 22nd of July the following notice.

"I have had a visit to-day from the abbot of the suppressed monastery of Roggenburg: and he tells me that the Directory of Ulm have prohibited the Redemptorists from labouring in their apostolic mission within the confines of Bavaria", which unhappily was quite true.

The Bavarian Government not having yet taken possession of the principality of Babenhausen, they could not prohibit the exercise of F. Clement's ministry in that province. And the labours of these "*Preachers of Penance*" as the people called them, being confined to this little principality, all the inhabitants of the neighbourhood flocked into Babenhausen and Weinried, so that our Redemptorists were overwhelmed with fatigue. The Bishop's Curia at Augsburg had given them leave to say mass and preach in the little church of the Hospital: so that on the 2nd of July, F. Antony Egle preached the first sermon and F. Clement set up the *Via Crucis* in this church, to the great delight of the sick. On the 3rd Sunday of this same month the Feast of the most Holy Redeemer was solemnly celebrated there with High Mass and sermon throughout the octave; while on the last day, F. Clement gave the people the Papal Benediction: to the immense consolation of the assembled crowds.

But the greater was their satisfaction with the missioners and the warmer their affection for them, the more indignant (we say it with sorrow) were the Parish priests And the one at Babenhausen never rested till he had got the authorities to prohibit the services in the hospital.

At last, on the 3rd of August 1806, the principality of Babenhausen by Royal Decree, was incorporated with the Kingdom of Bavaria. On this occasion, the good Prince Fugger, whose authority now only extended to minor cases, assured the Fathers that he would do his utmost to protect them: but he told them privately that he had very little hope of success: and advised them strongly to look out elsewhere for the future.

Father Clement felt terribly the coming destruction of a house from which he had hoped for so much fruit and all the more, from the eagerness with which the people had responded to his appeal. To increase his sorrow, bad news came also from Warsaw, where the house was also gravely threatened; and the Fathers besought him to return there and help them in their troubles. Clement, finding he could do no more at Babenhausen, resolved to return to Warsaw, leaving F. Passerat to preside over the Community at Babenhausen as long as it was possible to remain there. On taking leave of them, he exhorted them with tears to persevere in their holy vocation, even under the most painful circumstances and added: "Pray, my beloved Bretheren, pray earnestly that the Congregation may not perish. The times are evil, and who knows what will come next? Perhaps we may never see one another again: but in all circumstances, let us hope in Divine Providence".

On the 10th of August, after having received the vows of the Polish novice, Schulski, he started for Vienna with a cleric, Martin Stark, as his companion. On this journey we have heard of a fact which proves more strongly than ever the influence F. Clement had over men's minds and hearts, and the unlimited confidence he had in Divine Providence. They arrived one evening at an inn where they were to rest for the night, very tired and faint, for they had eaten nothing all day; but unhappily their purse was empty! Several times during their toilsome march, poor young Stark had complained of terrible hunger, and F. Clement had promised him food on arrival. But the innkeeper would give nothing on credit and there was only a little straw for them to lie upon. Stark reminded F. Clement of his promise, which the latter renewed. In the same room were two men gambling, and soon from quarrelling they came to cursing and swearing. This was more than F. Clement could stand: and rising from the straw, spoke to the men with such sweetness and charity imploring them not to offend the good God, that his aspect and words touched both their hearts and they not only ceased their bad language and threw up their cards, but they ordered a good dinner and to show their gratitude, insisted on F. Clement and his companion sharing it with them. F. Clement accepted; and turning to his young cleric said: "Now, do you see how God never abandons his servants!" On many other occasions besides this one, F. Clement showed an extraordinary power in couverting souls. One day, he was travelling in a carriage with a young man who was very ill both in body and mind: and in spite of all F. Clement's tender charity and kindness, he did nothing but swear at and insult him. Finding that his loving remonstrances were unheeded, he resolved to bear it all in silence. When they arrived at the inn where they were to get down and dine, the young man tried to do so, but was so weak that he could not move. Then F. Clement, forgetting the insult he had received, carried him in his own arms tenderly into the inn and after dinner, with a like charity, carried him back into the carriage. This extraordinary kindness and generosity touched the young man to the heart and he made a public apology to our Saint, exclaiming: "If I had known such a priest sooner, I should not have fallen into so miserable a state as I am in now!"

On the 3rd of Septbr. F. Clement arrived in Vienna and met his dear companion, F. Thaddeus, who had come from Warsaw on purpose to explain to him by word of mouth the grave perils with which their house in that city was threatened: so that they stayed some weeks in Vienna to try and find a refuge in Austria for their persecuted Congregation. But from the sad condition of that country after the disastrous war with France, they found there was no hope of making any foundation there for the moment· so that in December they both returned to Warsaw, where F. Clement, was received as an Angel of consolation.

CHAPTER XIV.

THE REDEMPTORISTS ARE DRIVEN FROM BABENHAUSEN AND TAKE REFUGE IN SWITZERLAND.
A short notice of F. Clement's first disciples.

[From 1806 to 1807.]

WHILST Father Clement was occupied in Vienna with the troubles of his Warsaw House, affairs in Babenhausen went from bad to worse. On the Feast of the Exaltation of the Holy Cross, a Royal Commission took possession of the Principality. The following day the Government officials took the oath to the King of Bavaria; and two days later, the Redemptorists received notice that in a couple of months they must leave Babenhausen. F. Clement having received this sad news on the 4th of Oct., wrote to F. Passerat desiring him to try and find an asylum in Switzerland. On the 9th, F. Passerat started accordingly, and went to Coire, Rheinfelden and other places, but without any result and so returned on the 27th of the same month to Babenhausen.

Divine Providence, however, did not forsake them. On the 19th of Novbr., a letter arrived unexpectedly from Coire, in which Baal, the Chancellor of the Bishop of Coire, invited the Fathers to take refuge in the deserted Convent of St. Luke, which had been occupied by the Premonstratensians, who had been lately dispersed, after having lost all their possessions in Vorarlberg and in the principality of Lichtenstein. They had ceded their monastery, by permission of the Holy See, to the Bishop of the Diocese for the use of his Seminary; but, later on, this Seminary had been transferred to Meran. This Bishop of Coire was a rare gem of the Episcopal Order—namely, the holy and excellent Count Buol-Schauenstein; who was delighted at the idea of having these good Religious for his church and schools in the place of the dissolved Premonstratensians. And he was still more pleased when he found that the Redemptorists asked for no reward for their labours. He only exacted, as a condition, the consent of their Vicar General, so that F. Passerat wrote instantly to F. Clement, who accepted the offer with joy. F. Passerat started accordingly for Coire to make all the necessary arrangements, taking with him F. Hartmann and the laybrother Bonaventura Stoll. Having settled everything with the Bishop and his council, F. Passerat returned to Babenhausen to fetch his remaining subjects, who were in a very critical position and only not violently expelled thanks to the energetic remonstrances of good Prince Fugger.

The Bavarian Government, to avoid the odium of a violent expulsion, but to ensure the departure of the Redemptorists, put out the following decree:

"In the Name of His Majesty the King of Bavaria."
&c. ... &c. ... &c. ... &c. ... &c. ...

"According to the Report received regarding the Redemptorists residing in Babenhausen, where they had been of late tolerated though not regularly established, the Governor of the Principality is hereby informed:

1. That he is not to insist on driving them away hastily, but graciously to concede to them six month's indulgence, reckoning from to day, and that on account of the coming winter. Which indulgence must be immediately communicated to the Redemptorist Fathers, enjoining them, at the same time to make immediate arrangements for evacuating the Royal States at the required time.
2. The said Fathers are strictly forbidden, under the most stringent penalties, to admit into their order any individual whether as priest or laybrother.
3. They may not in any case, or on any pretext, render any service in the cure of souls, whether it be by preaching, hearing confessions or visiting the sick. Their ministrations must be limited to saying mass.

4. A Register must be kept of the said Redemptorists, showing their nationality, their physical state, and the time of their entrance into and profession of their order.
5. They must be taken away from the Hospital which was confided to their care, and send in a report to the undersigned of the condition of the said Hospital.
6. The Governor of the Principality will draw up a protocol of these conditions to be submitted to the Redemptorists and the said protocol only signed by the Superior and two other members of the Congregation (in proof of having received it) shall be sent to us within eight days.

Ulm, 19th of December 1806.
Kingdom of Bavaria territorial direction in Switzerland.
(Signed) Baron von Leiden.

The Parish Priest of Babenhausen, with a zeal worthy of a better cause, hastened to carry out the execution of this decree by prohibiting the Fathers on Xmas Eve from administering Holy Communion. As to the "*Gracious*" concession of the Government to allow them to protract for six months their stay in Babenhausen, it is needless to say that the Fathers did not take advantage of it: for to prohibit them from preaching, hearing confessions, or visiting the sick and thus condemning them to total inaction, was like depriving fish of water and birds of air. Accordingly on the 3rd of Jan. 1807, F. Hofbauer and the clerics started for Coire, and two days later, F. Passerat with F. Louis Czech, who had taken the habit before their departure. The few that remained on at Babenhausen had much to suffer: for on the 22nd they received an unexpected visit from the Royal Commissioner, Baron von Leiden, with a Secretary, who made a rigorous inquisition into the state of the house and accused the Fathers of having encouraged the young men not to submit to the new military levy. Under Prince Fugger this species of conscription was unknown: but was put into operation as soon as the Bavarian Government had taken possession of the principality. It was, therefore, not to be wondered at that it was only submitted to unwillingly and by force, and whenever possible the youth resorted to emigration to avoid it. "Very willingly", they said, "will we serve our King: but we are not disposed to shed our blood for a foreign Sovereign like Napoleon." The Redemptorists were made responsible for this reluctance, and it was even asserted that they had publickly preached against this new military law. It is needless to state that the whole accusation was a palpable calumny and that they had never been guilty of such an act of imprudence. But the Commissioners pretended to have proofs of their assertion and so the Fathers were subjected to a rigorous examination as to their habits, works and way of life. F. Hofbauer submitted a quantity of pulpit notes to the Commissioners, who after having looked them over returned them, saying that they had been certainly calumniated.

Another accusation against the Fathers was, that they practised medecine and had a pharmacy in their house. This was partly true: for in the country, where a Doctor was not always at hand, they used to give certain simple medecines to the people and had learned what to do in case of sudden accidents. But this, which was one of their works of mercy, was imputed to them as a crime. The whole house was searched; but no pharmacy was found.

Again the Fathers were accused of having private confessionals now that they were forbidden openly to hear their penitents. But again was the house ransacked to find these confessionals and in vain! The Royal Commission, therefore, was compelled to acquit them and declare their innocence of the different charges brought against them: but with the usual injustice of persecutors, they forbid their living together any longer in community. Upon this decision being made known, Prince Fugger advised the remaining Fathers to depart immediately, although, he was grieved to lose F. Sabelli who was the Tutor of his sons. On the 11th of Febr., therefore, the whole community with their students, left Babenhausen, amidst the tears and heartfelt regrets of the good. And it was very lucky that they started when they did, for two days later came an order from the Governor refusing them passports! The poor people had clubbed together to find money for their journey and had moved their furniture for them in carts to Bregenz, where they were deposited in the Capuchin Convent.

Thus, after four years' arduous toil, the house in Germany had to be given up: but F. Clement had sown the seed: the Congregation had become known to and loved by the people: faith had been revived in thousands of souls, and he had had the consolation of forming a number of apostolic men as his disciples, who, later on, were to do much for the glory of God and the good of souls.

We will only say two or three words here of some of the fathers he had thus gathered together.

The first, *F. Martin Stark*, was his secretary and inseparable companion. After F. Clement's death, he became the first Recter of the Vienna House, and in 1846, was sent to America to consolidate the Congregation there.

Another favourite disciple was *F. Joseph Forthuber*, called by F. Clement *"The good Joseph"*, destined to be Superior of the Bucharest mission. Then there was *F. John Kaltenbach*, a man of extraordinary piety and insatiable in good works: *F. Joseph Hofbauer*, the first priest who joined the Congregation in Germany: *F. Martin Schöllhorn*, Rector of the first French House of the order: *F. John Sabelli*, who, in 1822, was made secretary to the Father General and was the Confessor of Maria Teresa, Queen of Naples: *F. Antony Egle* whose labours were chiefly in Switzerland; *F. Sebastian Heberle and F. Bonaventura Stoll* who became excellent missioners and zealous confessors. But of all these, none was more esteemed by F. Clement than *Father Louis Czech*, the pearl of the Babenhausen students, who won all hearts by his sweetness and prudence. He was still alive when the cause of F. Clement's beatification was brought forward in 1864, and was invaluable as a witness of his holy life in community at Warsaw and in Germany. Devoted to our Lady he died on the Feast of the Immaculate conception in 1868, being 79 years old.

In addition to these, there were many other fervent disciples of F. Clement whom he imbued with his own spirit, although it was given to him only to sow the seed in tears which was afterwards to bear such abundant fruit: *"Euntes ibant et flebant, mittentes semina sua"*. 125. Psalm.

CHAPTER XV.

THE REDEMPTORISTS IN COIRE. THEIR TROUBLES AND PERSECUTIONS. DRIVEN FROM THENCE, THEY TAKE REFUGE IN THE VALAIS.

[1807.]

WE have seen that F. Passerat, who had obtained the acceptance of his Congregation by the Bishop's Council at Coire, was only waiting for the consent of Father Clement, which the latter hastened to send to the Vicariate in the following terms: "Your Reverence has had the great kindness to promise to the Father Rector Passerat, a temporary refuge for his exiled Fathers from Babenhausen.

In your obliging letter of the 5th of November, of which the Rector sent me a copy, I see with great pleasure that you have deigned to offer us the use of the Convent of St. Luke for the space of half a year or more. On this occasion, I wish to fulfil my first duty by thanking you with all my heart for this act of truly Christian Charity, which has relieved me from a great load of anxiety. May the Good Jesus hear my prayers and be Himself your eternal reward.

I hope that our Congregation, by the grace of God will give no displeasure to the Bishop's Council, since my earnest wish is to give all its labours for the benefit of the Diocese, for the glory of God and the good of souls: and that, not for a year only but for ever.

If the Diocese should desire to establish a seminary for the formation and education of priests, our Congregation would be most happy to undertake it at St. Luke's and to train the students in accordance with the teaching of the Church.

As to the maintenance of its members, that will be no burden upon any one: for by the conditions of our constitution, we are forbidden to beg. As to the maintenance of the students, we leave that to the wise decisions of the Diocesan Chapter.

I beg leave to assure your Reverence that the main object of our institution is to be in no one's way: but to strive, on the contrary, to be of all the use we possibly can and to edify the people in word, deed and intention.

Our house in Warsaw, called St. Bennone, which is now in the 20th year of its existence, has founded an Orphanage containing 40 boys; a male school of five classes; a female orphanage; and a large public Poor School, where instruction is given gratuitously to all. These different works have been founded one by one almost imperceptibly and have been maintained by the mercy of Divine Providence, which never fails to assist men of good will who correspond with His grace. Only in case of extreme necessity does our rule permit us to make known our need to certain persons: but habitual *quêtes* are forbidden, our holy founder being convinced of the danger attending mendicant orders, from the disorder which arises, in consequence, in community life. I hereby give the Father Rector Passerat, all necessary faculties for the acceptance of the Convent of St. Luke and for all the business which may have to be transacted with the Bishop's Council, as also for the erection of the seminary if desired. And all that he shall have settled and decreed I shall consider as having been done by myself; as I cannot be present and as I have the fullest confidence in the ability and capacity of the Rector regarding the matters in hand. In conclusion, I beg instantly to recommend this affair to your Reverence, so that if it be God's will, (as I cannot doubt) it may be speedily settled for the glory of God and the prosperity of Holy Church. May St. Charles, who is the patron of this Diocese, bless your zeal for this good work.

I remain, with respectful veneration
your Reverence's devoted and obliged servant
John Clement Mary Hofbauer
Vicar General of the Cong. of SS. Red.

This letter shows us all F. Clement's gratitude to his benefactors, his love for his brethren, his zeal for the glory of God and above all, his disinterestedness and strong faith in God's Providence. Like another St. Cajetan, he trusted in God without seeking human aid and only accepted spontaneous offers of charity. Yet Coire was a small town, the inhabitants of which were mainly protestants, and from whom, therefore, small help could be expected. But he never lost his hope. How admirable is our Lord in His servants!

For a letter to reach Coire from Warsaw in those days and especially in the winter season took a long time. But at last it arrived and the Convent of St. Luke was at once given over to the Redemptorists. On the 19th of February 1809, the last of the Babenhausen Fathers arrived at Coire. In all, they consisted of eight Fathers, five clerics and four laybrothers. Only a portion of them could live in the Convent: the rest took a house in the town. Their poverty was very great: the few bits of furniture they could bring from Babenhausen only fitted up two or three rooms and for want of beds, half of them had to sleep on a board wrapped up in their cloaks. The spring was bitterly cold: they had hardly any wood: and the only stove they had, burnt so badly that it only served to prevent their actually freezing and was not able to warm any of them. They had an equal scarcity of food: and that consisted generally of a soup of hot water and potatoes and a dish of milk. But as they were filled with the spirit of mortification which F. Clement had so carefully instilled into them by his own example, they were all happy and contented and began instantly to preach and to hear confessions. Their simple and practical expositions of the Word of God produced at once a most favourable impression and their church was soon crowded not only by Catholics but by Protestants and even by Calvinist Ministers.

Hence the Devil, foreseeing their success, determined to raise a fresh tempest against them. They had hardly settled in Coire, when there came a letter from Ulm from their old enemy, Baron von Leiden, addressed to the Governor of the Grisons, in which he stated that, for grave reasons, the King of Bavaria had been compelled to exile the Redemptorists from his realm: and therefore that if the Governor of the Grisons permitted them to settle in their Canton, he must take care that they did not draw near the Bavarian frontier.* The Governor answered that the affair would be referred to the Council and that in the meanwhile he would take all the required measures of precaution. He further begged to know for what reason the Bavarian Government had exiled these religious?

On the 25th of February the Council communicated this despatch to the Coire Municipality, inviting them to make further enquiries regarding the Redemptorists. F. Passerat

---

* Vorarlberg and the Tyrol then formed a part of the Kingdom of Bavaria. —

was consequently summoned immediately before the Municipality, where he went, accompanied by F. Joseph Hofbauer. He was questioned as to the number of his subjects, the names and nationality of each and on various other points: and he was severely reproved for having established himself at St. Luke's without the consent of the Civil Authorities. To this F. Passerat did not answer, leaving it to the Bishop to justify himself, as he had an undoubted right to call in the assistance of any priests he chose into his Diocese, without consulting any civil authority. The Fathers, however, were courteously treated by the Council who permitted them to remain at St. Luke's and did not prohibit their receiving any fresh members. Hence Joseph Forthuber was soon after admitted into the Congregation.

On the 4th of March, however, the municipality wrote to the Vicar General expressing their surprise that he had allowed the Redemptorists to establish themselves in Coire without consulting the City whose territorial rights were thereby infringed. This the Vicar General flatly denied, asserting that they had only taken the place of the Premonstratensians, who had never required the permission of the State to occupy St. Luke's: and that the continuance of Divine Worship in that Convent depended solely on the Bishop and his Council. As to the questions of *nomination* and *investiture* he would not enter into them, as the Convent was ecclesiastical property and consequently Catholic, although situated on City ground. However as, two days later, a public Commission of the State was to meet in Coire to discuss the question of the Redemptorists, the Vicar General wrote to the Syndic, Rudolph of Salis-Soglio, to recommend their cause, and the Catholic members of the Commission drew up a collective statement justifying the admission of the Redemptorists. But notwithstanding this strong recommendation and the Catholic protest, the Commission decreed their expulsion; and that in spite of the

Syndic: the Protestant members of the Commission pretending to refute the reasoning of their Catholic Colleagues. The Bishop, they said, might certainly call simple priests into his Diocese, but not a Congregation and especially not the Redemptorists, whose sojourn in Coire would involve them in grave difficulties with the Bavarian Government: and all the more, because they came from Prussian Poland where even the Jesuits were tolerated.

On the same day (12th of March) the Catholic members of the Commission demanded that the execution of the Decree should be postponed till confirmed by the Great Council. But all their efforts were fruitless: and the Redemptorists received notice to quit the Canton in eight days unless they wished to be expelled by force.

The notice of this cruel measure produced great irritation in the minds of the Catholic population especially in the neighbouring Commune of Ems, where the Fathers had often gone to exercise their ministry. The inhabitants rose and resolved to prevent the execution of the Decree by force of arms, imploring the Fathers to take refuge with them, as they would know how to defend them. But neither the Vicar General nor the Redemptorists would hear of any armed intervention. However, this energetic movement on the part of the Catholics produced a certain effect. The unjust decree was not carried out at that time; and on the 19th of March the Syndic wrote to F. Passerat that he and his Fathers could remain, at any rate, till after Easter. Two days later, he wrote to the Vicar General saying that the Redemptorists would be tolerated in the Canton provided they would consent to separate themselves.

On the 20th of March arrived the answer from the Bavarian Government to the Council of Coire, signed by Baron von Lerchenfeld. In this despatch it was stated that the Redemptorists had been expelled as a useless corporation contrary to the maxims of the Government as regarded monastic orders: that their preaching was contrary to the meek and humble spirit of Christianity: and that they were suspected of having provoked the resistance to the military levies. Such accusations were only to the honour of the Redemptorists, for certainly their maxims were very different from those of the Bavarian Government, who had acted in defiance of all right and justice and arbitrarily suppressed all the monasteries in the Kingdom. This government, in fact, persecuted the Church and all religious institutions, while the Redemptorists stood up for all sacred rights. The preaching of these Fathers naturally displeased the Freemasons and the pretended "Illuminated" members of the Government, whose only aim was to destroy the Catholic Faith. As for all the alledged "suspicions" regarding the levies, it is useless to add more than that Baron von Leiden himself had owned that it was a pure calumny.

On Easter Day, F. Passerat and his brethren ran the risk of being forcibly expelled from St. Luke's: but the Syndic averted the fatal blow. However two days later, an order appeared dissolving the Community and dispersing its members. The Syndic however, gave leave to the sick to remain in the house and look after their poor furniture. In three days, the Fathers were dispersed as Chaplains in different parishes in the neighbourhood of the town. On the 1st of May the Grand Council of the Grisons was assembled and the question of the Redemptorists was again brought forward. Triumphant answers to the accusations brought against them were made by several eminent persons especially by the Prefect Vieli, who, fearing a hostile decision, suggested that the whole matter should be referred to the General Diet. But the Bavarian Government had written to Reinard, the Swiss President, to warn the Governor of the Grisons against any measure in favour of the Redemptorists. The result was that the decree of expulsion was confirmed and they were forbidden to reside any longer in the Canton. Thus the Grand Council yielded to the unjust pressure put upon them by the Bavarian Government, which, having taken possession of Vorarlberg and the Tyrol, tried to destroy all ecclesiastical institutions in these countries. But the noble Tyrolese people rose as one man against these enemies of their Faith and in the end, the Bavarian Government was shamefully defeated and compelled to yield.

On the 23rd of May the Governor of the Grisons communicated the fatal decision of the Grand Council to the Vicar General of Coire. The Vicar General referred him to the Prince Bishop, then residing at Meran in the Tyrol, adding that the Catholics had implored his mediation and begged that the matter might be referred to the Federal Diet.

All this time, poor F. Passerat was in the greatest anxiety: not knowing where to turn for refuge. The Vicar General had given him a magnificent testimonial in which he stated that "The Redemptorists had edified the whole country by their exemplary lives: that they had shown the most devoted zeal in the salvation of souls and by their readiness in helping every one with their gratuitous services". He gave them letters of recommendation also to the Prince Bishop of Sion, Joseph Antony von Blatter, whom he thought would be prepared to give them an asylum.

With these documents in hand, and trusting in Divine Providence, F. Passerat started on the 25th of May (accompanied by F. Casimir Langanki) for the Valais, climbing over the highest mountains by the most dangerous paths. Arrived at Vissach, they were warmly received by the Parish Priest, Adrian von Curten, whose parishioners came forward at once with offers to receive the Redemptorists and give them a house. The Bishop was equally propitious.

During this time, the Catholics of Coire had appealed to the Federal Diet assembled at Zurich to intreat that the

Redemptorists might remain in their Canton. But the Diet refused to entertain the question, saying it was not a general but a cantonal one, and the Bavarian Government, who had sworn death to the congregation, were even more enraged at the dispersion of the Fathers in different houses, as thereby their influence was only increased; and declared it would be better they should be once more reunited in Coire, *provided they were forbidden to exercise their ministry.* Father Passerat, having left F. Langanki at Vissach, came back alone to Coire with the joyful news 'that a house was guaranteed to the congregation. And on the 8th of July, he sent Fathers Francis Hofbauer and Sabelli to begin the new Foundation. The rest celebrated solemnly at St. Luke's for the last time the Feast of our Lady of Mount Carmel and of our Holy Redeemer.

If Father Clement had been rejoiced at the foundation of Coire, we may imagine his disappointment and distress at the result of the persecution they had endured. He wrote two letters to thank the Vicar General for his protection of their house which we will give in extenso.

In that of the 6th of July 1807 he writes: "O! how difficult it is in these days for our Lord's workmen to labour in His Vineyard! If God does not bless the anxious care which your Reverence has shown on our behalf, I fear that the enemy of souls will again hinder the sowing of the seed by our poor Congregation; although that seed promised to bring forth such abundant fruit. But, I will not cease to ask of the Most High, through his great mercy, to remove all obstacles if it be His holy will. May God bless your Reverence for the protection you have granted to our brethren!. I humbly beg of you to direct them, in this difficult moment, by your wise counsels. I trust that all the subjects of our Congregation will have always at heart the glory of God and the good of their neighbours: and that their conduct will be such as to give no cause of complaint to any one. If they should no longer have the good fortune to be under your orders, I beg of you to forward to them the enclosed letter".

On the 18th of July he writes again: "Convinced of the good will and kindness of your Reverence, I venture once more to trouble you with a few lines. I was very much touched by a letter I have received from my spiritual sons saying that had it not been for your energetic protection, they would have been innocent victims of the persecution now raging against them. My sorrow has been greatly relieved by this announcement; and I hope that He in accordance with Whose Holy Will we are striving to walk, will direct all things to His greater glory. I can do nothing further than instantly pray to our Lord to fill you more and more with his love and to grant you health and strength to labour for Him. I shall be always happy to hear that my persecuted sons are promoting the honour of God and the salvation of souls under your Reverence's prudent guidance.

With profound veneration I commend your Reverence to the protection of the most High; and recommending myself to your fervent prayers, I shall never cease to be your Reverence's unworthy but grateful servant

Clement Mary Hofbauer
Vicar General of Cong. S. S. Red.

On the 5th of August the sad news reached Coire, that, in the brief space of ten days, three of the Fathers had died in Warsaw, Father Hausner, Vannelet, and Hübl; under which sad circumstances, F. Langanki with brother Norbert Spitznagel were recalled to Warsaw.

All this time, the poor Redemptorist Fathers continued to be an eyesore to the Protestants and Free-masons by whom they were surrounded, and the Diet having decided that it was a Cantonal business, the Governor of the Grisons renewed his orders to the Vicar General to dismiss them at once, adducing as a reason that F. Passerat had written to his Superior at Warsaw complaining of the conduct of the Bavarian Government. This the Vicar General, after conferring with F. Passerat, emphatically denied: and he likewise intreated the Governor to defer their expulsion, at any rate, till the winter was over. But the Governor was inexorable and would have driven them out by force had they not spontaneously departed. In fact, F. Passerat, feeling that all reasoning was worse than useless, had already sent off his last Fathers and students to Lucerne, which they reached towards the end of November; he having certain clerics who were to be ordained by the Nunzio there. After winding up all their affairs at Coire, he rejoined his spiritual children at Lucerne, and soon after undertook with them the journey to their new home in the Valais.

This journey has remained a memorable one in the Annals of the Congregation, not only from its extreme difficulties and dangers, but also as a manifest proof of the special protection of God towards His faithful and persecuted servants.

To arrive at the Valais, it was necessary to cross a high mountain called the Grimsel. F. Passerat with eight of his companions, principally students, undertook this ascent in the middle of December, a proceeding which proved an exceptional courage and faith in God. The beginning was practicable enough: but as they went on, the depth of snow rendered their progress almost impossible. The evening of the first day they arrived more than half frozen and thoroughly exhausted at a wayside inn where they were to halt for the night. A violent hurricane came on which heaped up the snow on their path to an extraordinary height. The posts which should have indicated the right road were all buried: while a whirlwind of snow blinded our poor travellers and increased their peril, as they sunk up to their knees at every step. Their guides, who were entirely bewildered and did not know which road to take, flatly refused to go any further. In this emergency F. Passerat suddenly exclaimed: "My sons! fall upon your knees. Prayer alone can save us!" All knelt down in the snow and with outstretched arms repeated five Paters and Aves. The two Protestant guides were so struck at their faith, that one of them cried out: "Forward!! When men pray like that, there is nothing to fear." And this man put himself at the head of the little band, dashed through the snow which came up to his waist, and discovered the right road, which brought them, though in a terribly exhausted state, to Obergestellen, the first village in the Valais. Our Lord having thus preserved His servants from such great perils, provided them also with the necessary restoratives. When they arrived at the inn they found a newly married couple who were holding a nuptial Feast. Being good and earnest Catholics, they were at once deeply interested in the condition of our poor travellers and considered themselves most highly honoured to have such holy Religious as their guests. They received them accordingly with every demonstration of charity and affection and treated them most loyally to the best the house could produce. F. Passerat and his companions accepted with gratitude this unexpected kindness which only the more confirmed their confidence in God. Rested, refreshed and well fed, they continued their journey and on the 30th of December 1807 arrived safely at Vissach.

In the mean while, the Bavarian Government in its blind rage, had expelled by force the Bishop of Coire from the Tyrol, of which the western portion had unfortunately fallen under their temporary jurisdiction, and without asking the leave of the Holy See, they ordered that the Diocese should henceforth be under obedience to the Bishop of Augsburg instead of Coire. The Professors of the Seminary at Meran, not choosing to submit to so schismatical a proceeding, were sent into Switzerland and, followed by the students, took up their residence at St. Luke's, so that a few days after the departure of the Redemptorists, the Diocesan Seminary was established there.

CHAPTER XVI.

FATHER CLEMENT AN EXAMPLE OF ALL RELIGIOUS AND DOMESTIC VIRTUES TO HIS BRETHREN.

IT is time now to return to the subject of our biography and to consider how it was that in spite of such continual trials and persecutions, he was able to effect so much for the glory of God and the good of souls.

Let us cast a glance at F. Clement in his own room at St. Bennone, where, through a little window, he could look down upon the Blessed Sacrament. At this window he passed long hours in loving colloquies with our Blessed Lord. Whom he contemplated, and adored and loved and consulted in all the difficulties of his life. Here he prepared the sermons which so touched the hearts of his hearers: here he found light in his doubts, consolation in adversity, courage in persecution and fire to kindle his zeal for God's service. It is not wonderful then, that when speaking of Jesus in the Blessed Sacrament he seemed inflamed with love, and that when offering the Holy Sacrifice he was often wrapt in ecstasy; while after Holy Communion abundant tears flowed down his cheeks. Everything in this little room was simple and poor; there was nothing ornamental whatever. Everywhere Evangelical poverty made itself felt, which F. Clement looked upon as the very foundation of the spiritual life. When, in the beginning of their foundations, at Warsaw and elsewhere, the absolute necessaries of life were wanting, F. Clement was never disturbed or put out; but always cheery and merry over their privations, thus encouraging the others to bear them bravely; and declaring that such poverty was, in reality, a rich treasure. And when the misery ceased and comparative comfort supervened, he still never lost sight of this principle and was as moderate in prosperity as he had been gay in the time of need.

He guarded the rule in this respect with the greatest vigilance and never tolerated any infringement of it either in himself or others. On one occasion, one of the Fathers, from inadvertence, had lined his cloak with silk. F. Clement discovered it and insisted on the lining being taken out, while he reproved him sharply for thus breaking the rule of poverty. In the same way, being once given a silk handkerchief to cure a bad sorethroat, he could not be induced to wear it, though he gratefully accepted a woollen one in its place. "It is quite impossible", deposed the Jesuit Father Frederick Rinn, "to be poorer than Father Clement in fact and deed. He called poverty the first Beatitude; and the only path pointed out to us by Christ, from his cradle in the stable to his nakedness on the Cross and His deposition in a sepulchre intended for another." So greatly did he esteem Religious poverty and an entire detachment from all earthly possessions, that he could not bear to hear any one talk with admiration of any worldly article. One of his Fathers was describing some beautiful jewels he had seen which had been put into his hands. F. Clement interrupted him by saying: "And you and I have had in our hands this very morning the inestimable presence of Our Lord in the Blessed Sacrament! how can you glory then in having handled what is, after all, but dust and ashes?"

In proof of his zeal for the exact observance of poverty in the Congregation, we will mention another fact. In the General Chapter held at Nocera dei Pagani in 1802, a mitigation in the rule on this head was proposed and carried. No sooner had F. Clement heard of it, than he wrote by F. Thaddeus to the Father General, expressing his sorrow at the change and his fears of the result. He wrote: "I have heard with horror that, in future, Rectors will be permitted to keep a chest in which their subjects may deposit their money. Such a regulation was unknown to our Congregation in the Pontifical states and is destructive of the vow of poverty. It would deal a deadly blow to the spirit of our Institute; for such a clause would open the door to innumerable abuses." Our Lord, however, consoled the heart of His faithful servant by not permitting that this new statute should be approved of by the Holy See, and thus the wishes of the holy founder of the Congregation were not infringed by the proposed relaxation of the rule.

Even more fondly than poverty, however, did F. Clement, esteem and love the virtue of purity, which he justly considered as the very essence of sacerdotal life. This precious jewel was guarded by him with jealous care. His grave and modest exterior, his pure and careful words, his very movements, which, without affectation or singularity were always regulated on the same principle, caused an eye-witness to exclaim: "His whole person shines with angelic purity, so that his very look inspires chaste thoughts."

In a general way, he kept his eyes cast down, so that his intimate friends declared they never knew their colour. He was even more cautious and reserved with women, although he was never uncourteous or uncivil. His intercourse with them was generally serious and brief: and people used to declare that he knew them by their voices more than by their faces. In the tribunal of Penance he was very sparing in his questions as to certain sins and only listened to what was absolutely necessary for the integrity of the confession. And as he knew that purity was a celestial gift more than a virtue acquired by laborious exercise, he continually and fervently recommended himself to God and to His Immaculate mother; and never ceased to strengthen his petitions by fasts and penances and by bearing patiently the many pains and discomforts which are the portion of almost every one in this life at one time or the other. He showed the same extreme anxiety to infuse this love of chastity into the minds of his students, imploring them never to cease their watchfulness over themselves and their natural affections.

When asked how they were to deal with women? he used to reply: "Recommend all good women to our Lord": meaning, "Think of them in your prayers, but not otherwise". He often quoted the example of the holy Job, who had made a compact with his eyes never to think of a virgin: and he continually warned his young priests of the great dangers they might run from keeping up intimacies with the other sex. "Women remain always women", he would say, "and unless they have overcome their natural tendencies, like St. Teresa and other Saints, they are always dangerous to us".

The third stone in religious perfection F. Clement would call obedience. It was true that he was Superior from the time he left Rome till his death; but with what humility and veneration did he write to the Father-General! Every word revealed the true spirit of a son, nor can we find any where a trace of independence, of self-will, or of contradiction. In whatever work he undertook, he never stirred without consulting his superiors, to assure himself that he was thereby following the Divine Will: nor did he ever begin any important business without first seeking the approval of the F. General and the Papal Nunzio.

To know the spirit of obedience existing in a Religious, there is no better test than to watch how he observes the rule of his order: and of this F. Clement was a notable example. One of his sons, who had continual opportunities of watching him at Warsaw and elsewhere, wrote "that even in the most minute things, F. Clement's humble obedience to the rules of the congregation was most remarkable, so that no one could complain if he exacted the same from his subjects. He was always the first at all community exercises, especially in the morning and never allowed fatigue or overwhelming occupations of other kinds, to interfere with his regular observance of the rule; in fact he would never make exceptions for himself; but behaved as if he were the lowest and youngest of the community. In his paternal admonitions and fervent exhortations, he dwelt often on the importance of this virtue. One day one of his Fathers came late to church and gave as his excuse "that he had remained to hear another confession". F. Clement replied: "What you did in that way, you did for the Devil;" punctuality being one of the points of obedience on which he strongly insisted.

And now, what shall we say of his penances and mortifications? The Jesuit Father Sebastian Wittmann writes on this head: "F. Clement was a St. John the Baptist in the desert, a preacher of penance, both by word and example; and thus converted thousands of sinners and led them in the paths of Christian perfection." In truth fasting and abstinence were his inseparable companions. In the morning he would be the first to rise and begin a day which was always so hard and fatiguing to his poor body: and at first he never took any thing for breakfast, although later he was compelled to take a little soup at 10 o'clock, that is, after he had passed many hours in ministerial work and hearing confessions etc. He would not take a cup of coffee after his mass like the rest; and as long as he remained in Warsaw, he never touched wine. Only in his later years was he forced to take a little when he came back, tired to death, after his visits to the sick; when he would thank God, who, by this gift, recruited his strength for fresh work. It was a real marvel to every one how, with so little food, which he often took so hurriedly, he could do such an amount of labour. But besides his constant mortification as to food and drink, he used disciplines, slept on a hard bed and exposed himself to cold and heat, wind and rain, snow and hail without seeming even conscious of the state of the weather. He never would use an umbrella till he became an old man, no matter how it poured. He always declared that such little mortifications were necessary to him; and often encouraged them in his disciples, although he would make them act with discretion and in proportion to their health and strength. "You see, a missioner must be mortified", he would say, "so as to be able to bear unexpected fatigues". It always pleased him when his young students, although not of an age to fast, would deprive themselves of their breakfast on Fast Days to give to the poor. However, he was very careful not to impose the same rule on all: and would often say" that what would be good for one would be bad for another", especially in the matter of corporal penances: and that nothing should be done to injure the health or diminish the strength, which was so needful for the work of the apostolate. While recommending, therefore, great discretion in external mortifications he laid far greater stress on internal ones, and especially on the abnegation of self and fighting vigorously against our dominant passions. He would say to his students: "Disciplines and hair-shirts and other instruments of penance are not absolutely necessary, nor even difficult, to some natures. But the mortification of our own wills, of our natural inclinations, and above all, of our pride, is absolutely necessary and a far more arduous task."

But some people may ask: "How is it that F. Clement with his life of continual prayer, mortification, and toil, could speak of himself constantly to his subjects as having passions and evil inclinations to fight against?" It is because, even in the holiest souls, there is still some vestiges of the old Adam, some cause for them to humble themselves before God. F. Clement was, by nature, irascible and violent: and this natural irritation would crop up from time to time: so that to avoid giving way to it, to conquer any outward sign of anger, and to subdue any internal feelings of it, was a matter requiring continual watchfulness and struggle. Looking at this defect with an eye of faith he would sometimes say: "I thank God that He has left me this natural irritability, which helps me to practise humility and be patient with others: besides preserving me from pride."

With the most persevering energy he would fight against this unhappy inclination and receive in silence the gravest injuries, so that one of his companions wrote: "The most unjust treatment did not disturb his external tranquillity and sweetness, which were the honest expression of his heart. It is true that sometimes the struggle would be seen in his face; but a single look upwards would restore his habitual calm". If however, he did not succeed in conquering himself at once, an act of humility and contrition instantly followed and gave him fresh wings to renew the combat. In addition to the virtues of his private character we must add a word of the extraordinary talent God had given him for the office of Superior, he being able to govern with such success communities composed of such different elements, hostile nationalities, and directly opposite tastes, habits and inclinations. Whoever has lived in similar communities will know well the difficulties of government in such cases. But this great servant of God had the secret of knowing how to guide and direct each soul so as to contribute to his own sanctification and the good of the community. Whether in prosperity or adversity, all came to him for direction and counsel, and no one went away dissatisfied or discouraged: for his words were full of Divine Wisdom and uttered with such paternal kindness and sweetness that even when they were bitter to the inclination they touched the heart and inclined each to follow the advice given. His wonderful humility made him abstain from ever making his authority painfully felt: nor was he ever imperious in his orders. Without distinction of persons, he would listen to the humblest lay-brother with the same patience, sweetness and charity that he would show to his best Fathers. He was always at the service of any one of his subjects and never disdained the humblest offices; as, for instance, helping the cook if inefficient and teaching him how to prepare the food, or anything else. His sweetness and charity as Superior did not however, prevent his being firm and even severe when necessary. He loved his spiritual sons too well to pass over things which really required correction: but he knew how to choose the moment to prove their spirit. He watched especially over the finest characters amongst them, encouraging them to practise heroic virtues. This was especially the case with F. Passerat, whose singular generosity of spirit was frequently put to the proof by his wise and loving Superior, who was determined that he should attain to uncommon perfection and not be content with the beaten track. And the result justified his fondest expectations. With weaker natures, however, he was firm though patient. He was very fond of F. Martin Stark, who often accompanied him on his travels: but having discovered a little boyish vanity in him, he continually mortified him, in imitation of St. Philip Neri; one day sending him to fetch water at a distant well: or to go and buy milk in a public square: or other similar humiliations. In the same way he corrected his inclination to elegance in his dress. With all that, he was wonderfully considerate of people's feelings and if ever he had exceeded in finding fault in any way, he would hasten to remedy it for fear of wounding personal susceptibilities. "One day" relates a student of his, "I received a reproof from him which, with my natural sensitiveness, I felt bitterly and thought was unnecessarily severe. I went to my own room, but a minute or two later, he came in, with a piece of music in his hand and said to me: "You wanted to have this hymn, did you not? Let us try it together": and forthwith he began:

"Or Maria salutero" "A suoi piedi m'inchinero &c." I remained quite confused at this proof of his sweetness and gentleness, which he evidently did because he feared he had hurt me by speaking too strongly."

Happy indeed were those who had such a Superior over them!

Another remarkable characteristic in Father Clement was, his devotion to the Congregation. Father Tannoia wrote: "What his devotion was to his Order and what care he took to preserve its spirit, I cannot find words to express! Yet no one knows what he went through and suffered in his efforts to establish it in different countries. And this tender love he transmitted to his spiritual sons: and the result was that each one of them was ready to sacrifice everything and even life itself, rather than lose his vocation."

Another proof of the affection he bore for the Congregation was given by F. Clement in his intense anxiety for the beatification of St. Alphonsus. Not only did he carefully search for every single circumstance which would help the cause, but when it was solemnly proclaimed, he gave a large sum out of his poverty to enhance the splendour of the function.

The intense love he bore to the congregation will give us a measure of his grief at the disastrous events and persecutions we have to record regarding his new foundations.

CHAPTER XVII.

GREAT ANXIETY AS REGARDED THE HOUSE AT WARSAW. THE DEATH OF F. THADDEUS HÜBL.

[From 1806 to 1807.]

WHILST F. Clement was using every means to plant his Congregation firmly in Germany, his enemies combined to destroy it in Poland. Under the Prussian Government the influence of the Socialist and Fre-mason sects increased daily. Guided by a certain instinct, they felt that of all strongholds of religion and morals, St. Bennone was the most to be dreaded: and therefore they determined to combine for its destruction. Their first method was by various calumnies to irritate the Government against the Congregation: and although these allegations were judicially disproved and no pretext was found for any proceedings to be taken against them, the Government, in order to curry favour with the Free-masons, directed that the church should be closed an hour earlier than usual. But this did not satisfy the sects, who trumped up a variety of fresh accusations against the Fathers: so that the King, Frederick William the 3rd, ordered that the Superior of St. Bennone should be sent for to Berlin to answer the charges brought against them.

F. Thaddeus Hübl was at that time Rector and being very ill, he sent his Father Minister, Iesterheim to defend the Congregation, who was furnished with the highest recommendations from all the principal inhabitants of Warsaw. The different points of accusation were read out to him, and he, with perfect calm and tranquillity, begged the Court to read the documents he had brought with him and which contained the most complete justification on all the counts which had been brought forward. The judges were thoroughly satisfied, and F. Iestersheim was received with marked kindness by the king and his ministers, who sent him back in peace to Warsaw, with orders to the authorities there to watch over the safety and honour of the Redemptorist Fathers, and not to molest them any more. This happy result was due partly to the absurdity of the accusations and partly to the threatened war with Napoleon, when it behoved all nations to be united among themselves.

The war fell indeed heavily upon Prussia. Bonaparte's Generals, Murat and Davoust, entered Warsaw with their victorious troops on the 13th of November 1806, and on the 19th of the following month Napoleon himself made a solemn entry into the capital of Poland. By the treaty of Tilsit (9th of July 1807) Poland was taken away from Prussia and made into a separate Grand Duchy under the King of Saxony, Frederick Augustus, a nephew of the late King of Poland, Augustus the 2nd.

On F. Clement's return to Warsaw in 1806, he found the French masters of the city and his poor Fathers in great tribulation. It was true that by the Concordat of 1801, the Catholic Religion had been reestablished in France. But unbelief and hatred of Christianity continued just the same and all religious orders suffered endless vexations wherever the French arms were victorious. It is true that the King of Saxony was a good Catholic and personally attached to F. Clement and to his Congregation. But as Grand Duke of Warsaw, he had scarcely the authority of a prefect, being obliged to obey Napoleon's orders in everything. Hence the enemies of the Congregation were enchanted at the change of Government which they felt, would ensure their victory. From this moment, F. Clement and his Fathers were subjected to every species of insult and ill-usage: so much so that he was heard to say later: "That no one could imagine what he had suffered in Poland, the whole of which would never be known till the day of judgment".*

During this terrible time, F. Clement was an angel of consolation towards his brethren. Not that he undervalued

---

* One of the witnesses in the cause of his beatification relates the following: "After the death of F. Clement, a servant of a noble Polish family came into the sacristy of the Ursulines in Vienna and seeing there a picture of the servant of God exclaimed: 'I knew this holy man well and what he suffered in Poland. He was once thrown into a damp and subterranean dungeon, where his hands and feet were so tightly bound that he could not defend himself from the rats, who ran all over him. By the energetic intercession of my Mistress, the Countess, he was, at last, set at liberty." This confirms the rumour among the people of the tortures and outrages to which F. Clement was subjected in Warsaw.

the greatness of the dangers which surrounded them: but his courage and calm only increased in proportion. His example and exhortations so raised the spirits of the Community that they were ready to meet whatever calamity might befall them. And in truth, hell itself seemed unloosed against the unhappy Fathers. Not content with the most hideous calumnies, ribald songs were composed against the "*Bennonites*" as they were nick-named and distributed far and wide among the people. In the theatres, they were travestied in their religious habits and the most sublime mysteries of our holy religion were infamously represented on the boards. Those even who came to their church were insulted in the public streets. Vile cowards besieged the doors, and when any of the Fathers appeared, to visit the sick or perform any other ministerial function, the word was passed down the street and a rabble of half drunken men armed with sticks and stones would load them with blows and insults. They had a special spite against F. Blumenauer, because by his magnificent preaching, he had converted so many people; so that they threatened to murder him and several times came with loaded pistols into the church, but did not dare carry out their sacrilegious designs. So grave was the danger, however, that it was considered more prudent for him not to leave the house. In the midst of all this persecution, for which they could obtain no redress from the authorities, F. Clement remained calm and resigned and did his best to tranquillise his companions and prevent any acts of imprudence or retaliation. One would have thought that under such circumstances our Lord would have specially consoled His faithful servant. But, in the inscrutable decrees of God, He chose this moment to inflict on him the deepest, sorrow. Death carried off his dearest friend, F. Thaddeus Hübl, who for 24 years had shared in all his joys and sorrows. He had been his main stay in the first start of the Congregation. He had been F. Clement's adviser in the most critical circumstances. In fact, he was half of himself, and yet God called upon him to make this sacrifice at the very moment when he was most needful and when F. Clement was in such grievous want of so tried and faithful a friend!

CHAPTER XVIII.

WHO FATHER THADDEUS WAS. AND HOW HE WAS ESTEEMED AND REVERED BY ALL. HIS SOLEMN FUNERAL.

UNTIL his journey to Rome in 1803, F. Thaddeus was in delicate health; but nevertheless he never gave way or spared himself in any manner, but laboured incessantly in our Lord's Vineyard. Besides his arduous work as Rector of St. Bennone, he was continually appealed to by the Archbishop and the Professors of the seminary to solve difficult questions in theology, as every one considered him a wise and profound theologian. Endowed with rare talents, he had acquired an extraordinary knowledge of the writings of the Fathers of the church, of profane and ecclesiastical history and of dogmatic and moral theology. He was also an indefatigable student. The Archbishop had so high an opinion of his science and prudence that he would not give faculties for confession to any priest unless previously approved of by Father Thaddeus, whom he also compelled to act as his Clergy Examiner—an office which he filled with scrupulous fidelity and salutary severity. In the latter years of his life he rarely preached, not so much on account of his continual occupations as from the weakening of his physical powers: but he was untireable in his assiduity in hearing confessions. He was the Director of people of every class; Prelates, Canons, members of the highest nobility and again of the poorest among the peasants. As he spoke and understood six different languages his confessional was frequented by all the strangers who passed through Warsaw. He resembled F. Clement in many things: and especially in the strength of his faith, his zeal for the salvation of souls and his sweetness and affability towards every one with whom he came in contact. His rare qualities and eminent virtue not only won all hearts, but even drew forth admiration from the French Authorities; so that if the implacable enemies of the Congregation did not succeed as quickly as they hoped in their iniquitous designs, it was mainly owing to the great influence of F. Thaddeus.

A work of heroic charity was the actual cause of his death. In the French army, which at that time occupied Poland, there was an Italian Regiment, who from overfatigue and other causes, were mostly in Hospital and ardently wished for the consolations of their faith. They spoke only their native tongue and none of the chaplains of the Hospital understood them. The Archbishop wrote to F. Thaddeus telling him of this and imploring him to go and assist them: and he, though very suffering at the time, at once hastened to the hospital and with the greatest charity administered the last sacraments to all who needed them. His presence softened the last moments of these poor fellows, who did not know how to find words to express their gratitude and full of hope and consolation, passed to a better life. They left, however, behind them a sad legacy and that was the infection, which he took during his constant attendance on the dying. In consequence, he was seized with malignant Typhus Fever which carried him off after a 15 days illness, borne with admirable resignation and patience. On the 4th of July 1807, this noble soul returned to its Creator. Father Clement had never left him during his illness and had the melancholy comfort of closing his eyes when all was over. This victim of christian charity died full of holy consolations and celestial joy; but to his brethren, his loss was simply an irreparable one; for so great was his tenderness and solicitude for each of his spiritual sons, that F. Clement called him "*The mother of the Congregation*". To Father Clement himself this misfortune was the greatest that could have happened to him. In a conference held shortly after, he exclaimed: "Our last hope is gone. God knows what we may yet have to suffer!" Used as he was to every description of trial, this blow was the heaviest of all. Writing to a friend at Foligno he says: "I feel convineed that our beloved F. Thaddeus is already triumphing with Christ in Heaven: but I cannot get over the immense sorrow which his death has caused me. I am doing my utmost to resign myself to God's will and protest that I desire nothing but Its accomplishment: but I own that, since his death, I have never known a happy hour. To him the change is all gain: but our loss is simply irreparable". He then begs his friend to have a mass said in the Church of St. Clare of Montefalco on behalf of his dear friend.

On the 9th of January 1808, writing to F. Blasucci, then Superior General, he says: "I find myself pretty well in health since the death of our beloved F. Thaddeus: but I cannot get over my sadness and sorrow". As long as he lived, he entertained the same strong love for this dear friend and wore his picture on his breast. Later on, he lost this print in Vienna, which was a real grief to him.

To return to the funeral of F. Thaddeus. No sooner was the sad news of his death made known, than all the Catholics of Warsaw, from the Archbishop downwards, hastened to St. Bennone to express their sympathy with F. Clement and to do honour to his cherished remains. The Superiors of all the other Religious Houses in the town came likewise and finding the poor Redemptorist Fathers overwhelmed with grief, undertook to make all the necessary preparations for the funeral. The Archbishop wishing to show his extraordinary gratitude and veneration for this model of priests, ordered that, for the three following days, all the bells in the town should be tolled; and determined that his obsequies should be attended by all possible pomp. All day long the carriages of the Warsaw nobility drove up in succession to the door of the house, every one craving leave to look once more on the face of their spiritual father and best friend.

The whole of the interior of the church was hung with black by the sacristans of the cathedral and the bier of the poor Religious was adorned as if it were that of a Bishop or a Prince. More than 500 candles, weighing each four or five llbs. burnt continually round the bier, being brought by the faithful from every quarter. The Religious of every order joined in singing the office for the Dead in the Redemptorist Church and this pious ceremony went on without intermission for two days. The mourners who crowded the church were of every class, rich and poor, Poles and foreigners—all felt that in him they had lost a common father. The Secular Clergy joined the regulars and during the interminably long procession, all following with lighted torches, the finest orchestral music played funeral marches which expressed the hearty sorrow shown on every countenance.

This magnificent and gorgeous funeral was entirely carried out at the expense and by the spontaneous impulse of the people; for the poor fathers of the Congregation had done nothing; nor contributed in any way to the triumph of this their humble though most worthy Superior.

The holy death of Father Thaddeus was announced to F. Passerat and his brethren in Switzerland in a curious way. They were all saying their night-prayers together one evening in Coire, when suddenly they felt a great shock like an earthquake which shook all the windows and a loud noise was heard as of something falling, which made them hasten to go over the house and see what had happened. But finding nothing whatever either broken or displaced, they began to think there was something strange and supernatural about it, and all the more when they heard that precisely a similar sound had been heard by their Fathers in another house. They noted down the day and hour in both cases, and after some time, the sad letters came from Warsaw announcing the death of F. Thaddeus at that very moment. In the same way in 1787, the death of St. Alphonsus had been made known to Father Clement and Father Thaddeus.

By the extraordinary honours paid to him, the people of Warsaw showed not only their veneration for the departed Superior, but also bore witness to their love and devotion to the Congregation. All the lies and calumnies and all the insults and persecutions of their adversaries had not lessened the esteem in which they were held by all the right-thinking among the population. The Church of St. Bennone was more frequented than ever; and the number of Communions in 1807 exceeded a hundred thousand: so that in that way, by the goodness of God, F. Clement was a little consoled amidst the tribulations and difficulties which beset him on all sides.

In two letters which he wrote on the 9th of January and the 24th of February 1808 to the Father and Procurator General, F. Clement expressed himself as follows:

"Our church is almost always full to overflowing. The confessors of the King and Queen of Saxony who frequent it and sometimes sing High Mass there, are quite amazed at seeing every mass so crowded and more than a hundred persons at Holy Communion at each mass. A great many Protestants have likewise been received into the church. We have a pious King and a very holy Archbishop. At first they had been prejudiced against us: but now they are only anxious to confide to our care all the missions in Poland. I have given up one house in the neighbourhood of Warsaw hoping to obtain a better one from this new Archbishop. The new Vicar General of the Diocese of Warsaw (Gregory Zacharyassewicz) is a man full of prudence and zeal, the greatest friend of the Congregation and really a true Father to us all. The only complaint he makes against us, is, that we are not sufficiently numerous. We have now nine novices and two good clerics. If the Prussians had not so cruelly oppressed us, our numbers would be very much larger. It is, however, a perfect miracle, how in these wretched times, when the country is so exhausted and ruined, we are able, without begging, to maintain so numerous a family, being, with our orphans, upwards of 64 persons." In this same letter (of 9th of Jan. 1808) F. Clement reports the work of his Congregation to the Superior General and not knowing that his Fathers had been already sent away from Coire he writes:

"In the Canton of the Grisons our Fathers have made great progress in virtue and science, and your Reverence would certainly allow them to be worthy sons of our holy Father, when we consider that in spite of all the hardships and persecutions they have undergone, one and all have been faithful to the Congregation. God only knows what they have had to go through; but everywhere they have spread the good odour of their virtue and sanctity. The enemy of the human race was quite determined not to allow us to found missions in Germany, but nevertheless he was the cause of our doing much there. In some places we were only allowed to stop a few months: but during that short time, there was a most extraordinary change for the better in the people, so much so that many fathers of families declared they did not know their children again. Everywhere they introduced the frequent reception of the Sacraments and heard innumerable General Confessions. People came to our missions from a distance of 50 and even a 100 miles. On the mountains and in the vallies of Switzerland as in

Germany, we hear the peasants singing our hymns and chaunts. The young Fathers, especially, work perfect miracles in the way of conversions, and if God will permit the foundation in Switzerland to continue, they will convert thousands of Protestants."

Thus, F. Clement in the midst of all his trials, rejoiced in the happy result of his labours: while his whole heart and soul were bent on the glory of God, the salvation of souls, the conversion of sinners and heretics and the propagation of his dearly-loved Congregation.

CHAPTER XIX.

THE CONGREGATION IS DESTROYED IN WARSAW AND THE FATHERS BARBAROUSLY DRIVEN AWAY.

[1808.]

THE clouds which hung over the horizon could not induce F. Clement to slacken in any way his apostolic labours: on the contrary, he determined to carry out a new work which, at first, he had only vaguely thought of. Feeling that not enough had been done for the education of girls in Warsaw, he resolved to call in the assistance of the Redemptoristine nuns and in order to obtain the King's consent had recourse to the mediation of the Court Confessor. Nor was the important work of giving missions in any way neglected, as appears by a letter of F. Clement's to the Father General in May 1808: so that the fatal blow found the Fathers of St. Bennone in the full fervour of their holy operations; a circumstance which redounded to their glory, to the eternal shame of their enemies. On the 16th of April, which was Holy Saturday, the solemn celebration of the Resurrection, according to Polish custom, was held in St. Bennone between nine and ten o'clock at night.* During the solemn procession carrying the Blessed Sacrament round the church, a French officer in plain clothes scandalised the people by his indecent behaviour with two women, which compelled one of the priests to admonish him. The officer was furious and hurried out to find a companion to avenge, as he pretended, this grave insult. And when, after the function was over, the people were passing out by the little door near the sacristy, two men dressed in plain clothes who afterwards turned out to be also French officers strove to enter the church, and this being difficult owing to the narrowness of the corridor and the multitudes who were coming out, they forced their way in by blows and violence. Such mad behaviour, as may easily be imagined, produced great confusion and indignation among the people, so that the two officers were roughly handled by the Poles and driven back outside the church. The officers in return wounded and illtreated several of the congregation. The confusion momentarily increased, when a Polish officeal came up and instead of reestablishing order, added fuel to the fire by accusing the Poles of having insulted the French officers. The Father Rector came out of the house to try and quell the disturbance and reason with the Polish official; but was seized by the French officers and loaded with blows and insults. The Superior told them that for such unworthy conduct he would report them to Marshall Davoust. After this, one of the Frenchmen again got into the church to seek the women with whom they had previously misbehaved. In the mean while, some one had run to the Guard-House to seek the protection of the soldiers. But these only came to take parts with their officers and forcing their way into the Sacristy, drove out the frightened people and illtreated the Fathers

* The details of this affair are taken from a printed correspondence in Polish written in 1816 by Monsg. Ignatius Raczynski, Prince Bishop of Gnesnia and Administrator of Warsaw.

there. The Polish officials however, intervened, turned out the soldiers, reassured the weeping people and exhorted them to go away quietly, while he begged the Fathers to close the doors of the church so that no more French people could go in. After this, he went with a laybrother to the Guard-House in the old city, leaving four soldiers to protect the house. Then the Commandant returned with a larger body of men, examined the passage and the door, went to the F. Rector and heard the whole account and reassuring them with kind words, left them in peace. The day after Easter, the Minister of public worship wrote to the Vice-Administrator of the Diocese complaining bitterly of the Fathers for their ill-treatment of the French officers and demanding that they should be punished. An enquiry was set on foot and a statement drawn up in writing of the facts of the case which was forwarded to the Minister of public worship by the Vice-Administrator on the 18th of April, together with a letter in which he set forth the innocence of the Fathers in the strongest possible light.

"These Fathers", he wrote "who would have fallen victims to a furious rabble had it not been for the active protection of the Commandant, have indeed reason to complain of their treatment, although they are unwilling to prosecute their offenders. The enclosed accurate statement of what happened has been drawn up by them solely at my express orders and is confirmed by all impartial witnesses. If they came out of their House, it was but to pacify the irritation of the people and to preach forbearance and peace. The absurd accusation of a Redemptorist having fought with a French officer, is refuted by the universal testimony of all who know the gentleness and sweetness of these venerable Fathers, who are models to us all. You may reflect how little fit their accusers are to judge dispassionately in the matter, they being filled with such bitter prejudice and hatred against them."

I can produce as many witnesses as you please who will confirm the statement I have now made: and if you thereby recognise the innocence of the Fathers, the affair may be considered as at an end inasmuch as they, for the love of God, are quite willing to forget the injuries they have received, nor do they exact satisfaction from any one. I beg and intreat of you, in the name of all the Clergy of the Diocese, to order that the civil and military authorities may prevent that our churches, consecrated to the service of Almighty God, should be desecrated by the behaviour of persons, who seek solely to gratify their evil passions and lustful eyes even in such holy places. If they wish thus to indulge in their vices, let it be elsewhere, where they may not give scandal to holy and devout persons who frequent the church to pray."

This energetic defence of the Fathers on the part of the Vice-Administrator had no good result, although the authorities were compelled to allow their innocence of the charges brought against them. Nor would they examine the proposed witnesses, as then the odious calumny would have been even more flagrantly exposed. But all the papers in the Rector's room were seized and ordered to be examined by the civil and ecclesiastical authorities. The latter were added to try and deceive the people by making them believe that there was some blame attached to the Fathers. But the Vicar General, seing that he was thus being made an accomplice of the persecution, refused to appoint the priest proposed by them to make the ecclesiastical enquiry: and the papers were consequently examined by the civil authorities alone, without, however, their being able to find a single thing which could criminate the Congregation, whose innocence, in consequence, only shone the brighter in the eyes of all men. But, like the Fable of the Wolf and the Lamb, all this was but a pretext to give an appearance of justice to the brutal destruction of the congregation. In fact, six weeks before the suppression, a high masonic dignitary had said to a priest friend of his, "that the Bennonites would be very soon driven away from Warsaw". The priest replied "that he was sure that the King would never consent to the expulsion of a body of men who had done and were doing so much good". But the Free-mason named a minister, who was a noted infidel, who had im- immense power and had resolved on their destruction through the influence of Marshall Davoust, and added "that the King would be compelled to give his assent to the sentence".

It happened exactly as he had foretold. Davoust obtained from Napoleon the authority which the sects so earnestly desired. And an order came from Paris to the King insisting on the suppression of the Redemptorists. With tears in his eyes the King was compelled to sign the following iniquitous decree:

Frederick Augustus,
By the grace of God King of Saxony and Prince of Warsaw.

"We have waited till now for the papers regarding the affairs of the Bennonite Fathers, wishing to examine into them ourselves and especially as to the incidents connected with the functions at Easter. This long delay has now been removed owing to certain confidential reports from the French Court, founded on the complaints of the authorities of Warsaw, who consider that it would be dangerous for the Principality to allow the continued residence of those Fathers in the City, seeing that they have mixed themselves up with political matters, although contrary to their rule and vocation. Hence we order:

1th That the Bennonite Fathers shall be immediately removed from the Principality of Warsaw.

2nd That it shall be lawful for them to carry away with them all their personal property.

3rd That the Minister of the Interior shall provide them with the necessary means of transport for their journey.

4th That the Minister of the Interior and the Police, in concert with the French Authorities, shall sequestrate all the papers of the said Fathers, which must afterwards be examined by a commission chosen by the Minister and the French Council.

5th That the Church of the Bennonites shall be closed till further orders.

6th The Ministers and the French Authorities shall determine the time and the mode of execution of this Our Decree. But we command that the Minister of the Interior and the Head of the Police shall send us in without delay a report of the execution of this our will.

Dated from our Palace of Pillnitz, 9th of June 1808.

Frederick Augustus.   Stanislaus Breza,
                       Secretary of State.

With regard to this Decree, the Archbishop, Count Racynski, rightly remarked: "Any one who reads the Decree for the expulsion of the Redemptorist Fathers must see that they were punished in spite of their entire innocence: for if their enemies had found the shadow of a real fault in them, they would not have failed to publish it as a crime and allude to it with malicious words in the Decree itself."

What the King signed with tears, was carried out in a most lamentable way. The good Fathers, as malefactors, were surprised and literally dragged out of the City: so that it might be said by them as by their Divine Master: "You are come out as it were to a robber, with swords and clubs to apprehend me." (26. St. Mat. 55th verse. Our Lord, however, would not leave His faithful servant, Clement, without a warning of the coming blow. One day, during the octave of Pentecost, (which fell that year on the 5th of

June, he was repeating before the Blessed Sacrament the 87th Psalm and came to the words: "I am poor and in labours from my youth: and being exalted, have been humbled and troubled," when he felt a violent shaking, accompanied with a loud noise which made him tremble all over. Whilst he was thinking over this and wondering what it could possibly mean, he felt another equally severe shock. He recognised then a supernatural agency in it all, and looked upon it as a warning of some great misfortune. He humbled himself before God, resigning himself entirely to His holy Will and offering himself as a perfect holocaust: after which, his habitual calm returned and he was in perfect peace.

The following day, an agent of the police, dressed in plain clothes, came secretly to F. Clement, told him that the Decree for the suppression of the Congregation had been signed, and that if he had any private or important papers in the house, he had better burn them at once, as the secret police had orders to allow nothing of that sort to be taken out of the house. F. Clement thanked him for the warning and at once set to work to dispose of everything. He summoned the Rector, F. Iestersheim and made him burn all the letters without giving him the reason. Then he called him and all the Fathers into the Refectory and after having imposed silence upon them, made them a short and touching allocution and then announced to them the sad news. All responded to his words with tears and sighs. They did not weep for their own fate, but for the irreparable harm which would be done to innumerable souls in that unhappy city. F. Clement consoled them as well as he could with loving words and then gave orders that all the chalices, vestments and other valuable ornaments of the church should be hidden in a safe place. Time pressed and at any moment they might expect the execution of the fatal Decree. The valuable relics were distributed among the priests and every one was warned to take into his own room the linen, clothes and money required for the journey. Having thus made all the necessary dispositions, they returned to their respective employments, expecting from one hour to another the conclusion of the tragedy. At last, the hour came when God permitted the enemies of the Congregation to do what they willed with the house and its inmates. Any one who witnessed the warlike preparations which preceded the expulsion of a few harmless monks might have imagined that a revolution was impending or that an invading army was at hand. The Governor, fearing lest the Poles should look upon the expulsion of the Redemptorists as an attack upon their religion and that they would consequently fly to arms in their defence, occupied all the corners of the streets with troops.

On the 20th of June (being the Monday after the Feast of Corpus Christi) the Government agents arrived very early in the morning at the House of St. Bennone, while, at the same time, the church was entirely surrounded by soldiers. Seals were affixed to the Sacristy, the Library and the Rector's room, and then all the Fathers and Brothers were summoned into the Refectory. One was just finishing his mass: another was in the confessional, a third was preaching and had to break off in the middle and leave the pulpit. The congregation could not, at first, understand, why one Father was called out after the other and looked at one another in mute surprise. Then a few wished to leave the church; but found all the doors closed and guarded by the troops. Hearing the noise of the carriages and the soldiers outside they at last understood that the dreaded catastrophe was at hand. Then followed a burst of indignation and sorrow from them all and many bursting into tears, exclaimed: "O! my God. They have taken away our good Fathers and we shall never be allowed to see them any more!"

In the mean time, all the members of the community

being assembled in the Refectory, the principal Commissioner delivered to F. Clement the Decree of suppression and the list of the proscribed saying: "Here, Sir, is the Decree of the suppression, and all the persons named in this list are desired to leave the house with us without reply."

No one made any answer: but at a sign from Father Clement, each went to his cell and quickly returned with his respective bundle ready for the journey. The Commissioners were taken completely aback at their readiness in obeying the orders so arbitrarily given; and could not understand who had warned the Fathers of the issuing of the Decree. They feared, however, that some resistance would be made during the journey. The perfect calmness and serenity of the persecuted Fathers touched then deeply: and one or two of them were so moved that F. Clement himself had to encourage them to carry out their instructions. So true is it that virtue such as theirs draws the homage even of the impious!

In the mean time the carriages were drawn up at the door of the house, into each of which three of the religious, with one commissioner, were ordered to enter; the commissioner being appointed to prevent their escape and to provide the necessary expenses of the journey. The carriages were then closed and started off, escorted by a strong body of cavalry.

We may fancy the grief of the Fathers at being thus forcibly carried off from their beloved monastery: but still greater was their dismay when, on reaching the gates of the City, they discovered that they were all being driven in different directions: nor could they imagine what was to be their ultimate destination.

When the Police saw that the carriages had driven off and that the Fathers were actually outside the City gates, they opened the doors of the church and let out the congregation. Then calling a neighbouring priest, they ordered him to remove the Blessed Sacrament to the nearest Parish Church, and closing that of the Redemptorists, they affixed to the doors the government seals.

The indignation of the people at this impious proceeding was deep and menacing: so much so that bands of soldiers were ordered to patrol all the streets of the City and the sentrys were every where doubled. Marshall Davoust, in order to calm the inhabitants, put out a French proclamation, which was afterwards translated into Polish by the adjutant Szymanowski, who had the command of the troops at the moment of the expulsion. When the cause of Father Clement's beatification was first introduced, he was living in Rome, where he soon after died. When questioned as to the facts we have just narrated, he deplored his blindness at that time with many tears and could not be consoled at the thought that, in his youth, he had lent a hand to and been made an instrument of so iniquitous a proceeding. Soon after the suppression of the Warsaw house, the same fate befell those in other parts of Poland and Russia. Thus was Father Clement's great and arduous work of 20 years brutally destroyed in a few hours, and the Religious whom thousands of persons venerated as their best friends and benefactors, were cruelly exiled and despoiled of all their possessions to satisfy the hatred of the enemies of Christianity.

If the Royal Decree of expulsion were in itself severe and unjust, its execution was to the last degree hard and cruel. By the terms of the Decree, the proscribed Fathers were to be treated with consideration; they were to be allowed to carry away with them all their personal property, and were to be provided with money for their journey and freedom to go where they liked outside the principality. But in its execution, not one of there conditions were observed. They were carried off and treated as the worst of malefactors and not allowed to speak to any human being.

Great was the exultation of the sects at this unexpected triumph. On the evening of the day of the Father's expulsion, the Free-masons made a great banquet in their principal lodge and passed the night in firing off pistols and other insane demonstrations of joy. Their newspapers determined to justify the action of the Government and for several days were loud in their denunciations of the supposed crimes of the Redemptorists. But all who were not in their camp, knew well the value of such calumnies, and the Catholics saw clearly enough in the outrages showered on the victims, the best proof that could be given of their innocence.*

But leaving the base intrigues of F. Clement's enemies for a moment on one side, let us turn to the evidence given by a noble Polish Lady, Mary Cecilia de Cholomiewska, afterwards superior of the Salesian Nuns of Kaminiec, driven out of Poland as the Redemptorist Fathers had been and who is now living at Lemberg though 92 years of age. She writes:

"I always have before my eyes that venerable priest with his noble and dignified yet simple bearing, who seemed to spread a kind of holy peace and divine love wherever he went. His conversation was always simple: he never used long words: but what he said impressed one strangely and at once excited one's confidence. His great Love of Our Lord showed itself in every action; yet he had not a vestige of singularity or of affectation. His face literally beamed with purity and with that peace which is the fruit of holy joy and intimate union with God. The Holy Spirit had

---

* There were found, however, many loyal and honest men publickly to refute these vile calumnies, and among the rest Archbishop Raczynski wrote: "They took very good care to exile these good Fathers *without a trial*, nor could any one understand for what reason men were thus cruelly and ignominiously treated who had won the universal esteem of the whole country and whose admirable free schools had trained so many hundred youths in science and piety. But it was from their eminent virtue and usefulness that they drew down upon themselves the odium of the bad."

given him a special gift to guide souls. He worked without intermission to bring about the salvation of men, seeking out the most miserable and abandoned of God's creatures and exhausting himself on their behalf without ever thinking of rest.

His principal devotion was towards the Blessed Sacrament of the Altar and this he endeavoured to excite in the hearts of all; together with an ardent desire for the frequent reception of Holy Communion. He would exhort his penitents so to labour as to be worthy to communicate daily: and in order that Jesus in the Blessed Sacrament should be duly honoured, he introduced the Solemn Adoration in Warsaw, where he had found a great want of such devotion. The daily visits to the Blessed Sacrament which he established, were made in the most solemn way in the Church of St. Bennone and produced the most salutary results. The multitudes of people of every rank who joined in this devotion were daily drawn nearer to God, and the Fathers in their sermons dwelt long and often on the efficacy of prayer before the Blessed Sacrament and increased the desire of the faithful to frequent the church for this purpose. Confessions, which used to be very rare, became frequent and the same with communions. In that Church of St. Bennone it seemed as if a continual Feast were being held—or rather a continual Mission. The church was always full and the confessionals besieged by penitents. Under F. Clement's directions also, a multitude of pious associations and confraternities were formed especially among young men, which produced extraordinary fruit. After the expulsion of the Fathers these associations were gradually dropped: but many afterwards entered into religious communities and gave great edification by their lives.

F. Clement was loved and honoured by every one. His sweetness and amiability attracted quite irresistibly all who knew him intimately. He would bring spiritual subjects into conversation so sweetly and simply that they never seemed forced or out of place. In the first talk I ever had with him, he asked me "if I frequented the Sacraments?" I named my French confessor, when he was silent: but on his next visit, said to me: "Go on making your confessions to him: for I have found out he is not a Jansenist". Very often, however, I went to confession to F. Clement, who always exhorted me to greater charity and gentleness and admonished me to preserve purity of heart by a frequent reception of the Blessed Eucharist. His goodness knew really no bounds. When any one spoke of a noted sinner, he would say: "Send him to me". And it was extraordinary what conversions he effected, even among some of the worst of the Free-masons, inducing them to break their bonds and free themselves once and for all from the tyranny and terrorism of the sects. If ever he found Jansenist books in a house, like Nicol's, for instance, he would turn them out with disgust. It was not only the Salesians who were so greatly indebted to him but all the Warsaw nuns. Those of the Blessed Sacrament were all his penitents: so also were the Carmelites, the Canonesses of St. Augustine, and many others: "It is not to be wondered at, then", writes Canon Prusinowski, "that the Apostolic life of so holy a man and the spirit which animated both himself and his companions, shoult have won all Catholic hearts to the Congregation."

As Warsaw, when F. Clement walked down the street, every one would follow him with love and veneration; and mothers would present their babies to him to implore his blessing. F. Clement himself always retained the greatest affection for Poland: and only two years before his death he was seriously engaged in a project to reestablish the Congregation in that unhappy country, regarding which he seemed occasionally to have extraordinary revelations from our Lord. One morning, in particular, when he was making his usual thanksgiving after mass, he seemed, all of a sudden, as if wrapt in a kind of ecstasy. Then his face changed: he sighed heavily and tears coursed one another down his cheeks; but he did not utter a word. After a little time, he seemed to wake out of a deep sleep and exclaimed with deep sorrow: "O! Unhappy Poland! What miseries are about to fall upon thee! What crimes will bring about thy ruin! Thou art bathed in thy blood!" More than that could not be heard. And he never spoke of it again. At other times, however, he seemed to hope for a happier future for that distracted Kingdom, which had given such illustrious Saints to the Church and was ever fruitful in grand and generous souls.

CHAPTER XX.

FATHER CLEMENT WITH HIS BRETHREN DETAINED AT THE FORTRESS OF CÜSTRIN. HIS JOURNEY TO VIENNA.

[1808.]

FROM fear of the people in the neighbourhood, the Fathers, as we have said, were divided on leaving Warsaw and driven in different directions: but their separation, which had been an addition to their trial, was not to last long. One place had been chosen for their exile; so that nearly at the same moment, all their different carriages drove up to the Fortress of Cüstrin on the Oder, in the Province of Brandenburg in Prussia*: and there F. Clement, full of sorrow at the treatment of his sons, could at least rejoice in having them all round him once more.

The arrival of these unexpected prisoners produced a

---

* After the Treaty of Tilsit the French occupied the Fortresses of Prussia, leaving only the Civil Administration in the hands of the Prussians.

great sensation among the Protestant population of Cüstrin. Everybody asked who they were? and for what crime they had been exiled from a Catholic country? and however much the soldiers tried to keep away the people, the latter would continually crowd round the fortress and whenever any of the Fathers appeared, would be never weary of admiring their calm and dignified aspect and their quiet resignation to their unmerited imprisonment. They declared they had never seen criminals of that sort. When they found out that they spoke German, the sympathy for them was only increased. "They seem such good people!" they exclaimed: "how is it they are thus treated?" Others said: "We do not treat our own ministers so, even if they have committed grave crimes!" And when they had ascertained that the only sin of these poor Religious was, that they had shown too much zeal for religion, public sympathy was openly manifested, together with a real veneration towards the Fathers; and many said: "O! our pastors would never have made such a sacrifice for their Faith!"

The Governor, however, who knew the truth, did his best to compensate the Fathers for their unjust imprisonment by treating them as well as he could. He gave them each a room provided with every necessary, and besides that, a large apartment decorated with holy pictures, in which was an altar and every thing that was required for saying mass. He behaved towards them invariably with great kindness and made them hope that the King of Prussia would allow them to open another house in a Catholic part of his dominions. But Father Clement knew the Prussian Government too well to entertain hopes of that nature.

After they were a little settled, he introduced once more the regular life of the monastery and no one hindered them. On the contrary, full liberty was given to them, even to go out of the house. In the mean time, the sympathy of the people increased daily and all the more, as they also had suffered so terribly from the French. They were especially delighted with the devout hymns which were heard so often from the windows of the Cüstrin Fortress: for F. Clement was a great lover of holy songs and promoted them on all occasions. Besides, he was anxious to do everything he possibly could to keep up the courage and cheerfulness of his spiritual sons: so that in the midst of their tribulations, they sang daily the praises of God and maintained a quietness and even brightness of spirit which greatly impressed the Protestants around them. F. Clement's favourite Hymn at that time may thus be literally rendered:

> Ah! Thou listenest, at last, O! Heaven!
> To our ardent sighs and tears,
> And without veil or other hindrance
> We shall see our Lord appear.
> To the throne of God Almighty
> Will our voice and heart ascend,
> With desire and affection
> Shall our hearts in union bend. . . .

But the ardent desire he felt to be once more at work in our Lord's Vineyard, made F. Clement address the following letter to the Prince Archbishop of Gnesnia:

"Most gracious and Reverend Prince!

The gratitude of your sons to so loving a Father, makes it a duty to write and offer you our homages. But we must temper the expression of our feelings, so as not to sadden too much your paternal heart. Although we are not worthy to be called your sons and your sheep, yet in you we recognise both our Father and our Pastor: and therefore we venture to lay at your feet the expression of our deep gratitude for all the benefits you have heaped upon us, the memory of which will always remain engraved in our hearts and will render it incumbent on us continually to lift up our prayers to the Father of mercy, that He may crown you with every blessing and consolation.

As for ourselves, we are resigned to the fate which has befallen us in accordance with the holy will of God. Suffer is sweet when there is no remorse for that which has not been our fault. The decree was communicated to us without any previous trial or enquiry: but its execution was far harder than the tenor of the decree. The decree gave us the right to carry away with us our own property: but we were exiled so precipitately that this was not possible. The pretended examination held before certain priests was so abominable as not to be mentioned. Here we are separated from all and we cannot imagine the reason why. We have been placed in this Fortress and God alone knows what fate is reserved to us. The signatures which were extracted from the Poles in Warsaw were contrary to their conscience. But in all these things we recognise the will of God. May He be for ever blessed! for He hath permitted all this to happen to us, doubtless because we were not what we should be.

Now, all we can do is, to turn to your Highness and to implore your mediation with His Majesty the King. If we are not to be allowed to return into the province of Warsaw, at least let them give us back our own things: and we crave further the liberty to go either into Saxony or Alsace.

We recommend ourselves, as unworthy servants, to the benevolent consideration of your Highness.

Clement Hofbauer, Vic. General,
with all the Congregation of the S. S. Redeemer.

Cüstrin, the 28th of June 1808.

In spite of the sympathy of the Archbishop, it was however, found to be impossible to obtain the King's consent to a new foundation in Saxony or Alsace: for certainly they had not been driven away from Warsaw for the purpose of transplanting them, as a compact and strong body, into another place: but in order to weaken and disperse them.

But their sojourn at Cüstrin was not to last more than a month, and then came an order that the community were to be separated and that each of them should repair to his native country. One reason which induced the authorities to shorten their stay in Cüstrin was, that every day the Fathers acquired greater influence over the Protestant population, who, edified by their conduct and touched at their pious songs, openly showed their sympathy towards them. The Protestant Pastors became very much alarmed at the tendency many showed to become Catholics; and urged the Government in consequence to remove the Fathers as soon as possible.

The day came when these poor Religious found themselves compelled to separate from one another: and their parting was the more sad as they foresaw the possibility of never being again reunited in community, which unhappily was the case. But resigning themselves in this, as in all else, to the holy will of God and after receiving the blessing of their much-loved Superior, they started for their different destinations.

F. Clement obtained leave to take with him the young cleric, Martin Stark, with whom he marched towards Vienna. The journey was a very difficult one: for in their passports, the route they were to follow was minutely prescribed. But as F. Clement was most anxious to say mass every day, he sometimes had to deviate a little from the route to be able to find a Catholic church. In Upper Silesia, however, they ran a great risk. French troops occupied the country, and a sentinel stopped them and asked for their passports, which unhappily Stark had lost on the way. Being brought before the Commandant, they where severely reproved and roughly handed; and he not believing that they had lost their passports threatened to shoot them then and there, as spies. But most fortunately while this subject was being discussed, a Polish officer came in who knew F. Clement well and instantly made himself his guarantee. Nevertheless, they were detained in a convent until an answer could be received from Cüstrin, which affirmed that they had actually started with their passports; but that they had certainly deviated a little from the prescribed route. After a good deal of annoyance, F. Clement and his companion were allowed to proceed on their journey, but not without having received a very sharp reprimand.

In this way F. Clement arrived at the frontier of a country which he had loaded with benefits. But even in the land which he was now entering he was not well received, but loaded with unjust suspicions and endless vexations. They had hardly crossed the frontier when they were again imprisoned because they had no Austrian passports, and they were obliged to wait till a Polish Lady could obtain them from Vienna. With this they continued their journey by Olmütz, Brünn and Tasswitz, where F. Clement paid a visit to his sister, Barbara, who had received the church ornaments safely which had been despatched from Warsaw. After a short stay in his native land, F. Clement hastened to reach Vienna, meditating all the while on fresh undertakings and anticipating still more arduous labours.

Who that saw this poor priest's way-worn entrance into Vienna, could have guessed that he was to be the great instrument chosen by God to revive piety in that city and to save innumerable souls not only there but throughout Austria? Who would have imagined that a poor and humble Religious already well-advanced in years, was to be the spiritual physician sent by Providence to infuse a new life into the Church, which for so many years had languished and well nigh perished in that country? Yet so it was: and the words of the Apostle were once more verified that "*The foolish things of the world hath God chosen that He may confound the wise: and the weak things of the world hath God chosen that He may confound the strong. And the base things of the world and the things that are contemptible hath God chosen, and things that are not, that He might bring to nought things that are. That no flesh should glory in His sight.*" 1st Cor. 1. chap. 27. 28. & 29. v.

Which words received a fresh confirmation from Father Clements life, as we shall see in the following book.

THE THIRD BOOK.
FROM THE ARRIVAL OF FATHER CLEMENT IN VIENNA IN 1808 TILL HIS PRECIOUS DEATH IN 1820.

CHAPTER I.

HIS ARRIVAL IN VIENNA. HIS RESIDENCE NEAR THE ITALIAN CHURCH, IN WHICH HE EXERCISES HIS ZEAL AND GREATLY PROMOTES THE WORSHIP OF THE BLESSED SACRAMENT.

[From 1808 to 1813.]

NO sooner had F. Clement arrived in the Austrian capital, than he had to suffer the petty persecutions of the Police. But sufferings, outrages and persecutions were his birthright and assuredly they did not fail him in Vienna. First, he was taken to the Police station, and there detained several days. Various accusations were made against him: among the rest, that he had taken with him to Poland two youths of Znaim and Tasswitz, without permission of the Government: that he had secretly left the Dominican Convent in Cracow where he had been imprisoned: that he had crossed the frontier and returned to Warsaw: and more than all, that he had with him certain monies and rich vestments which could not be considered the lawful property of a poor Religious. He had to justify himself upon all these charges one by one; and had no difficulty in proving his innocence. The money he had about him he had received for masses from the Royal Family of Bourbon in Mietaw: the vestments came from Warsaw. To these undeniable facts, was superadded the mediation of many distinguished personages, so that after three days he was set at liberty, though under the supervision of the Police for some time. F. Clement and his companion, however, after the example of the Apostles *"went from the presence of the Council, rejoicing that they were accounted worthy to suffer reproach for the name of Jesus,"* and even augured well for their future missions, from the very fact of the persecution they had endured.

The first thing to do was to find a house in which he and Martin could live and serve God in silence, till a way was opened to them to work publickly for the salvation of men. First, he went and stayed with a friend in the Alservorstadt; but soon after, he found a little lodging in the town adjoining the Italian Church, of which Baron Penkler was the secular administrator. The house assigned to him was very small, but suited F. Clement well, he having for many years had intimate relations with the Rector of the Italian Church, Don Luigi Virginio, an Ex-Jesuit, who used to be his interpreter between Rome and Warsaw, as we have before related. He had also several warm friends in two or three others of the Clergy attached to that church, such as Count Simeon de la Tour, Don Pietro Rigoletti, Comte Guicciardini, Lantieri and Stampfer.

F. Clement would at once have commenced his labours in that church, both by preaching and hearing confessions, but prudence compelled him to remain for a time hidden and retired, as the Police were on the watch to spy out every step he took. Added to this, in 1809, the French entered Vienna and exercised also a hostile influence. On the 13th of May that capital fell into the hands of the French. On the 6th of June the battle of Wagram was fought near

Vienna; and on the 18th of October the Emperor Francis I. concluded a peace with Napoleon at the Castle of Schönbrunn.

The French had always been hostile to the Congregation of the Redemptorists and banished them from Bavaria, Poland and Switzerland, and hence F. Clement, as Vicar General, could not venture to act openly, so as to attract their attention. Therefore, even from that motive, he was condemned to quiet and silence.

However, though precluded from preaching or administering the sacraments, he did not remain idle. Two weapons remained to him, penance and prayer, so that the heart of God might be moved and a door opened to him to resume his apostolic labours. In the mean while, his companion, Martin Stark, prepared himself to receive the Priesthood, which he did on the 14th of Oct. 1810 from the Apostolic Nunzio, Severoli, in the Nunzio's own Chapel.

They both lived at that time in the greatest poverty, F. Clement resuming the trade of cook and preparing what poor food they could find, unless they were asked out to dinner.

F. Clement was especially well received in Vienna by the bakers, as he had formerly learnt their trade. Almost every Friday and Saturday they dined with the baker, Weyer, at the "Iron Pear", where, as a boy, F. Clement had worked. At other times, they dined with another baker named Apprich, in Rauhenstein Street. Their hosts looked upon these days as seasons of great joy and edification; for F. Clement, as usual, though he eat little, would interest his friends so much with his stories, which always had a devotional turn, and told them so many edifying facts with such a charm and sweetness of manner, that they were too delighted to have him. His little house corresponded exactly with his life and was a perfect model of poverty. It was situated just behind the high altar of the Italian Church, the altar of the Blessed

Sacrament being close by; so that he could, as at Warsaw, make himself the Guardian of the Divine Tabernacle and enjoy sweet communion with his beloved Lord and Master. He had been also given the permission to go from his own room by a little covered passage to the Oratory of the Archduchess Beatrix (Mother of Francis IV. Duke of Modena), where he could satisfy his ardent desire for prayer. In this chapel, in fact, he passed many hours of the day and often part of the night.

Another favourite place of pilgrimage with him was the Church of "Mary Help of Christians" in the suburb of that name, where the mother of God was specially revered.

But this strict retirement was not permitted to last long. For in the year 1809 Don Luigi Virginio, the Rector of the Italian Church died, a victim of charity, as F. Thaddeus had been two years before in Warsaw, having caught the typhus fever whilst attending to the French sick in the Hospital. Until his successor could be appointed, F. Clement was intreated to take the office of his deceased friend and act as Rector.

In this way, he resumed his priestly functions sooner than he expected, and even when a successor to the Rector was appointed in the person of Don Clemente Caselli, he, being an old man, implored F. Clement to undertake all the functions in the church, which F. Clement accepted with great pleasure. And so a new field of operations was opened out to him which his zeal made as fruitful as possible. First of all, he determined to try and make the sacred offices of the church as perfect and beautiful as he could, so as to attract the faithful and supply the want of preaching. And in truth the magnificent functions at the Italian Church soon produced a marvellous effect. To see that venerable Priest offering up the Holy Sacrifice, or assisting at processions, or reciting litanies, or still more, carrying the Blessed Sacrament at an exposition with such overwhelming reverence and love, touched the most indifferent among the congregation. His modest reverence, his tender devotion, and the deep humility which shone in his whole countenance produced a marked and salutary impression. But of all the Feasts, the one he celebrated with the greatest joy was that of the "Forty Hours", in which the Italian Church had the precedence of all the churches in Vienna: and this solemn function was so dear to him that even in after years he never would miss it if he could help it. He would go the day before expressly to help in making the necessary preparations and generally sang the High mass on the occasion. When he had to officiate in the church of the Mechitarists he would take equal care to celebrate this function with the greatest possible splendour.

After a time, he resumed his labours in the confessional, hearing both Germans and Italians. Every Saturday he repaired to a church in the suburbs very early in the morning to hear the confessions of the poor, and often made them a little address in honour of the Divine Mother. In this way, he became, by degrees, well known and the good began to flock to him for counsel and assistance from all sides. He formed around him a kind of Congregation of young men of every class, who looked up to him as their father and best friend: and the more they knew him the more they were attracted by his wonderful sweetness and charm of manner and were led on by him to the practice of every heavenly virtue.

Nor were women excluded from his paternal care. Among the first who placed themselves under his direction were the two sisters Biringer, who gave such valuable evidence of his sanctity at the time when the cause of his beatification was brought forward. Their father had met him several times in the baker's (Apprich's) house and was so edified by his manner and conversation that he made up his mind to entrust to him the religious education of his daughters. He hardly, however, dared ask him such a favour: but at the first hint he gave, the servant of God showed himself most willing to undertake this charitable office and hence became a constant visitor in the house, heard the first confessions and gave their first communion to his children and became the friend and adviser of the whole family, both in temporal and spiritual matters. In the same way, F. Clement instructed in Catholic Doctrine the little Countess Caroline Zichy, prepared her for her first confession and communion and guided her in the paths of virtue till his death. Up to the year 1865, the pious Countess remembered a number of little incidents regarding his teaching. Among others, one day she asked him with childish simplicity "if in Heaven she would have beautiful frocks?" "Little goose that you are!" exclaimed the good Father. "The most beautiful dress you can have in this world will appear but as dirty rags in comparison with the glory you will have in Paradise!" The wholesome influence he exercised over the young Countess may be abundantly seen in the earnest wish she had all her life to dedicate herself to God in a religious life, although, family duties, especially towards her aunt, Countess Zichy Ferrari, prevented her doing so. But hardly had she breathed her last in 1866, than her devoted niece although 60 years of age, entered the Convent of the Salesians at Brussels.

Innumerable were the conversions effected by F. Clement during the period of which we are now speaking, especially those of the Brothers Weit: but we will conclude this chapter with the words of Francis Hemmerich who saw him at that time and wrote as follows:

"In the years 1811—1812 I used to attend the Italian Church then served by Father Clement. His extraordinary humility and devotion edified me so much that I felt as if I were watching an Angel from heaven. I wanted very much to speak to him: but such a crowd of young men surrounded him when he left the church that I could not get near him. I never saw any man like Father Clement in my life; neither in Vienna nor in Würzburg, which is my native country."

CHAPTER II.

HE WAS NAMED CONFESSOR AND DIRECTOR OF THE URSULINES. DEPLORABLE STATE OF THE CHURCH IN VIENNA. WHO WAS ARCHBISHOP HOHENWARTH. THE DAILY OCCUPATIONS OF FATHER CLEMENT.

THE great good effected by F. Clement in the Italian Church and the visible blessing from Heaven which seemed to accompany all his works, had not escaped the notice of the Archbishop, Count Sigismund Von Hohenwarth; and the post of Confessor to the Ursulines falling vacant in 1813, he nominated F. Clement to that office, which the latter accepted. It is true that the direction of nuns did not enter into the sphere of action prescribed by St. Alphonsus to his sons: and far rather would F. Clement have been employed in preaching and giving missions. But the times and circumstances were such, that he felt it was a simple duty to accept the charge. In fact, the very name of a "Mission" infuriated the present Government: while the office of Confessor to the Ursulines offered him a favourable opportunity for working wonders in the salvation of souls. The Ursulines had a thousand children in their schools and had also higher classes for day-scholars; and an Institution for training School-Mistresses. An increase of fervour in the nuns would necessarily influence all those under their instruction and by raising the tone of the whole Community, would procure the salvation of very many souls outside the monastery. The Confessor of the nuns was likewise Rector of the Church, where he could preach, hear confessions, and perform all other sacerdotal functions. Hence this appointment gave F. Clement an opportunity of labouring for the people and promoting their spiritual welfare more easily than in any other position.

On the 31st of May 1813, on the Feast of St. Angela Merici, the Foundress of the Ursulines, F. Clement entered upon his new office and lived in a little house in the *Seilerstätte* street, adjoining the monastery. To arrive at his apartment one had to climb up to the 2nd floor of an old, poor, and mean-looking house.* There he had but one room, with a tiny sort of dressing room on one side which held various little necessaries: while his one chamber served as his study, bedroom, dining-room and even oratory. The furniture consisted of two old wardrobes, a table of common wood, an old sofa, two or three chairs, a bed, a kneeling-stool with a Crucifix and the image of the Madonna above it, a pendulum clock of no value and some old prints stuck on the walls. On the floor above, F. Sabelli lived, and when he was sent to Switzerland, F. Stark took his place, though he slept near the Italian Church. A very small room alongside was inhabited by a young student named Srna, whom F. Clement educated and provided for and to whom we are indebted for this description of his home. From thence to the monastery, which was in the street called St. John, there were only about a hundred steps.

The church of which F. Clement now had the care was not only poor and simple, but, we must own, was terribly neglected. It was so dirty and ill-kept that hardly any one would come to it. There were no sermons ever preached there except at Christmas, Easter and Pentecost, and when the Litanies were recited on Sundays and Festivals there were literally not above two or three people to make the

---

* This house was bought and rebuilt in 1850 and is no longer as it was in F. Clement's days. The number is also changed, being formerly N. 989 and now N. 11.

response "*Ora pro nobis*". We can easily imagine F. Clement's sadness at the first sight of this church, and the worst of it was that almost all the churches in Vienna were in a similar state; i. e. deserted, stripped of their ornaments and deprived of all solemn functions. It could not be otherwise: for external worship being the expression of internal Faith, when that was wanting, the other would necessarily be abandoned. When Faith in the Real Presence, for instance, is strong, the churches will be carefully adorned and everything provided to do honour to the solemn Mystery therein contained. But when Faith and love wax cold, there is no longer any interest in the matter.

Now at the time F. Clement arrived in Vienna the Catholic Church was, as it were, dead, mainly owing to the Emperor Joseph, who had done his best to destroy it. But even before he came to the throne, Protestantism had sown tares among the wheat and Gallicanism had made open war against the Holy See. But the faithful Catholic of Austria could have made head against these two hostile powers if the Emperor, blinded to his own interests, had not, by his arbitrary laws, played into the hands of these subverters of the Faith.

Infatuated with the idea of being Head of the Church, every one of his ordinances bore the stamp of schism; while, to take away the old Faith from the hearts of the people, he attacked the Hierarchy and Liturgy of the Church in the most furious manner, and thus endeavoured to destroy the visible authority and external form appointed by God Himself. Hence the cry was, "no longer the Church, but the State": no more reference to the Pope but to the Emperor: no longer the Bishops but the Ministers were to regulate the services in the churches and administer to the spiritual wants of the Dioceses! "Thus", writes Henry Hurter, in the life of his Father Frederick, "the whole organisation of the church was well nigh destroyed. All Catholic works were stopped, such as Confraternities, Associations of prayer, and the like, and almost all the convents were suppressed. Processions and pilgrimages were prohibited, and so likewise were the common devotions in use among the people in the churches, such as Benediction, the Rosary, frequent exposition of the Blessed Sacrament, the Sepulchre on Holy Thursday, sung Vespers and in fact every external expression of Catholic Faith. To supply the void, an imperial ordinance prescribed certain services which by their cold monotony alienated the piety of the Faithful; and no sooner were these dismal functions over, than the churches were closed for the rest of the day. The multiplied expressions of Christian Piety being thus cut off from the people and the admirable organisation of the Church destroyed, only a handful of individuals had the courage to substitute private devotions, while the masses became an easy prey to the seducers."

In the same way and with the same object, the seminaries were suppressed, together with all the schools of Theology; and all those who aspired to the Priesthood were obliged to study in the Royal University, where, under the guidance of masters who were professed Rationalists and who hated the Holy See, the students lost both their Faith and their love of God and of the Church

Hence, all those who distinguished themselves by marked anti-Catholic tendencies were rewarded by promotion to the most important posts, such as Councillors of State, Ministers in the Public Offices, or Canonries and other dignities in the Church. Then, if they proved themselves sufficiently subservient to the state, they were made Bishops and Archbishops, and the Holy See found itself compelled to preconize them for fear of worse consequences — i. e. an open schism, with which that unworthy Ambassador, Cardinal Herzan, menaced Pope Pius VI. Hence these Bishops not only published the pernicious decrees of the Government and insisted on their observance by their priests, but they went so far as to declaim in their pastorals against all the ancient ecclesiastical institutions, which they impudently denounced as abuses and superstitions.

It is fair to say that Archbishop Hohenwarth, who then administered the Diocese of Vienna, was not of this class of Bishops, but a man of proved virtue and full of earnest Catholic sentiments. Born on the 2nd of May 1730 at Gerlachstein in Carniola, he entered the Society of Jesus in 1748 and was employed in the instruction of youth and in giving missions. Five years after the suppression of the Society, he was summoned to the Court of the Grand Duke of Tuscany to undertake the education of the Archduke, afterwards Emperor under the title of Francis I. In the year 1792, he was made Bishop of Trieste and six years later was translated to the Bishopric of St. Hippolitus. But in 1803, the Archbishop of Vienna, Cardinal Migazzi dying, Francis I. promoted him to the Archbishopric.

Hohenwarth lived a simple and austere life, dividing all his revenues among the poor and punctually fulfilling all exercises of piety. He loved F. Clement and still more, his disciple Frederick Werner, whom he received into his own house for a year and in whom he placed the most entire confidence.

In spite of his admirable personal qualities, we must say that he did not know how to cope with the evils of the times: nor how to fill aright the first Metropolitan See in that vast monarchy. Besides, being appointed to the Archbishopric when he was 73 years of age and having filled that post till 1820, the feebleness of his physical powers incapacitated him from governing the Church with vigour and energy, however much the circumstances of the times may have required it. For this reason he was liked by the Government, who left him free to govern his vast Diocese with his Canons, (many of whom were sadly unlike himself) and who knew that they would be spared any inconvenient complaints or protests. If occasionally the Archbishop would complain of the sad state of the Diocese, he never brought his complaints before the Government, being fully persuaded that his remonstrances would be worse than useless. There were very few, in fact, who had the courage to declare themselves openly to be Roman Catholic: for such a declaration was ascribed either to weakness of intellect or to a want of patriotism. It was simply impossible for a really honest Catholic priest to obtain any ecclesiastical dignity. To become even a Professor at the University, an Aulic Councillor, or a Canon, indubitable proofs would have to be given that the candidate was thoroughly imbued with what were called Josephin principles. Nor could any strictly Catholic books be published, because, though the censorship was in the hands of ecclesiastics, even these inexorably cancelled any writings which did not coincide with the pretended "new lights" of the day. What moral courage, then, did it not require of any man to own to his Catholic principles! For want of this bravery it happened that the great majority ended by denying their Faith, and the neglected and deserted condition of the churches was the strongest proof of the incredulity which unhappily was then dominant throughout the country.

But this courage, so wanting in Vienna, was amply found in F. Clement: who, without caring for the opinions then in vogue, showed himself a truly Catholic Pastor. For that reason he was looked up to with the greatest admiration by the good, although dreaded by the followers of the new doctrines. He became a centre of Catholic movement and influence and a rallying point for the feeble and down-hearted. The seven years he passed at the Ursulines, however much they might be concealed by his humility, and by the obscure nature of his office, were in reality, the most fruitful in his Apostolic life: for during that time he managed to rouse once more in Vienna and throughout Austria a truly Catholic spirit.

And as the life he led during those seven years was uniform, we will here give a sort of Horarium of his daily occupations, reserving the account of his brilliant spiritual triumphs to another chapter.

He rose very early in the morning, often at three o'clock, according to the evidence of one of his devoted disciples Emanuel Veith, who sometimes slept in his room. Then he would at once say the following Hymn of which we here give a rough translation.

> All for the glory of my Lord and Saviour
> And for His honour, will I act this day.
> Whether in labour or repose
> All will I consecrate to Him.
> I give him body, soul, and life,
> And only ask His grace and aid.
> Bless us, O! Lord, in this our strife,
> And save us from all mortal ills.
> O! Mary! help us in our needs,
> And plead thou for us with thy Son.
> Eternal God! To Thee I bring
> This offering of my daily life.
> Thou, the beginning and end of all,
> Direct my steps and guide my path.
> Accept me, Lord, without reserve,
> For Thine I am, in life, in death, in all!

Then he said his morning prayers and made half an hour's, meditation: after which he began his ministerial work, from which no physical suffering or bad weather ever deterred him. Once or twice a week, he went to the church of the Mechitarist Fathers to hear the confessions of the poor and then he returned to the Ursulines to hear the confessions of the Nuns and others who were waiting for him there. But before seating himself in the Sacred Tribunal, he would kneel with profound humility on the steps of the altar and there, before Jesus in the Blessed Sacrament, pray for light and grace to fulfil this difficult part of his ministry. He heard confessions till 10 o'clock but sometimes till $^1/_2 11$, so great was the crowd around his confessional. Then he said mass with a devotion and compunction which edified all who were present at the Holy Sacrifice.

After this tremendous fatigue, he would come home, transact the business of his Congregation with Fathers Sabelli and Stark, answer certain necessary letters, and give counsel to any who might be waiting to seek his advice. At midday, he made, with his Fathers, an examination of conscience, according to the Rule of St. Alphonsus and recited the Litany of our Lady: after which the simple dinner provided by the Ursulines arrived. But this, Father Clement would scarcely do more than taste, as he never would sit down at table, but served the rest, only taking a mouthful now and then. Sometimes he would eat nothing at all, but spent the time, while the others were dining, in reading or in holy conversation.

In the afternoon he always paid a visit to some church. Either to that of Mary "Help of Christians", or to one in which the Blessed Sacrament was exposed, as he never, when he could help it, missed assisting at the "Fortry Hours" adoration. Then he would visit the sick, who had sent for him even if they lived in the most distant suburbs of the city, and above all, the *"pauvres honteux"*— i. e. people who had seen better days and were ashamed to make their distress known and to whom he secretly conveyed money and food. Whenever he was wanted, he would come back in the afternoon or evening to the Ursulines to hear confessions. But his immediate disciples and especially his confraternity of young men, used to come to the little room adjoining his own for their confessions. In fact, towards evening his house was full and especially of students, to whom he gave little conferences which produced extraordinarily good fruits. When they were gone, he would read a chapter of Holy scripture and often one from the old Testament, or from the Acts of the Apostles. Then, when he was sure of being alone, on the days appointed by the Rule, he would take the discipline and spend the rest of the evening in prayer: after which he would go to bed and take the brief sleep which so arduous a day required.

Once or twice a year, he left all these exhausting occupations and passed eight days in retreat alone with God, going through the spiritual exercises, and to be more sure of solitude, he literally lived in the church, where he retired whenever pressed by importunate visitors.

Thus his holy days were passed. Cardinal Rauscher writing of him says: "F. Clement was incessantly occupied in our Lord's service and in labouring indefatigably for the eternal salvation of his neighbour."

Not only his days but his nights were so employed: for if any sick person sent for him, he would curtail his short rest to watch with him and often sat up night after night with the dying. Neither did he ever dream of making up for it by resting a little longer the next day: but went straight from the sick-bed to the church, where he resumed his usual task in the confessional. Well may F. Clement be called "that good and faithful servant" whose whole life was spent in the service of his Lord, and who never let slip a single moment without employing it to the honour and glory of God!

CHAPTER III.

F. CLEMENT BY HIS FAITH AND ZEAL INFLAMED THE VIENNESE WITH A LIKE ARDOUR.

THE humble baker would certainly never have become the Apostle of Vienna had he not been animated with that same spirit which filled the poor fishermen in Galilee and transformed them into Apostles; so that they were enabled to found, in the midst of the vice and corruptions of the great Roman Empire, a Christian Community which should endure to the end of time. Magnificent indeed were the proofs given of F. Clement's heroic Faith during the process of his beatification. One wrote: "The Faith of F. Clement was stronger than the iron rock and in matters of Faith he never would yield a single inch." "This venerable servant of God" added Cardinal Rauscher, "embraced with the most vivid Faith every truth revealed by the mercy of God and all that the Church proposed to him to believe." He very often was heard to thank God for having been born and bred of pious and Catholic parents and still more for having been so carefully educated by his pious mother in the true religion and in the holy fear of God. He often said he had no merit in believing so fervently, for that he had never experienced the smallest temptation to do otherwise, and on the contrary it would have been a violent effort to him to doubt any revealed doctrine. Hence, speaking of infidels, he would often exclaim with sorrow: "Unhappy men! what a multitude of errors must they believe, not to be able to believe the Truth!" "The light of Faith", wrote an Ursuline nun, Sister Jacqueline of Welschenau, "guided F. Clement in all his operations. In the pulpit and in familiar conversation he would continually allude to this great gift and say: "To one who has not faith, even the most sublime Truths of our holy religion appear as fables," or again: "If I could understand the most sublime mysteries of Faith by opening my eyes, I would rather close them, so as not to lose the great merit of Faith", and again: "I do not myself believe my eyes so much as the infallible oracles of holy Church, for she can never err in matters of faith, while our eyes are subject to a thousand illusions." One day he was pasting a print on the wall and exclaimed, alluding to this topic: "I am more persuaded that God is One in Three Persons than I am that this picture is sticking on the wall." Canon Greif declared "That so marked was this characteristic in F. Clement, that he considered he was specially chosen by God to revive the languishing Faith of the Viennese and rouse those whom the evil spirit of the times had filled with doubts or indifference."

It would be too long to quote all the evidence given by his disciples on this subject: but Father F. Rinn mentions the joy with which he used to relate a story of St. Louis King of France, who, when he was told one day that Jesus was actually visible in the Blessed Sacrament and urged to run and see it, answered: "Let unbelievers go and solve their doubts: as for me, my Faith does not need either miracles or arguments." With joy would F. Clement have shed his blood in defence of this or any other Truth. He had one thing ever before his eyes and in his heart, and that was, the thought of God and Eternity. This simple rule for all his thoughts, wishes and actions could not be disturbed by anybody or anything. In converting or directing souls, he had no other weapons save the simple Catholic Faith and the practice of the Church. He had a great esteem for human learning and natural sciences: but he would often say that he preferred the science of the Saints and added: "*Quoniam non cognovi litteraturam, introibo in potentias Domini*". (Ps. 20. 16 v.)

Father Czech, speaking of F. Clement's burning Faith, wound up by saying: "Such was the power of his reasoning and the evident conviction with which he spoke, that he persuaded the most incredulous; and even enkindled the flame of Faith more brightly in the hearts of his spiritual sons."

He would exclaim sometimes to the nuns: "I cannot understand how a man can live without Faith. A man without Faith is like a fish out of water." At other times he would say: "I am proud and vain and a great sinner, who knows nothing: but one thing I possess, by the grace of

God, and that is, to be a *thorough-going Catholic*. I would not exchange my Faith for that of any one. Of no other thing can I glory save that of being a Catholic!"

This living and ardent Faith was clearly shown in the following prayer, which, if not actually written by him (as we believe) was printed and distributed by him whenever he had the opportunity. We will here translate it as closely as we can.

"O! my Redeemer! Is it possible that that terrible moment is come in which few Christians remain who are filled with the spirit of Faith? that moment in which Thy wrath will be provoked into withdrawing from us Thy holy protection? Have the vices, the evil habits of Thy children irrevocably moved Thee, in Thy justice, to take vengeance on our sins? O! Divine Author and Consummator of our Faith, we intreat Thee, in the bitterness of our humbled and contrite hearts, not to permit the grand light of Faith to be quenched within us. Remember Thy mercies of old. Cast a look of compassion on the Vineyard which Thou hast planted with Thy right hand, and which Thou hast irrigated with Thine own precious Blood and with the blood of so many thousand martyrs, with the tears of so many generous penitents, with the sweat of so many apostles, with the prayers of so many confessors and innocent virgins. O! Divine Mediator! behold those zealous souls who lift up their hearts incessantly to Thee to obtain the preservation of their most precious treasure, the true Faith. Suspend, O! Just God, the decree of our reprobation: turn away Thine eyes from our infidelities and fix them on the precious and adorable Blood, which was shed on the cross to purchase the salvation of men and which is daily offered up for us on our altars. Keep us all in our true Catholic and Roman Faith.

Let sickness and sorrows and troubles come upon us, if Thou wilt—but leave us our holy Faith. For, if we possess that precious gift, willingly shall we bear all sufferings, and nothing can affect our happiness. On the other hand, without this treasure of Faith, our miseries would be unspeakable and illimitable. O! Good Jesus! author of our Faith, preserve it to us pure: keep us within the bark of Peter, make us faithful and obedient to his Successor and Thy Vicar here on earth, so that the unity of Thy Church may be preserved, her holiness promoted, the Apostolic See protected and the Universal Church extended to save the souls of all men.

O! Jesus! Author of our Faith, preserve and enlighten our Sovereign: convert and humble the enemies of Thy Church: concede to all Christian Princes and to their subjects the spirit of peace and true unity. Comfort and preserve us in Thy holy service, so that in Thee we may live and in Thee die. O! Jesus! Author of our Faith, for Thee I live, for Thee I die!"

F. Clement exhorted likewise his penitents to pray specially for perseverance in the Faith and for this purpose he recommended to them the following prayer:

"O! Father of mercy, look upon the face of Thy Christ, who in the days of His flesh offered up unto Thee strong prayers and supplications and tears for Thy spouse and our mother, the Church. Behold, O! Father, that bloody sweat, that crown of thorns, those pierced hands and feet, the wounds of our Brother Jesus Christ. Listen O! Father to the groans of Thy Beloved Son on the Cross; the heavens were opened, the rocks were rent, and will not Thy mercy be moved towards us? Preserve in Thy holy Faith all those who confess to Thee with a sincere and contrite heart. Defend them from false prophets, who go about in sheep's clothing, but inwardly are ravening wolves. Blunt the edge of their weapons so that their evil counsels may come to nought and they themselves be covered with confusion. O! merciful God! grant to those that believe in Thee, the grace to live in unity and concord: to love Thee with perfect charity: to follow Thee faithfully unto death, ever persevering in Thy holy service, and finally to praise and bless Thee for ever in eternity. Amen.*

In the strength of his Faith, F. Clement did not much care for a multiplicity of arguments wherewith to prove it; on the contrary, he wished that our weak reasoning should hold itself at a respectful distance from the sublime mysteries of Faith rather than strive to investigate their depths. His disciple F. Madlener, relates "that he considered the arguments drawn from reason to prove any particular truth in religion, were only useful for beginners: and that more solid arguments could be drawn from the history in which God has revealed himself. The Catholic Church was to him the most culminating fact in history." On this point Cardinal Rauscher remarks: "The heralds of infidelity in these days do not like religious disputes and pretend that these are antiquated subjects, which modern progress should consign to oblivion. Yet, they often dispute themselves, especially on the preambles of Faith, which they either combat with new sophisms or elude with insidious interpretations. F. Clement despised all such artifices. One day when I was speaking to him about the proofs of Christianity, he replied that he thought the very existence of the Church was an abundant proof in itself of its truth. And I am convinced that the example of his fervent and undoubting Faith, acting as it did with such charity, had far more effect and worked far more conversions than others did with the most learned and subtle arguments."

"He hated", added another witness, "the vain disputations of which the Germans are so fond and by which they searched at a distance for the Truth which God has put within reach

---

* Sister Thaddeus Taxboeck, a laysister among the Ursulines, heard these prayers from the mouth of F. Clement himself, by whom they were indelibly impressed on her memory.

of all. For this reason, his sermons and exhortations were supremely simple and straightforward; and with peculiar pleasure he would quote those words of our Lord: "I confess to Thee, O! Father Lord of heaven and earth, because thou hast hid these things from the wise and prudent and hast revealed them to little ones." (XI. St. Mat. 25. v.) And this simplicity and humility in F. Clement was not without its reward: as such supernatural lights shone forth in his reasoning that he seemed imbued with extraordinary knowledge. He always declared, in his humility, "that he had never learnt anything": but all those who heard him were in admiration at his profound wisdom and learning and very justly believed that God, by a special grace, and in some supernatural manner, had infused into him such treasures of knowledge that he could instruct the most learned among his auditors.

"In fact", as F. Kral attests, "he had scarcely any time for study as a boy: then a long period of his life was spent as a baker and also a portion as a hermit, so that during that time, he lost the little knowledge he had acquired as a youth. Even his philosophical and theological studies were made in an incredibly short time: and no sooner had he been ordained priest than he found himself overwhelmed with work and charged with such laborious functions that the marvel is how he could ever have acquired the deep science which excited such admiration in all who knew him. The most learned Theologians would often propound difficult questions and doubts to him: yet he always answered clearly and correctly. If any writings were submitted to him or any new book of which he was asked to give an opinion, he would point out at once, in a few brief words, what he considered the imprudent or doubtful passages; and sometime would smilingly add: "*You know I have a keen Catholic nose.*" With this joke or another he would always pass off any comments on his extraordinary wisdom, and thus hide the particular lights which he had undoubtedly received from Heaven."

Another of his disciples, Canon Veith, whose acute intelligence was well-known in Vienna, thus speaks on the same subject:

"Father Clement, with admirable acumen and promptness, would, when necessary, give the clearest judgment on any literary production whether poetry or prose; as well as on dogmatic speculations, mystical doctrines or learned hypotheses. Nor could he althogether conceal the fact that these extraordinary supernatural lights on such scientific and difficult subjects came direct from God: which I can prove by certain words which now and then escaped him inadvertently, especially when he raised his finger towards heaven." There were also certain cures which were attributed to clairvoyants and mesmerical influences, which he absolutely condemned and rejected.

"I cannot imagine", wrote another witness, "where F. Clement made his studies: but I know that in all theological matters he was profoundly versed and looked upon as a real authority. I and my friends used often to listen with surprise at his vast knowledge and still more at the ease with which he would unravel the most intricate theological questions."

The strong Faith which we have mentioned as Father Clement's characteristic, and which captivated his intellect to the obedience of Christ, produced the most salutary effects on his own heart. All that was noblest and grandest, when viewed in the clear light of Faith, became the object of his thoughts and wishes: hence arose the great consolation he derived from prayer; his extraordinary recollection of spirit; his profound respect for everything pertaining to God — in a word, all the virtues which are summed up in that one expression — *A Life of Faith*. "In that great servant of God" as Father Kral writes "the words of the Gospel were fully verified: 'Where your treasure is there will your heart be also.' As God was the continual subject of his thoughts, whenever he was not occupied in works of charity, he was always praying or meditating." Even when he was walking in the streets of Vienna he would say his Rosary, which he held hidden under his cloak: and even when he had a companion with him he would speak little and only when charity required it. One day, when he was going to see a sick person, after having walked a long time in silence, he turned to F. Kral, who was with him and said: "Do you know what I have been doing? Saying the Rosary. Won't you do the same?" "He would also" (as Cardinal Rauscher relates) "often repeat the Rosary of our Holy Redeemer, which is composed of 33 'Paternosters' in honour of the 33 years which the Son of God passed on earth. In fact, according to the Apostolic precept, he prayed without ceasing. His mind had no difficulty in raising itself from external things to the God with whom he was ever so closely united: and he seemed only to come back to the interests of men whenever charity required it. Very often I have seen him seated in the midst of his young men with his eyes half closed whilst they were reading some edifying book. He was meditating on Divine things all the while: but from time to time he would interrupt the reader to make some wise observation or call their attention to a particular point which he thought might be edifying or instructive." Another witness states: "Whether F. Clement were in the town or in the country and whether it were winter or summer, he would walk without a hat, covering his head only with a little black "beretta", out of respect to the presence of God and his Angel Guardian.

The anxiety he felt to walk always in the presence of God and to offer up to Hime very action and word, was only equalled by his solicitude to renew continually his purity of intention in all his works. Not only was he devoted to this particular exercise, repeating continually the words, "*All for the glory of my God*", but he tried to induce every one around him to practise the same. We have a little formula for this purpose drawn up by him and which he taught to Sister Thaddeus, of which we will here give a translation.

"My Creator, my Lord and my God! my desires are not hidden from Thee, nor are my groanings of spirit unknown to Thee. Yet, as the necessities of this life do not permit my thoughts to be directed continually to Thee, I make this compact with Thee, which I pray may avail for the whole week.

1. Whenever I lift up my eyes to Heaven, it is with the intention of glorifying and blessing Thy divine perfections, Thine omnipotence, Thy infinite wisdom, Thy goodness and Thy justice.

2. Whenever I open or shut my eyes, it is with the intention of magnifying and praising all the actions and works of Thy only-begotten Son and of all Thy Saints and of the Just (whether past, present or future', if done to Thy glory, of which I earnestly desire to become a participator.

3. Whenever I breathe, it is with the intention of offering up the life, passion and blood of our Holy Redeemer Jesus, together with the merits of all the Saints, to Thy eternal glory, for the salvation of the whole world and as a satisfaction for all sin.

4. As often as my heart beats in my breast, so often do I curse and detest each and every sin, whether of my own or of others, committed, since the beginning of the world, against the glory of Thy holy Name, which I would wish to be able to wipe out with my blood.

5. Finally, whenever I shall move hand or foot, so often do I intend to submit myself entirely to Thy most holy will, desiring only that it may be done in all things.

So that this five-fold compact should never be broken, I

confirm and seal it with the Five Wounds of Jesus Christ; and I will that it may always be valid even should I not remember each intention at the time myself. Amen."

This formula abundantly expresses the generous and living faith of F. Clement and marvellously confirms the wise judgment formed of his character by Cardinal Rauscher.

CHAPTER IV.

THE DEVOTION OF F. CLEMENT FOR THE MYSTERIES OF OUR REDEMPTION. HIS ZEAL FOR THE WORTHY CELEBRATION OF THE DIVINE OFFICES.

THE fruits of a lively and healthy faith are always seen in the practices of piety used by holy souls. These practices vary according to different natures and dispositions. Thus, one has a special devotion to certain mysteries in our Faith: another to some special operation of God's love and mercy: a third will venerate some particular Saint in Heaven, and so each and all of these practices of devotion contribute to form that beautiful many-coloured vestment with which our mother the Church is adorned by her faithful children.

With regard to F. Clement, all the witnesses in the cause of his beatification were agreed on one point: and that was, that his special devotion was given to the sublime mysteries of the incarnation, passion and death of our Holy Redeemer: and to the Blessed Sacrament on the altar.

In fact, his devotion to the mysteries of the Sacred Infancy were peculiary strong and tender. Each time that he watched by the Crib, he was filled with the sweetest feelings of joy, gratitude, humility and compassion, contemplating the Divine Majesty reduced to such poverty. Advent and Christmas-tides used to fill him with holy exultation. He never lost an opportunity of striving to kindle in other hearts some of the burning love which filled his own: nor could he refrain from bringing forward the subject to his intimates; or from dwelling in the pulpit on the feeling which abounded in his own heart. He would point out to his hearers how wonderfully our Lord had honoured human nature even beyond the Angelic one, seeing that He himself assumed it for us, although the "*Seed of Abraham*" understood it not. On Christmas Day he took care to explain to the people the significance of the three masses which each priest celebrates on that day, namely, to honour the triple generation of the word: the eternal, the temporal and the mystic. "The first mass", he would say, "is said at midnight when all is dark and nothing is to be seen: so, to our poor intellect, the eternal generation of the Son in the bosom of the Father, is utterly dark and incomprehensible. The second mass is said at dawn, that is, when darkness and light are mingled: this denotes that the temporal birth of the Son of God in the womb of Mary though partly incomprehensible to our intellect, is in part made clear. The third mass is said in the morning, when everything can be clearly seen: for equally clear to our minds is the spiritual birth of Jesus in our hearts, producing in us so sensible an amendment."

But to understand still better his Christmas feelings, we will again refer to some devout exercises given by him to Sister Thaddeus for Advent.

1. "Excite continually in your heart a lively faith in the mystery of the Divine Incarnation.

2. Adore the Son of God for us made man and now present in the Sacrament on the altar, with the same sentiments and affection with which the Blessed Virgin adored Him when she had conceived by the Holy Ghost. Do this in a special manner during Holy Mass, when, at the Creed the priest kneeling, says the words: '*Et incarnatus est de Spiritu Sancto.*'

3. Thank the Divine Father who deigned to send His only begotten Son: Thank the Son of God, who made himself

man for our salvation: and thank the Holy Spirit, through whom the Blessed Virgin became the Mother of God.

4. Say the '*Angelus*' on your knees when you hear the sound of the bell and renew these exercises. Many are the indulgences granted by the Sovereign Pontiffs to a devout recitation of the '*Angelus*'.

5. Make some special act of humility, to honour the humility of the Son of God.

6. Practise some act of mortification during the Fridays in Advent, according to your state or position.

7. Offer yourself to God every morning in union with the Sacrifice of Jesus for our salvation."

The love which F. Clement bore the Infant Jesus induced him to have an engraving done on copper of His image in the Crib which he afterwards distributed everywhere. This was the first holy picture that had been seen for ages in that country, as the use of them had been entirely forgotten. Later on, he had another done of the Sacred Heart.

The next great devotion of F. Clement was to the dolorous passion of our Saviour Jesus Christ.

He could not even think of the agonies He suffered without being filled with the deepest sorrow and the tenderest compassion; so that when he had to preach or speak on the subject he was often unable to continue from sobs and sighing. He exhorted all his penitents to meditate continually on the Passion of Jesus and to accept all suffering willingly for the love of Him.

Father Pajalich writes: "That he would continually remind his hearers how our Lord by His sufferings had sanctified all our sorrows and all our actions, if only they be offered up in union with the actions of Jesus."

No less striking was the devotion of this servant of God towards the admirable Sacrament of the altar which has never failed, since its origin, to draw holy souls so powerfully to itself. Even when he was a lad he would remain in the church of St. Saviour's in Vienna to serve every mass from six o'clock till midday: then at Warsaw and later on, at Vienna, he would spend hours in humble adoration before the Blessed Sacrament; and when It was exposed, would pass the whole night before It. When he was offering the Holy Sacrifice, at the moment of Holy Communion, tears of love and tenderness would course down his cheeks. And the older he grew, the more fervent he became: so that instead of tepidity in this devotion, each year saw him more tender and ardent.

If he came into a church or passed before the Blessed Sacrament, he would kneel instantly and adore His Redeemer for several minutes with the utmost fervour. Towards the middle or end of his sermons, he would exclaim with ardent love: "O! admirable Sacrament! O! tremendous mystery! before which the Angels prostrate themselves with trembling, we adore Thee!" He insisted besides on the Ursulines praising and adoring Jesus in the Blessed Sacrament every hour exclaiming: *"may the most holy Sacrament of the altar be praised and exalted by me and every other creature now and in eternity!"*

He would speak of this august Sacrament in the most moving way from the pulpit and exhorted every one worthily and frequently to receive Holy Communion. His tender devotion to this mystery would be shown by frequent and almost unconscious ejaculations such as: "O! good Jesus! O! great and most amiable Good! O! Sacrament most holy! O! Sacrament Divine! All praise and all thanksgiving be every moment Thine!"

He made a point of visiting the churches in which the Blessed Sacrament was exposed during the 40 hours and exhorted every one to practice this devotion and thereby gain the indulgences attached to it, besides praying there for the conversion of poor sinners.

When he was himself in adoration before the Blessed Sacrament exposed, he appeared like a man transfigured: and when he had to bear It in procession, or to the sick, his extraordinary recollection and the evident love he felt towards Him whom he carried, struck all who watched him. When he blessed the people with the Blessed Sacrament, his face was so transfigured that it touched every one and it seemed as if he saw Him whom he loved, not under the veil of faith, but actually face to face.

His greatest happiness was to give Communion to a large number of people and to take it to the sick. He implored every one who passed by a church to raise their hats as an act of reverence towards the Blessed Sacrament within: and still more did he inculcate spiritual communion several times a day and a visit to Jesus in the Blessed Sacrament, as an efficacious means of maintaining oneself continually united with God.

Frequent Communion in those days was very rare and in fact, we may say almost unknown, especially among students: but F. Clement contrived to introduce it among his penitents and in that way drew many young men away from a wordly life and gained them entirely to the service of God. This success was the more marvellous because the clerical state was at that time very much looked down upon and consequently rarely embraced by young men of good birth or position. Most touching was it to watch F. Clement during the celebration of Holy Mass. Of this Cardinal Rauscher speaks as follows:

"If, in all the Sacred functions he performed we were struck with the great fire of charity which burned in his heart, still more remarkable was his manner while offering the Holy Sacrifice, when he seemed as it were, consumed with Divine Love."

And the Ursuline Sister, Welschenau, mentions "that this great servant of God, by his sacerdotal life still more than by his preaching, contributed in a wonderful manner to raise the dignity of his office and give splendour to all divine functions. His manner in church was such that it impressed the whole Congregation with increased reverence and devotion: and when he walked down the Aisle they spontaneously rose to their feet and regarded him with eyes full of respectful admiration. Then when he had vested for mass and walked up to the altar to offer the Holy Sacrifice, he appeared indeed full of majesty and dignity as a true Vicar of Jesus Christ. Faith and devotion shone in his face, so that he seemed as a Seraph burning with the love of God and entirely absorbed in the contemplation of His infinite perfections. No one could look at him at such times without feeling himself moved to increased devotion and having his mind impressed with a more exalted idea of this tremendous sacrifice. There was nothing in the least affected or exaggerated in his way of celebrating: but all came from his pure soul being so full of the God Whom he daily held in his hands.

"Many of us could not resist watching him", wrote Sister Giacomina, "but I was the most curious of all. One day I remained in the Choir in a little corner looking down into the church to see him go back to his house. He came out of the sacristy and thinking himself entirely alone and unseen, he prostrated himself on the altar steps and thence with inexpressible love and reverence threw a kiss to his hidden God in the tabernacle. Truly were the words realised in our holy spiritual Father: "*Where your treasure is there will your heart be also.*"

Canon Veith, speaking of this, added: "When F. Clement said the prayers before mass, he always recited them with such compunction that one felt he considered himself unworthy to offer the Holy Sacrifice." And another wrote: "One day after preaching, he went to say mass and when he came to the 'Confiteor' he repeated it with such an evident realisation of his own unworthiness that I never forgot it, although it is now 44 years ago. He seemed to feel contrition for all the sinners in the world." In spite of the tears he often shed during mass and while giving Communion, it never prevented his observing the rubric in its most minute details. With his really sublime dignity and devotion he exercised unconsciously the most salutary influence over his servers and many of his disciples and friends would strive to be near him in the chancel for their greater edification, among whom we may mention Monsignor Muzzi, who was then Auditor to the Nunzio* and who often came to the Ursuline Church for this sole purpose. Especially after the consecration and when he was making his thanksgiving after mass, his face was all aglow with Faith in the real presence of our Lord in the Blessed Sacrament; so much so that he was almost wrapt out of himself. Neither illness nor journies ever prevented his celebrating this august Sacrifice. Very often, with extraordinary humility, he would serve as Subdeacon to young priests who were celebrating their masses before the Blessed Sacrament exposed, to the great edification of the assistants. And the same anxiety he had shown in Warsaw for the highest possible honour to be paid to our Sacramental Lord, he did not fail to exhibit in Vienna.

When he first came to be Rector of the Ursuline Church, he found it deserted and neglected in every possible way: the chasubles were old and in rags and there were no ornaments whatever on the altars. But he determined at once to supply these deficiencies. First, he had the whole church cleaned; and then, with the help of a few generous benefactors, he, by degrees, obtained not only necessary but even

---

* Monsignor Giovanni Muzzi was sent later as Delegate and Vicar Apostolic to Chili, when he took with him a young priest as companion, Giovanni Mastai-Feretti, who afterwards became Pope under the title of Pius IX. Monsignor Muzzi died Bishop of Città di Castello.

beautiful things for its adornment. He was the first who had the courage to defy the Josephin decree as to the number of candles to be used at mass and in other functions; and to reestablish the good old Roman custom of illuminating and decorating the altars with as much splendour as possible, especially when the Blessed Sacrament was exposed.

In proportion to his love for our Lord was his anxiety for the decoration of His house, in which everything, in his opinion, should conduce to the glory of the Divine Majesty and awake in men's minds befitting reverence for all things pertaining to God. In no other church in Vienna not even in the Cathedral of St. Stephen, were sacred functions celebrated with half the dignity or pomp which was found in the Ursuline Church. On the Eve of each Festival F. Clement would announce it and preach upon it to the people; and to impress it the more vividly on their minds, he had paintings hung up representing the Mystery or the Saint in whose honour the Feast was to be celebrated. According to the spirit of St. Alphonsus he took great pains with the music also and insisted on plenty of candles and fresh flowers for the altars. In the same way, during Holy week he used to get a certain number of the students from the great Seminary to sing "*Tenebræ*" and help him with the functions, which contributed greatly to the edification of the Congregation. Above all, the Feast of Corpus Christi was kept (during the whole octave) with extraordinary solemnity. Every day there was a procession in the church, he himself bearing the Blessed Sacrament with the tenderest reverence and devotion: and at the end he would intone the "*Te Deum*" with a joy which led all the Congregation to join in it. It was the same with the "Forty Hours", when he would intreat the Apostolic Nunzio, to lead the procession. In this way, while satisfying his own devotion, he had the consolation of finding this church once so neglected and desolate, thronged with devout worshippers from all parts of the city. In no other church in Vienna, were there so many communions and confessions. A great many priests came also there to say mass, attracted both by the beauty of the church and the holiness of the Rector. Among these were the Nunzio, Cardinal Rudolph, brother of the Emperor Francis I., Cardinal Prince Odescalchi and many others, Lastly Dr. Grief, Tutor of young Prince Frederick Schwarzenberg often said mass in this church, served by this very young Prince, who became afterwards Cardinal and Bishop of the Church at Prague.

CHAPTER V.

HIS DEVOTION TO OUR LADY, TO THE SAINTS AND TO THE SOULS IN PURGATORY.

AS in so many other points, so in devotion to the Blessed Virgin F. Clement was a faithful imitator of his spiritual Father, St. Alphonsus. He delighted in speaking in the Pulpit of the glories and greatness of the Virgin Mary and it seemed as if on such occasions he had borrowed the fire of St. Bernard, so glowing were his panegyrics and so completely did he carry away the hearts of his audience by his words. Once, when he had come down from the pulpit into the sacristy, he went on unconsciously exclaiming: "*Ecce tu pulchra es Amica mea, ecce tu pulchra es.*" (Cant. 14.) He could not bear to hear her called simply "Mary", but said that there should always be added one of her titles of honour, such as Blessed, most Pure, Virgin full of grace, Mother of mercy, Refuge of sinners and the like. Once when a friend of his spoke of "Mary" in this bare way, Father Clement said quickly: "I suppose you mean Mary of Egypt?"

The mystery of her Immaculate Conception, her Dolours,

and above all, her Annunciation were objects of the tenderest devotion to Clement during his whole life. In whatever place or under whatever circumstances, he would never omit the "Angelus": and it was during its recital that he passed away to a better life. Like St. Alphonsus he had also a special devotion to Her under the title of our Lady of *"Good Councel"*; and in reward he received from her the most extraordinary Lights both for his own guidance and for that of others. But his great characteristic was his devotion to the Rosary. He called it *"his library"* and with reason; for he always found in it abundant material for meditation on the life and passion of our Blessed Lord and fresh thoughts for his sermons. Hence he carried continually in his hand a little Rosary given him by Pius VII. whether he were walking, or sitting in the Confessional. Having once accidentally lost it, he was quite unhappy and begged the Sisters to pray for its recovery: and when their prayers had produced the desired result, he said to Sister Thaddeus: "You have by finding this Rosary helped in the conversion of sinners, for whenever I have recited it for any particular person, I have always obtained his conversion." He consequently frequently exhorted the Ursulines and others of his Penitents to say the Rosary for special intentions of this kind. But he did it with even more devotion and faith when it was a question of the conversion of a dying person who had not made his confession for 30 or 40 years and who had refused to see or listen to a priest. How often he would come afterwards to the Ursulines, his face glowing with pleasure, and exclaim: "Our Lord has granted me another soul for whom I had offered my Rosary!"

He had a stock of very small rosaries which he would give to young men, so that they might hold them without being seen and would implore them to say them when they went out in the evening, so that our Lady might preserve them from all temptations against purity, which are so often met with in the streets of a great City.

"I am convinced", wrote one witness, "that F. Clement in that way stopped an innumerable number of sins and saved many souls". He had nothing more at heart than to diffuse this devotion to the Blessed Virgin; and so, in the pulpit as in the confessional, he would warmly recommend the invocation of her powerful aid together with confidence in her intercession.

O! how often would he repeat that "no one can enter Heaven save through her!" "Have recourse", he exclaimed, "in all your necessities to the Blessed Virgin, for she is the Mother of mercy and will obtain for you all you need from her Divine Son. The Son never refuses the prayers of His mother. She found grace before God and it never fails her."

"Beloved Children in Jesus Christ!" he one day said in a sermon, "if there be one among you who has lost the Faith or is in danger of doing so, make use of this simple and efficacious remedy. Say each day on your knees with profound humility and devotion an '*Ave Maria*' to our Lady and your perplexed souls will find peace".

At the same time, in dealing with sinners, he took care to remind them that the best and truest devotion to the Blessed Virgin consisted in the imitation of her virtues. In order, still further to show his love and veneration for her, he would constantly visit her sanctuaries. He had been to Loretto, to Altoetting in Bavaria, to Schoosberg on the confines of Moravia and Hungary; and, while at Vienna, he would go every year with some of his disciples to the sanctuary of *Maria-Zell* in the Styrian mountains. Seing the crowds of people from different nations, who were pouring out their prayers in their respective languages to this tender Mother, he would often exclaim: "O! come hither, ye pretended Philosophers, and tell me what induces all these poor people to come here from such great distances and endure such fatigues and such inconveniences? Who is it draws them and leads them to this spot? O! let us own, that it is simply their Faith, that mysterious power contained in the Catholic Church alone. Philosophers with all their fine arguments would never induce one of them to stir a foot beyond their houses, how much less so long and painful a pilgrimage!

O! if only the Holy Father in Rome could see this multitude of believers, what joy it would give him! I feel sure he would cry with consolation for what a splendid triumph it is for our holy Religion!"

He took the utmost care that those who made these pilgrimages with him should reap abundant spiritual fruits. Canon Veith relates that on one occasion he was very much distressed because he found in a little church at Dornau about a hundred Pilgrims waiting for mass, which he had already celebrated. All he could do was to speak to them and to hear the confessions of as many as he could.

Devoted as he was to the Queen of Angels, he honoured and venerated likewise the holy Angels and the Saints. Towards the Archangel St. Michael, as Patron of the Universal Church, he had a great veneration: and his reverence for his Guardian Angel was such that he walked continually whithout a hat out of respect to one whom he felt was continually watching and guarding him, at all times and in all places.

He had also a singular devotion to the Patriarch St. Joseph and implored his help in every need. "In all your necessities", he would say, "have recourse to St. Joseph, for he is the Father of the poor and the Orphans and a comforter in all human troubles: but especially invoke him to obtain a good and holy Death."

In the same way he felt a tender devotion to St. Ann; and to the holy Apostles, whom he called "The Fathers of the Church, who had illustrated her not only by their writings and their example, but who had sealed their Faith with their Blood." Above all, he honoured St. Peter, to whose successors, the Roman Pontiffs, he was so scrupulously obedient: and among the Apostles he had a special devotion for St. Thaddeus and St. James the Great, because in a time of great need, he had received special help from both. After the suppression of the monastery of St. James, the miraculous statue of that Saint was removed to the Church of the Ursulines and Father Clement never rested till he had solemnly placed it in a Side Chapel over an altar, where it is still venerated by the faithful.

He was also very devout to St. Catherine of Sienna, because she had done such great works for the Church and the Roman Pontiff: to St. Theresa for her magnificent revival of the Faith: to St. Athanasius for his heroic defence of the Divinity of Christ. He also had a tender affection for St. Clare of Montefalco, whose body is still incorrupt: for St. Barbara, the protectress of the dying: and for St. Luigi Gonzaga and St. Stanislas Kotska, those noble examples of youthful and holy purity.

He never let the Festival of the latter pass without saying mass in the room in Vienna, now turned into a Chapel, where St. Stanislas, being ill and not permitted to see a priest, received Communion from the hands of an Angel. Of F. Clement's great devotion to St. John Nepomucen and of his pilgrimage to Prague to venerate the shrine of that martyr and model of Confessors, we have already spoken.

We need not speak of the deep love and veneration with which he was penetrated for his Father and Founder St. Alphonsus; and in 1816, he had the great joy of seeing him raised to the altars of the Church. "I am doing all I can," he wrote from Vienna to the Procurator General in Rome, "so that the honour of our Father should be ever more widely spread. We practice private devotions, have books and pictures printed and do every thing so that our Lord may be glorified in the veneration we pay to the Blessed Saint under whose banner we are fighting".

By means of F. Passerat he transmitted all the money he could to Rome to help in the process of the Cannonization. Great was his delight when a miracle was wrought through the instrumentality of a picture of the Saint. It happened as follows. A man previous to leaving Vienna for Knittelfeld in Styria went to confession to F. Clement, who, on wishing him good bye, gave him a little picture of St. Alphonsus. The man put it in his trunk winding it round a little stick for fear of creasing it. Soon after his arrival at home, his house took fire and every thing in it was burnt. He was away at the moment and on his return anxiously looked amidst the ruins for this very trunk which contained a certain sum of money. But what was his astonishment when he found, that nothing had been spared by the fire, save this paper picture of St. Alphonsus! The two ends of the stick were burnt but the print remained untouched. The poor man ran to tell the Parish priest and to show him what had happened. And the priest having attested the fact, rang the Chapel bell and told all the parishioners (who hastened to obey the summons) of the marvellous preservation of the picture; which was afterwards framed with an account of its esape and solemnly exposed to veneration on the altar of the Church, where it remains to this day.

We have not yet spoken of the tender love F. Clement felt for the blessed souls in Purgatory. Earnestly did he offer up prayers and Sacrifices for these holy prisoners and exhort others to offer their prayers and good works as suffrages for this same intention. "Such prayers", he would say wisely "are never lost; they always please our Lord and bear a merit of their own. In fact, they are of double advantage; for they help the living who pray and the dead for whom the prayers are offered."

Hence he continually exhorted the Ursulines to acquire merit by good works so as to give them to the souls in purgatory and wished that they would offer up the mortifications, silence, fasts and other practices of their daily life in suffrages for them. And he taught them to use the following ejaculatory prayer. "My God and Heavenly Father! I offer Thee the precious blood of Jesus Christ and all that I do this day in union with Him, for the holy souls in purgatory." When any Sister died, he never rested till as many masses as possible had been said for her soul on that same day and it was marvellous how many priests he always found to say them. A Lady narrates that one day she came to see F. Clement and told him she had seen her defunct husband in a vision, apparently very suffering and miserably clothed. "Well", he replied: "perhaps he had not done in life as many charitable works as lay in his power. Hasten to clothe some poor person and offer it up in suffrage for his soul". The widow obeyed at once and soon after had the consolation of seeing her husband again, looking quite different and thankind her lovingly. She hastened with the good news to Father Clement, who said to her: "That is a sign that he is better: but go on helping him with your prayers and alms."

CHAPTER VI.

FATHER CLEMENT AS A PREACHER. HIS WAY OF ANNOUNCING THE WORD OF GOD.

WE have often spoken of the marvellous frint of Father Clement's preaching, both at Warsaw and in other places. When he became Rector of the Ursuline Church, the first question he asked when the Sunday came was, "the hour generally fixed for the sermon?" The answer was that except on great Festivals, they were not accustomed to have any sermon at all. Nevertheless, he ordered the bell to be rung and without any further preamble went into the pulpit and to the astonishment of the nuns began to preach to the very few persons present. This soon got wind; and the next Sunday a good many more came; till at last the church became much too small for the large audience, who even listened standing out into the street.

His method of preaching was very simple and apostolic; yet was not wanting in vigour and zeal and even at times, in holy enthusiasm. Cardinal Rauscher speaking of his sermons says: "He had never learnt any elegant oratorical arts or read any book of profane or classical elocution: nevertheless he proved himself a true disciple of one who spoke *as having authority*. I never heard any preacher whose words produced so much effect or who knew how to point out better the one thing necessary. You could not help carrying away some clear idea of his subject and so he often touched the hardest and most indifferent of hearers."

"When he preached", added F. Rinn, "you could not help being moved and filled with a kind of supernatural unction. I have heard very learned and eminent ecclesiastics as well as laymen say "that one word from his mouth would last them for meditation for a whole week". Often when beginning a discourse he would say: "To-day I shall try and speak with such clearness that I hope the smallest child may be able to understand me; so that before God's Tribunal, no one may be able to accuse me and say "I did not understand you".

Canon Veith adds: "There were no set divisions in his sermons, nor any flights of rhetoric: yet some of the most eminent Prelates of Vienna used to show the greatest anxiety to hear him; and a famous Professor, Zaengerle, who afterwards became Bishop of Gratz, exclaimed one day: "The Holy-Ghost alone could have inspired F. Clement's words this morning!"

The simplicity of his language did not in any way affect

the exactness and depth of his proofs: nor could he help revealing his intimate knowledge of Holy Scriptures and of the writings of the Fathers of the Church. He explained the sublimest mysteries of our Faith with such admirable facility that both learned and unlearned were equally satisfied. For instance one day, explaining the words which the Church sings on Holy Saturday, "*O felix culpa*" he set forth in simple but beautiful language how by the Incarnation of the Son of God, we became also sons of God, brothers of Christ and heirs of Paradise; so that human nature was more exalted before the Throne of the Divine Majesty than had it remained without stain in the terrestrial Paradise. So great was this mixture in him of simplicity and wisdom that F. J. Pilat used frequently to say: "If you wish to hear a great orator, go to this or that church. But if you wish to hear an Apostle, go to the humble Church of the Ursulines and listen to F. Clement Hofbauer". Some went to mock and ridicule his style: but his apostolic simplicity so won upon them, that they would often be converted on the spot and remain after it was over to lay down the burden of their sins at the feet of the preacher in the tribunal of Penance. One or two of his devoted friends and who became afterwards members of his Congregation, confessed that when they first came to hear him, it was solely with the idea of laughing at him. On one occasion F. Clement perceived a knot of students who, in this way, were turning his sermon into ridicule. He never lost his composure or his sweetness; but turning round to them said: "Laugh as you will: but remember that he laughs best who laughs last": and then quietly went on with his discourse, while the ashamed students knew not where to hide themselves from the indignation of the Congregation. Great as was his simplicity, equally strong was his zeal. On certain occasions he spoke with such vivacity and enthusiasm that every one felt how deeply he was penetrated with the truths which he preached. Canon Veith speaking of this says: "It was only in the pulpit that he let go the reins, as it were, of his fervour and then his face semed to be positively illuminated. His words rose like a flame and as a sharp sword, penetrated into the very hearts of his hearers. When he preached, the most perfect silence was kept by the crowd, who hung upon his words, which often led to instantaneous and marvellous conversions." The President of the Imperial Diet, Robert von Purkhardt, was so impressed by F. Clement's preaching that he spoke of it with admiration even in extreme old age. "Before 1820", he said, "there was great neglect of Church-going in Vienna. But one day when I happened to be passing by the Ursuline Church I saw a great crowd of people going in. I stopped and asked one of them the reason. He replied: "O! don't you know? F. Clement is going to preach."

I thought I would go in too and see what it was that attracted all these persons. The argument of the sermon was "that man only wanted a good and earnest *will* and that then God would give the strength and grace". F. Clement explained this with such zeal and fervour and spoke in so apostolic a manner, that I really felt as if he were inspired. Afterwards I found out that he was equally wonderful in the confessional and in visiting the sick, leading all men to a true view of Religion. I know a great many very learned and scientific men who cared nothing whatever about God or His Commandments before, but whom F. Clement converted in the most extraordinary manner."

We must not imagine that his zeal ever led him to use exaggerated gestures or expressions: on the contrary, he was always as dignified and calm as the lines in his face: but one felt he spoke from his heart and it was his genuine earnestness which so greatly impressed his hearers.

While most of the cotemporary preachers were so imbued with Josephin principles that they confined their teaching to very superficial moralities, he, on the contrary, taught Catholic Doctrine in all its extension and purity: "To form a true conception of the firmness in the faith of F. Clement", writes F. Frederick von Held, "we must remember the indifferentism on the subject which then prevailed in Vienna. It was the fashion, not only in public meetings, and in familiar conversations, but even in the pulpit to avoid any mention of revealed religion. The very words which expressed Catholic Truth or even Christianity in general, would never be heard or seen save in a vocabulary. Among the great preachers of the day besides F. Clement there was not one, save his two intimate friends Zängerle and Ziegler, who dared call Catholicism by its proper name or speak of its distinctive doctrines. To these must be added later Zacchary Werner, who became a faithful, humble and devoted disciple of F. Clement."

With equal frankness and freedom he preached on morals and customs and with the same intrepidity of soul with which the precursor of Christ spoke the terrible words to Herod *"non licet tibi"*.

But when he was thus compelled to open a wound and cut away the cancerous flesh, he did it with such prudence, delicacy and gentleness that he never raised a feeling of anger or disdain among his audience, but only sentiments of salutary shame and confusion and often of sincere and humble compunction.

Sister Thaddeus relates that, one day, preaching on St. John the Baptist, he pointed out so forcibly his spirit of mortification in spite of his innocence, as contrasted with the spirit of self-indulgence and the way in which worldly men run after pleasures, however guilty they may be, and refuse to suffer the smallest denial of their wishes, that he produced an electrical effect on his audience, many of whom melted into tears of penitence.

Notwithstanding this popularity, his preaching displeased those who thought it far more convenient to go with the spirit of the times; and the Government, who saw with an evil eye the results of F. Clement's teaching, sent certain secret Agents of Police to hear his sermons and report upon their tendency. Once only, however, did he say anything which displeased the authorities; when he received immediately an order to abstain from preaching in future. The holy man having read the order, burst into tears at the thought that he was henceforth to be deprived of so powerful a means of converting those who had gone astray. The affair became known in Vienna and caused a great sensation. The Sunday came and with it an immense crowd to the church, half of whom hoped he would preach, in spite of the prohibition; the other half curious to see what he would do. F. Clement at the usual time quietly went up into the pulpit and read the Gospel of the day. After which he simply said: "To-day I cannot speak to you to explain what I have read, for it is my duty to obey. But in the Holy Mass I shall pray to the Holy Spirit to say to the hearts of each one of you here present what I would have gladly preached." At these words, many burst into tears.

The indignation against the Government, however, was so great, that in a few days this unjust and arbitrary prohibition was withdrawn: and F. Clement was allowed to preach as before without regard to the perverse spirit of the times, caring nothing for the pleasure or displeasure of men and feeling as if the command of our Lord to his Apostles: "*Going, therefore, teach ye all nations*" was specially addressed to himself.

CHAPTER VII.

THE PRINCIPAL SUBJECTS OF HIS PREACHING. HIS MAXIMS AND SPIRIT.

FATHER Bartholomew Pajalich (a worthy disciple of F. Clement's) has left us certain interesting details as to his manner of preaching and the subjects of his sermons which we think may interest our readers.

During Lent, he would begin a series by dwelling on the infinite perfections of God and the end and dignity of man. In 1816 he dwelt principally on the works of God in creation and his mind was so full of beautiful thoughts and feelings that he was never at fault for want of words. His only preparation was to have read to him a short commentary beforehand on the beginning of the book of Genesis. The reader, however, was soon stopped by the words: "Enough! Enough!" The simple words *"Creavit Deus hominem ad imaginem suam"* or else *"Videbimus Deum sicuti est"* was material enough for the most moving sermon.

Among the perfections of God the one he would lay the greatest stress on was His extraordinary mercy and lovingkindness. Whenever, therefore, he had felt himself compelled to startle his audience by speaking to them of the terrible judgments of God, he would hasten directly after to awaken in them feelings of unlimited confidence in the divine mercy, representing to them in vivid colours the immensity of the love of Jesus Christ, and speaking of the precious blood shed for our salvation, the agonies suffered for us, and the maternal compassion of Mary. He was also indefatigable in his endeavours to encourage the weak, and to console troubled souls; while he infused into the hearts of sinners, feelings of unbounded confidence in the goodness of God, exclaiming at one moment: *"Jesus, Son of David, have mercy upon us!"* at another, Ezechiel's exclamation: *"Why will ye die, O! ye House of Israel?"*; while in the end, he would speak of the rewards God had prepared for the just and quote the consoling words spoken to Abraham by the Almighty: *"I am thy Protector and thy exceeding great reward."* As a primary motive for confidence, he would speak of the infinite merits of Jesus, whom, with St. Paul, he would always call *"that great Mediator between God and man."* Often would he express his grief at seeing the little confidence shown by Christians in the merits of our Lord and exhorted all to seek Him with a pure intention feeling certain of finding what they sought. If however Father Clement dwelt by predilection on the love and mercy of God, he did not omit speaking of His justice to proud and obstinate sinners, to whom he would often repeat the words of the Apostle: *"It is a terrible thing to fall into the hands of the Living God!"* and that in such a tone and with such emphasis, that the most careless were struck by it. "Ah!" he would sometimes exclaim, "in these days, when religion is fallen so low, one must speak with vigour. In the pulpit we must shake the nuts off the trees; though in the confessional, we may gather them up with sweetness and gentleness."

He was equally zealous for the honour of God and would speak of him as a "jealous God" and quote the words of our Lord: *"I am come to cast fire on the earth: and what will I but that it be kindled"*? (St. Luke XII. chap. 49. v.).

But his favourite subjects were the mysteries of our Redemption and especially the passion of Christ. In 1816, he was invited to preach, on good Friday, on the *"Seven words of Jesus on the cross"*: and his own emotion and burning eloquence made the most extraordinary impression on the immense crowd which had gathered to hear him. He added to the effect of his words by having appropriate music sung between the meditations of each word. He was never weary also of exhorting his disciples to enter into the spirit of the Feasts of the Church throughout the year. He would call priests "*the pupils of God's eye*", and on the Sundays preceeding the ember-days, he would intreat the faithful to join with him in earnest prayer that none but worthy priests should be admitted into the Church: and that they might be filled with truly Apostolic zeal and be ready to preach the Gospel to all nations and especially in Germany, where infidelity and indifference had made such rapid strides. "Think!" he would exclaim, "how by the means of good or bad priests, a blessing or a malediction rests upon a people! When, in the Old Testament, no punishment would avail to reclaim the Jews from their evil ways, God permitted false prophets to be sent to them. Therefore, conjure our Lord that He may raise up holy priests; who are the greatest blessing to any country and the means of saving each one of our souls. Honour them as the messengers of God, remembering the words of Jesus Christ: "He that honoureth you, honoureth me, and he that despiseth you, despiseth me."

He spoke with a like zeal of the reverence due to the head of the Church, the Vicar of Jesus Christ.

"Whoever does not honour the Holy Father", he would say, "dishonours the Church our mother. He who does not obey his commands, is equally disobedient to holy Church. A son who will not pray for his Father is looked upon as bad and perverse: and he who does not pray for the Pope is a bad Christian. He who has not the Church for his mother, cannot have God as his Father."

And we must remember that F. Clement spoke in this manner at a time when there was not a single preacher in Vienna who dared so much as allude to the Church of Rome in his sermon! In the teeth of this dominant heresy and indifferentism, he had the courage to exclaim openly: "Outside the pale of the Catholic Church there is no salvation." Preaching one day on the words of Ecclesiasticus, 3rd chapter, 11th verse: "*The father's blessing establisheth the houses of the children: but the mother's curse rooteth up the foundation*", he applied it so beautifully to the Church that the learned Adam Müller was profoundly impressed by it.

He underwent a real martyrdom for the precepts and rights of the Church; but no persecution availed to prevent his defending and observing them.

He inveighed one day with unusual warmth against those who quietly said: "O! what does it signify? It is only a precept of the Church!" and to dissuade his audience from ever treating such commands lightly, he would quote the examples of the Saints recorded in Holy Writ. He exalted the obedience of Abraham when ordered to sacrifice his son Isaac and added: "The heart of the holy Patriarch was filled with incredible sorrow at such a command: but did he hesitate to obey? And if our Lord asks so much less of us, how can we dare refuse Him? Should we not obey him willingly, even with joy in our hearts? and does He not speak to us through His Church? And he went on to make many other instructive observations on this particular subject; as for example, applying it to married people and exhorting them to imitate Abraham, who kept God's command a secret from all, so as not to throw any difficulties in the way of his obedience. His sermons always ended by a touching petition, in which he called down the blessing of our Lord on his hearers and prayed for every grace to be showered down upon them and especially that one of which each had most need. At the end he always promised to remember them in the celebration of the August Sacrifice. On certain solemn occasions in the year when the concourse was very great, he obtained leave to impart to them the Papal benediction. But first, he would make the Sisters in Choir recite the Psalm "*Miserere*", so as to move the hearts of the people to penitence and thus to enable them to receive the blessing with better dispositions.

Before concluding this chapter, we will give our readers certain maxims collected by Father Clement's illustrious and devoted disciple, the late Cardinal Otmaro Rauscher, who put them into writing whilst he was labouring at the cause of his beatification.

Sentences and Maxims of Father Clememt.

1. Temperance is the guardian of all other virtues.

2. A stone rolls easily down a hill: but to roll it upwards requires labour and fatigue.

3. In praying we must imitate the Jews when they were rebuilding the walls of Jerusalem: brandishing in one hand the sword and in the other the mason's trowel.

4. When impure thoughts come into our minds we should think of them as little as we do of the leaves which fall from the trees, or of the words of a scolding woman: that is, we must not dwell upon them for a moment and without heeding such suggestions from the enemy of souls, go quietly on our way.

5. Sadness is prejudicial to the body and does no good.

6. We must deal with God as a child does with its mother.

7. It is of no use to force our brains too much: for the tension of the nerves only weakens us and we do not advance in the least.

8. When we are conscious of having failed and done wrong, we must humble ourselves before God, implore His pardon, and then quietly go on our way. Our defects should make us humble, but never cowardly.

9. We must not force ourselves too much to preserve always a pure intention. If we make it in the morning in the best way we can, let us then go quietly to our daily duties without over-anxiety or scruples: like a little child who goes simply on its way and only cries out for its mother when it meets with some grave difficulty. God will find the means for our progress in perfection, if our *will* be only right.

10. We cannot obtain Divine grace by violence. Everything should be done gently. The Divine Mother suffered a greater martyrdom than any other woman, but she was always quiet and calm.

11. The best way to become a Saint is to plunge ourselves in the Will of God, as a stone is immersed in the water; and allow conselves to be tossed, like a ball, here and there, according to His good pleasure.

12. Let each of us try to engrave deeply in his heart a realisation of the sufferings of Christ. A meditation on the Passion after Communion or during mass, is the most fruitful of all devotions: for thus we learn the preciousness of our souls in God's sight and feel ourselves powerfully stimulated to make some return for such exceeding Love. But such meditation should not be forced; and should be done gently, as if we were thinking of a very dear friend to whom we owed a great debt of gratitude.

13. When we see a street full of people, let us think of the crowd which filled the streets of Jerusalem when our Lord was dragged from Pilate to Herod. If we have to go into a room where we expect to be badly received, let us remember how Caiaphas received our Divine Saviour with ironical joy and on whose face we might read the thought: "At last we have caught you, O! Great Master!"

14. He who is careful and watchful over little faults, will become perfect in a short time. Most of us want to do great things, like preaching or taking the discipline, and in the mean time we neglect little things. He who does not esteem what is small is not worthy of what is great.

15. We carry within us a serpent of which we should watch every movement, and when it shows itself, we should forthwith chase it away.

16. When we go in or out of the house, when we take any thing from one place to the other, whatever we do, in fact, let as make a good intention, on which all depends.

In this way the smallest actions may become great in the sight of God.

17. Let us strive in all things to seek only the approbation of God. Everything is done well which is done for Him.

18. It is a good and useful thing to practise constantly some little mortification: but this should be done without violence or anxiety. Do you want to look at something? Do so with half an eye. Do you care for any particular food? Take less of it than you would like: and that is enough.

19. In the pulpit we must knock down the nuts from the trees, but in the confessional pick them up very gently.

20. God needs no one for His work.

21. Only Children and madmen praise themselves to your face.

22. Whether men blame or praise us, we do not cease to be solely what we are before God.

23. Do not let us fear and be anxious about sins already forgiven, for those thoughts and images which previously brought about our fall, may easily return if we are disposed to dwell upon them. Habit has a great power over us and if we consent to such thoughts, we may be tempted to the same sin in our minds which we before committed in deed. Hence we must be very cautious, for we bear a precious treasure in a fragile vessel.

24. The misery of living for a single hour as the enemy of God is so great, that even the holiest penitent if not comforted by Divine grace, would die of despair.

25. At every moment, in some part of the world, Holy mass is being celebrated; and each mass is enough to redeem a thousand worlds and to empty hell itself, if mass could be offered for the damned. The very death of Christ would have been superfluous had it been possible to offer Holy mass before. Remember that he who is the friend

of God, may participate in all the masses celebrated each day and in all the merits of the Church militant all over the world.

26. In the last moments of our lives, we shall see clearly all we have done and thought and felt, as well as all we should have done and thought and felt, if we had been faithful to the grace of God. Then also we shall see the effect produced upon others by our actions and words and we shall judge ourselves rigorously for the imperfect intentions with which even our good works have been done.

27. Man after the fall is infinitely happier than he could have been before; for through Jesus Christ, he is become a Son of God and a participator in all Divine graces. One thing only is needful: and that is *his will*. Hence holy Church sings: "*O! felix Adae culpa!*" The angels look with astonishment at man, since their God deigned to clothe Himself in human flesh: and they would even envy him, if they were capable of feeling envy. Had Satan been able to foresee that God would save fallen man by so stupendous a prodigy, he certainly would not have tempted Adam to sin: for if even a single man were to participate in the redemption, Satan would blush for shame for all eternity.

28. Jesus willed to redeem us by an ignominious death and make thus so abundant an expiation, to prove to us the excess of His love which He has shown us in a manner truly divine. God could not do more than He has done to redeem man: and the reprobate will be forced to confess in the last day that they are lost by their own fault alone.

29. The world was created for the elect: and the bad are only instruments in the hands of God to prove and purify His chosen servants.

30. When Satan tried to tempt Jesus Christ, he was ignorant of the fact that He was the Son of God and never knew it until He had expired on the Cross. Nevertheless, he recognised that He was a most extraordinary person, and free

from every sin and imperfection. Hence he began to fear that He might turn out to be the promised Messiah. On the other hand, he could not persuade himself, that the son of a humble carpenter, sweating and labouring over his work and who was subject to Joseph and Mary, could really be the Son of God.

The Devil is more astute than all the sons of men and knows and comprehends all things save humility and obedience.

31. We dare not expose ourselves to the risk of committing a sin, even if thereby we could hope to empty hell and save the whole world.

32. If God sees that we love anything more than Him, He must hate us.

33. If the Saints in Heaven could be sad, it would be at the thought that they had not attained to the higher place which God had destined for them through the merits of Jesus Christ, had they only made use of the treasures of grace at their disposal. St. Theresa appeared to one of her sisters after death and told her: "That she would be willing to suffer the pains of martyrdom till the day of judgment if by this means she could augment her glory, as she might do by the recital of one Ave Maria".

CHAPTER VIII.

F. CLEMENT IS POWERFULLY HELPED IN HIS APOSTOLATE BY FREDERICK ZACCHARY WERNER. WHO THIS CELEBRATED ORATOR WAS.

HOWEVER vigorously F. Clement strove by his voice to waken the Viennese people from their lethargy, he could not do everything by himself. Among the old members of his Congregation, he had only two priests with him, Fs. Stark and Sabelli: and very often he was obliged to content himself with one, as during the first years of his mission in Vienna, F. Sabelli was in Switzerland: and in 1817, F. Stark had to accompany Cardinal Severoli to Rome. In addition to this, neither of these Fathers were good preachers and so were useless in the pulpit.

But F. Clement had not long to wait before he found what he wanted. In the year 1815, God sent him the very man for his purpose in the person of Frederick Werner, who having arrived in Vienna in the autumn of 1814, was instantly attracted by that great servant of God and became one of his most devoted friends and most faithful disciples.

Frederick was born in Königsberg on the 18th of Nov. 1768. From a boy he showed a great taste for dramatic poetry, so much so that in 1789 he published a book of poems, but filled with the spirit of the times, that is, with sneers against monks, nuns and Jesuits. He was then enthusiastic about Rousseau, and afterwards for Göthe, by whom he was much esteemed and distinguished from many others. He frequented Kant's lectures and when in Berlin maintained amiable relations with the heads of the new doctrines, having already been elected a free-mason. In the beginning of this century he was a Government official in Warsaw and as such very hostile to our Congregation. Removed to Berlin he was appointed one of the judges in the Redemptorist case when F. Iesterheim was summoned before his Tribunal; but in that instance he gave a just judgement. In the year 1807, he composed a drama called "Luther, or the Consecration of Force", which was performed in all German Protestant Theatres and was received with great applause.

In that same year he passed into Switzerland where he became acquainted with the Hereditary Prince Louis of Bavaria and also with Madame de Staël. From thence he bent his steps towards Italy and on the 9th of December 1808, he arrived in Rome. But he was hardly settled in the holy City than God determined to show His infinite mercy towards him, by calling one who had only thought of glorifying Luther and indulging in his senses, to become a faithful disciple of the Cross. And he who had called the mass "a celebration worthy of asses" and who had said that "he would not have "reason" made "to dance to the tune piped by a Pope" was to become one of the most faithful and devoted servants of the Holy See.

"It was in the city of Rome", as Werner writes to Dalberg "that Divine grace first touched my heart: and it was on Holy Thursday on the 19th of April 1810 that I came back to the Faith of my Fathers".

Professor Ostini was his guide in taking this great step, to whom he made a general confession. For three years and three months he continued under his direction: and as he felt himself called to the ecclesiastical state, he was dispensed from the irregularity of his previous life, when he had had three wives in succession, from all of whom he had been separated!

Ordained Priest by the Primate Dalberg, on the 16th of July 1814, he went to Vienna where he lodged next to the Servite Fathers. Here he made acquaintance with F. Clement Hofbauer and it was enough to see him and talk to him two or three times for Werner to be filled with respect and admiration for him. Very soon he implored F. Clement to take him under his spiritual direction, to whom he submitted with great humility and the simplicity and docility of a child.

F. Clement soon found out his extraordinary abilities: and exhorted him not to hide his light under a bushel, but to make use of the great talents which he had received from God to preach His word and save souls. In fact, Werner had a special power of influencing people of the higher classes with worldly tendencies, as he had already proved in Rome; and also the great gift of eloquence. His humility suggested the objection that having given such great scandal himself in old days when he was living in that society, he was unworthy to preach the word of God or to exhort others to penitence, when no one needed it so much as himself. F. Clement, however, having judged otherwise, Werner submitted at once; although, as he was suffering very much from his chest, he felt that this particular work would cost him a good deal.

When he appeared in the pulpit, very great was the impression he at once produced. The majesty of his figure, his great height, his pale, intellectual face, and the long grey hair which fell to his shoulders, added to the effect of his extraordinary eloquence. Being a born poet, he used the most graceful and magnificent imagery and drew what might be called word-pictures in a way which enthralled and enchanted his hearers. And although this flowery style might have, in some way, offended against the simplicity of F. Clement's apostolic preaching, yet every one felt that it came so naturally from his heart, that it produced a most salutary and lasting impression.

When, for example, he described the terrible scene of the last judgment it seemed as if it were actually present to him and a cold shudder ran through every one's veins. Hence F. Clement called him "The trumpet of the last judgment for Vienna". Again, when he alluded, to his past life, which was known to many of them, and of the great mercy of God which had saved him on the very brink of eternal ruin, he did so with such humility and such copious tears, that every one was moved to weep with him. He was equally eloquent in matters of Faith. Having gone through so many phases of unbelief himself, he demonstrated so forcibly the blessing and peace of being a son of the Catholic Church, and the blank desolation of Protestantism, together with the endless disunion and divisions existing among heretics and so-called philosophers, that he electrified his audience and powerfully moved a large portion of the Viennese to return to the bosom of the Church, thus vindicating her honour in the very city where she had been most contemned. He would constantly produce the Penny Catechism in the pulpit and show the people how in this little golden gook there was more wisdom and common sense than in all the big, learned volumes of pretended philosophers. Then he would lift up his voice and praise and bless God who had dragged him, a miserable sinner, out of Egyptian darkness and brought him back into the bosom of the one true Church in which he hoped to live and die.

The impression produced by these sermons was deep and lasting. Immense crowds flocked to hear him and especially during the Congress of 1815, when he had often Sovereigns among his audience. Very much against the grain, he was sometimes compelled to go into parties and *conversazione* at that time: and on one of these occasions, the King of Prussia wished to be introduced to him. He received him, however, somewhat coldly and said: "M. Werner! I do not like men who leave the Religion in which they have been born and bred."

Werner replied: "Neither do I, Sire! And therefore I left the religion of Luther."*

---

* We have, before our eyes, a letter of the 21st of Sept. 1818 written by Werner to the Secretary of Councillor Mayer at Dantzic, in which he expresses himself as follows: "Dear brother! let me speak to you and ask you in all seriousness: How is it possible that a man so highly cultivated and with such acuteness of intelligence as yourself, can give no thought to that which is most essential to man? How is it possible that one with such an amount of sound sense and ability as yourself should not, long ago, have doffed that absurd beretta called Protestantism and put on the glorious crown of the Catholic faith, the only one which deserves the name of Christianity?' O! I intreat of you to do now what you ought to have done long ago and for not doing which you will repent yourself for all eternity. Remember that the end of man cannot consist in seeking merely temporal things which are evanescent, but spiritual ones which are everlasting. Remember that truth is one . . . . For the love of God, then, make use of the leisure time now granted to you and

He preached sometimes in the Ursuline Church, but as he was not sufficiently grounded yet in dogmatic theology, F. Clement used to assist at these sermons and if any expression escaped him which was not strictly Catholic, he would at once tell him of it and oblige him to correct it, though prudently, the following Sunday.

The love and veneration felt by Werner for F. Clement was a singular proof of Divine mercy: for the latter could not preach to the highest society in Vienna, who yet needed instruction more than the poor, their minds having been thoroughly corrupted by heretical doctrines, infidel books, bad novels and worse plays. And as the Ursuline Church was too humble and small and Father Clement's preaching too simple to attract people of that sort, it was absolutely necessary that a man should be found of Werner's position, who should be able to preach in a fashionable Church to a fashionable audience and by his extraordinary gifts, and the brilliancy of his former position, rouse these people from their lethargy: and this Werner did so perfectly that it would really seem as if Father Clement had been divinely inspired and filled with supernatural wisdom when he urged him to undertake the task. In truth, heavenly benedictions never ceased to pour upon Werner's sermons; the conversions which ensued were as remarkable as they were numerous; and while every one was speaking of him with admiration, Werner himself never ceased attributing all these merits to F. Clement, whose instructions he eagerly followed. One day he was so moved at a sermon of his holy director's, that he rushed into the sacristy exclaiming: "He is quite unique: no one can be compared to him: it is the Holy Spirit Himself who speaks by his mouth!"

which death will soon deprive you of, to reflect that (except for those in a state of invincible ignorance, which you cannot pretend to be) there is no way of obtaining eternal happiness outside the fold of the Catholic Church", &c. &c.

Werner confined his labours to the pulpit and rarely heard confessions. And when any one came to him as a penitent he would say: "Go, instead, to my Master, F. Clement". This he also frequently expressed in the pulpit, speaking of him with the greatest reverence and saying that "he was a man whose shoe-latchet he was not worthy to unloose". And such praises from Werner's mouth greatly assisted in increasing F. Clement's influence even among the higher classes: so that these two valiant labourers in God's Vineyard, working together and in the same spirit produced such extraordinary fruit that they were universally and deservedly called: "The two great Apostles of Vienna."*

CHAPTER IX.

F. CLEMENT IN THE TRIBUNAL OF PENANCE. HIS ANXIETY FOR THE SALVATION OF SOULS.

A true missionary should always unite the Pulpit with the Confessional, showing the people in the former, the enormity of their sins and then leading them, in the latter, to confess and conquer them. This was eminently F. Clement's method and day and night found him occupied in hearing confessions, having no fixed hours but always accomo-

---

* Among the many wonderful convvrsions brought about by Werner's preaching we will mention the following:

Lorenzo Studach, born in Alstätter, in the Canton of St. Gall, was studying medicine in Vienna and went with all the world, to hear Werner preach. At first he listened from pure curiosity: but then something which he said touched him so much that he went to call upon him, made his general confession to him, gave up the study of medicine and determined to become a Priest. He became afterwards confessor of the Queen of Sweden and then Vicar Apostolic of Sweden and Norway. After the Reformation, he was the first Bishop of Scandinavia. He gave this account of his conversion through Werner's preaching in 1862, when he was consecrated Bishop in Rome.

dating himself to the convenience of his penitents and especially of the poor and labouring classes.

It often happened that God gave him special lights during his sermons so that he would break off in an argument and say sometting which struck to the heart one or other of his audience. The following is an instance.

One day, when he was preaching in the Ursuline Church on the torments of a bad conscience, it happened that a young man was present named Francis Hätscher, a native of Vienna, who, ever since he was a child, had been a great subject of anxiety and sorrow to his mother. All of a sudden, he disappeared from Vienna, and some said he had enlisted in the army and then deserted. The fact was, he had gone into France and it was believed that he went as a secret agent of the Police. For a long time he remained there; but when the Allied Armies entered Paris he returned to Vienna. As, however, he did not dare present himself to his mother, who was a very severe person, he wandered about the City without any occupation.

Chance, or rather his Guardian Angel, led him that morning into the Ursuline Church and F. Clement's sermon made such an impression upon him that he felt as if it were addressed solely to himself. The poor boy was so touched that he followed the preacher into the sacristy and implored him, for the love of God, then and there to hear his confession. F. Clement pressed his hand and said to him kindly: "This is not the moment for you to make your confession. Come along with me." So saying, he took him into his own house and kept him with him for several days, the only thing he asked of him being that he would pray every day for a short time before an image of our Lord scourged at the pillar, adding: "Here you must learn your lesson." In this way poor Francis was gently prepared to make a general confession of his whole life which he did with the greatest compunction. Then F. Clement asked him "what were his future plans?" And Francis having expressed his grief at not being able to go back to his mother, F. Clement answered cheerfully: "O! I will see about that!" The next morning F. Clement asked the mother to breakfast: and whilst the good woman was marvelling at this honour, F. Clement asked her about her children. She mentioned them, one by one, all except Francis, to whom she never alluded. "But you have surely another son, Francis?" asked F. Clement. "Where is he?" "O!" replied the mother angrily "he has been lost to us for a long while".

"People are not lost so easily" replied F. Clement smiling. "What if he were come home and converted?" And seeing that the woman did not believe him, he opened a little door and called Francis, who came with tears in his eyes to implore his mother's pardon. She, however, being still exasperated at his past conduct, began to scold him severely: but F. Clement interrupted her: "Now, that is enough", he said gently. "Let us breakfast together and rejoice over your meeting."

Very soon F. Clement found that this very youth had a decided religious vocation and great gifts for the apostolic life, so he admitted him into the Congregation. After being ordained priest, he was sent to Bucharest; and afterwards was one of the first missioners sent in 1833 to America, who with incredible fatigues converted the savages living on the banks of Loch Erie. Here the successor of Father Francis, Frederick Baraga (another of F. Clement's disciples) established the Diocese of St. Maria of Marianopoli. Bishop Baraga spoke often with great admiration of F. Francis, who finally died full of years and merits at Leoben in Styria on the 3rd of January 1863.

Very often, a single look of F. Clement's would be enough to touch men's hearts and bring about their conversion. A certain Schmidt relates that when he was a young man, he went one day to hear mass in the Ursuline Church more from habit than devotion and placed himself near the door: when, seeing two pretty looking girls higher up in the church, he left his place to get near them. At this moment, F. Clement who had been to take the Blessed Sacrament to a sick person, passed into the church close by the young Schmidt, and then, as if suddenly reading his thoughts, stopped and looked searchingly at him. This look filled him with salutary fear: he thought over his evil intentions, acknowledged his fault and went at once to confession. In 1868, when this very man was employed in a bank, he mentioned this little incident, attributing to it both his conversion at the time and his hopes of ultimate salvation.

In fact, Father Clement's very presence was sometimes enough to lead souls back into the right path. A comic actor of the Court Theatre used to come very often to a certain Herr von Pilat, to get theatrical articles inserted in the "Austrian Observer" of which he was the editor. Hence he often came across Father Clement, who was a friend of Pilat's, but the latter remarked that the moment F. Clement came in, the comic actor went away. At last he asked him the reason and the actor replied: "If I were to be often in that priest's company, I should have to give up my acting, which is my great delight, and go to confession and be converted; and I have not the courage for this!" However after a time, the poor actor was conquered and went to F. Clement and made his confession. But unhappily his conversion did not last long; and he was only another proof of how difficult it is to live a Christian life and continue on the stage.

When F. Clement was conscious of having failed in touching any unusually hardened heart he had recourse to more earnest prayer and additional voluntary mortifications. Sister Thaddeus related that one day having remained in choir whilst the other Sisters were at dinner, she saw F. Clement kneeling on the altar steps, who, thinking himself quite alone in the church at that hour, was pleading with God for the conversion of a sinner. "O! my Jesus!" he repeated, "my much-loved Saviour! Grant me the grace to win this poor soul! O hearken to my intreaty! If not, I must turn to Thy Mother, who certainly will listen to me!" Having thus prayed out loud with tears for some time he threw himself on his face on the steps of the altar till Sister Thaddeus was so moved at his evident grief that she could only mingle her tears and prayers with his.

If F. Clement thus rescued so many sinners, no less admirable was the way in which he trained them after their conversion to lead lives of consistent holiness. When President von Josch was asked whether he had ever seen a miracle performed by F. Clement? he replied: "I look upon his whole life as a continual miracle: because otherwise, it would be impossible to conceive how a man so simple could bring about so many astonishing conversions among people of every class and contrive afterwards to keep them always in the right path." And Dr. Alliroli, the celebrated translator of Holy Scripture and a great oriental scholar, expressed himself in the same manner. Canon Veith attests: "That the crowd round his Confessional was always the same. There you saw people of every class from porters and fruit sellers, up to nobles and literary men, who obeyed him with the same filial love and submission as if they were his own subjects and whom he guided with equal wisdom and charity. Among the women whom he directed, were some of the greatest ladies in Vienna: among whom were the Princess Jablonowska, Countess Constance Pyskiewicz (niece of the King Poniatowsky), Princess Bretzenheim, Countess Maria Szecheny, afterwards married to Count Bathyani (who founded a house of Sisters of Charity and took the habit herself after her husband's death), her sister Sophy, married to General Zichy, and another Countess Julia Zichy, whose maiden name was Countess Festetics and who at the time of the Congress of Vienna was considered to be not only the most remarkable, but, according to the Emperor of Russia, the most beautiful woman of her time. She died on the 18th of Nov. 1816 and had the happiness of being assisted in her last moments by F. Clement himself who speaks of her death as "that of a Saint".

Even the Apostlolic Nunzio, Monsgr. Severoli, afterwards Cardinal, became his penitent: as also Romano Zängerle, Prince Bishop of Gratz, who writes: "Under the guidance of F. Clement I made a sort of second novitiate (he was a Benedictine) to learn from him true asceticism." Cardinal Rauscher who became afterwards Archbishop of Vienna, never failed to assist at his sermons and was his penitent till F. Clement's death: as was also the Bishop of Baraga who writing to Pius IX. on the 10th of October 1865 thus speaks: "To Father Clement is due the revival of religion in Vienna, which, when he first came to the city, was well nigh extinct. Of this I was an eye-witness, as in my youth I was for five years in the Vienna University and had the good fortune to have F. Clement as my Confessor *which, till the last day of my life, I shall always look upon as one of the greatest graces and privileges granted to me by Divine Providence.*"

We should only weary our readers if we were to enumerate any more of his illustrious penitents, but we will mention one only, Lewis I. King of Bavaria, who during the Congress of Vienna remained with him nearly a whole night discussing spiritual questions and never missed an opportunity of going to him in confession. In addition to these eminent personages, there were endless students at the University, Government officials, Officers in the Army and even actors at the theatre, who flocked to him for guidance in all matters of conscience. Truly it was a remarkable thing to see this poor religious, deprived of all the natural gifts and accidents of birth and station which the world appreciates, thus leading men and women of the most eminent rank and learning as well as the poorest and most illiterate, in the paths of virtue and holiness: and still more marvellous was it to watch the implicit obedience and docility of certain persons towards him, whose habit it was to command every body else! We cannot help feeling that this extraordinary power was given to Father Clement as a special grace by Him who moulds the hearts of men and who chose him as a special instrument of His mercy. Many of his penitents became priests and being thoroughly imbued with his spirit did wonders as labourers in their Lord's Vineyard. Fathers and mothers, following his wise guidance, trained their children in the paths of purity and self-denial. In fact, among every class and in every state of life, his influence was felt for good, and Cardinal Rauscher spoke truly when he said "that the revival of religion in Austria could only be attributed to F. Clement, who thus paved the way for the future Concordat concluded by that Empire with the Holy See."

CHAPTER X.

WITH WHAT PRUDENCE AND CHARITY HE TREATED HIS PENITENTS.

CONFESSION is doubtless a penitential act, felt by every one to be more or less painful, but on some it weighs so heavily that they can not bring themselves to do it without a great struggle. It is, therefore, the business of a wise and prudent confessor to diminish this apprehension and remove the difficulty. F. Clement had peculiar tact in this matter and very often brought about the desired end in a singular manner. As an instance of this John Passy relates of his brother, Joseph, that having given himself up to bad and infidel reading, he, by degrees, lost his faith and finally became an actor. But the theatre affected his health, so that, after a time, he was obliged to give it up and to return from Prague to Vienna, where he was discontented and unable to settle to any thing. John brought him to F. Clement, who, instead of asking him to go to confession as John expected, begged him to come and see him in his room, and like a loving Father, began talking to him about his past life and what he had been doing. The more they talked the more Joseph felt inclined to open his heart to him; and, at last, he told him everything good and bad that he had done. When he had finished, F. Clement added gently: "Now, you see that without knowing it, you have already made your confession. Now kneel down and try and feel a real sorrow for the sins of the past." And so helping and encouraging him, he made the fullest avowal of his faults, received absolution and returned to his home at peace with God and man. His brother found him entirely changed and from that hour till his death he persevered in the practice of all Christian virtues.

Kind and patient as he was in the confessional, yet F. Clement never used many words or spent a moment more time with each penitent than was necessary. He did not fail, however, to convey in those few words the most salutary admonitions. He had the rare gift of instructing, correcting, advising and moving his penitents to sincere contrition and earnest resolutions in the fewest possible sentences, so that each person went away touched and satisfied. Occasionally his advice seemed hard: but those who took it, always found that the blessing of God rested upon their obedience. One day, a poor servant girl came to him in a beautiful silk dress. As she was leaving the confessional, F. Clement asked her: "Where she had got this dress?" The girl replied "that her mistress had given it to her and wished her to wear it". F. Clement replied, "Such clothes are not fit for your station. You should sell it or give it away in charity." The girl did so: her mistress was very angry and said that as she did not value her gifts, she should leave her service in a fortnight. The poor girl in dismay hastened to F. Clement and told him what had happened. But he comforted her and said: "Do not be auxious, you have done what was right and God will think of you and find you another situation." And so it happened. A noble Lady having heard the story, took her at once into her service; and also promised her a pension when she should be incapable of working, and so God rewarded the good servant's obedience.

It seemed indeed as if Divine Providence had given Father Clement a special insight into people's souls. On this point Sister Thaddeus wrote:

"We had in our convent a postulant who was much troubled by temptations as to her religious vocation. One day, in fact, the made up her mind to leave the convent, when she unexpectedly met F. Clement, who went straight up to her and said: 'Francesca, stay in this convent, for you are called to it by God.' Such words filled her with amazement, for to no one had she manifested her doubts and difficulties: and it was only afterwards that we any of us knew that she had decided to leave us. But F. Clement's words removed all her fears, and from that moment she remained in the monastery, where she was still living in 1868 when the cause of F. Clement's beatification was brought forward, though she was then 83 years old."

Sister Louisa Xavier von Pilat also relates: "One of our Sisters, who afterwards became Superior of the house at Gleink in Upper Austria, was a penitent of F. Clement's when she was in the world. After having heard one of his sermons, she felt herself suddenly inspired to become a Religious. But her Father having told her that he never would give his consent, she dismissed the idea and thought thereby she could satisfy her conscience. Although continually tormented by the idea, she took care never to reveal her struggles in the confessional. Great, therefore, was her amazement when one day F. Clement said to her, after she had made her confession: 'You must become a Salesian. I

will myself see that you shall be received.' She felt that
our Lord had revealed the thoughts of her heart to him and
at his words all doubts and hesitation vanished. As he had
said, the way was made smooth for her at once. She entered
the Salesian order where she has been for 50 years and has
never ceased thanking God for the grace of vocation and
consequent peace which F. Clement's words had thus procured for her."

The same testimony is given by several other persons. He seemed to guess the difficulties and temptations of each soul and often anticipated their disclosures. Sometimes, when he arrived rather earlier than usual at the Ursuline Convent, the Sisters would excuse themselves by saying they were not prepared. "Come all the same and I will help you", he would reply. And then he would make a little examination of conscience with them and mingle all with such salutary advice and holy consolations that the nuns often said they felt he could read their thoughts. "To go to confession and to die you should be always ready", he would say to his penitents, "for you never know the hour when God will call you."

Cardinal Rauscher, speaking of F. Clement's prudence in the direction of souls, writes as follows: "In all matters but especially in the Sacrament of penance, he showed extraordinary perspicacity and prudence. In a few simple but efficacious words he would judge at once what was expedient for each soul. He was very circumspect in leading the souls confided to him in the paths of perfection. He would put a curb on that impetuosity of spirit which accompanies certain conversions and insisted on everything being done quietly. When I was moved by his example to become a priest, he would not let me be anything but a Secular: and as my parents opposed even this strongly and made every sort of difficulty, he advised me to do nothing which looked like intemperate haste, but to yield to their wishes for a time and go on with my legal studies. He could not bear extremes in anything. He tried to lead all his penitents by ordinary ways and would hide as far as he could any extraordinary gifts received from God as being a less safe method. With all his tenderness and loving-kindness he knew how to humble his penitents when necessary, well knowing that the path of humility is that of humiliations."

One day when instructing Sister Thaddeus, F. Clement said: "If ever you fall into your old faults and weaknesses, do not lose heart; but trust in God and only try and serve Him better in future. Up to the very last days of our lives we must watch and pray. And as man, by himself, can do nothing to merit Paradise and as all our strength comes from God, so we should exercise ourselves greatly in prayer. For prayer in the fountain of all graces and virtue, the nourishment of the soul, the light of the intellect, a medicine against temptations and a secure refuge against the assaults of the enemy of souls. Let prayer then be your daily bread and pray with as much fervour and devotion and recollection of spirit as you possibly can, repeating often: "Lord may Thy will be done in earth as it is in heaven."

He managed admirably to infuse into others that confidence in God with which he was himself filled. He was also a wonderful consoler of troubled and anxious souls and of those who were tormented with scruples. One of his Congregation F. Joseph Forthuber, had this spiritual infirmity and at mass he never seemed to finish purifying the particles on the patens, to the annoyance of the assistants. One day F. Clement was serving him and seeing what he was doing, went up to the altar and whispered: "Leave something for the angels!"

There was a certain John Kraus, a spirit merchant in Vienna, who tried F. Clement's patience in the same way, although a simple, good, pious man, who subsequently became a priest. This Kraus owned to having heard F. Clement exclaim one day: "One Kraus is enough, two would certainly be the death of me!"

F. Clement showed his gentleness and evangelical prudence also in the imposition of sacramental penances which were never long and often very short. Cardinal Reisach relates that the wife of a certain Adam Müller when she made her profession of faith, was very much afraid that her sins would entail upon her some terrible penance. And when F. Clement gave her the easiest one possible, she expressed her surprise to him; but he answered: "Well, if you do not think it enough accept as a penance the trial God is about to send you." She had hardly reached her home than she was seized with a most violent toothache and felt that this was the penance prophesied by F. Clement; so that she accepted it courageously feeling it was sent for the good of her soul. In this apostolic manner F. Clement went on his way never resting till he had found the sheep that was lost. Sister de Welschenau adds to this picture of his labours, the following words: "O! how happy he was when he had succeeded in saving one or two souls! with what love would he welcome them! with what tenderness and paternal affection would he gather them, as it were, to his bosom! On such occasions his face would really be lit up with a supernatural smile and his eyes sparkled with a light which seemed to me to be the reflection of that great Light which enlightens every man who cometh into the world. He laboured without intermission in this work, hunting up the most miserable sinners and never resting till he had obtained their conversion. His exceeding love and his horror of Jansenism, made his piety amiable to all and opened the hearts of the most obdurate sinners who, in his hands, became docile and gentle as little children. God only knows what were the fruits of that Confessional in the humble little Ursuline Church!"

CHAPTER XI.
F. Clement as Director of the Ursuline Nuns.

F. Clement being himself a fervent Religious, it is easy to understand how much he had at heart the welfare of Convents and the practice of all monastic virtues. A well-regulated Convent was to him as worthy of veneration as the House of God. So, he one day said to a Salesian Sister: "When I pass your monastery I lift my beretta twice, once out of respect for the Blessed Sacrament and once to reverence the spouses of Jesus Christ."

He would often say "that Religious never realise till they come to die how great is their dignity and how signal a grace has been their vocation to a religious state: no human glory can he compared to it." Often would he speak in the pulpit of the excellence and advantages of a religious vocation, calling it an *Extraordinary Grace* and one which when received, must be followed, in obedience to the Will of God, in spite of all human considerations. As an example he would quote our Lord Himself, who, when only twelve years old, remained in the temple unknown to His parents: and when gently reproved by His mother, answered: "Did you not know that I must be about my Father's business?"

Whenever he saw any sign of a religious vocation among his penitents, he cultivated it with the utmost care, so that from a small spark, he might develop it into a living flame. Many were the souls whom he thus led into the highest paths of perfection not only in Vienna, but in Prague and in Gratz and in many different orders. It was remarked, however, that if present as a Clothing, he only said a few words. One who knew him well, replied: "The great joy he feels on such occasions really deprives him of the power of speech. When I announced my intention of leaving the world he was delighted and expressed himself warmly and eloquently on the subject: but when I was professed, he scarcely spoke; yet any one looking at his face could see the great joy which filled his soul when any one left the world to choose God alone for her portion."

It is impossible to speak in sufficiently strong terms of the great good he effected during the seven years that he directed the Ursuline nuns. At the end of 1813 regular discipline had been much relaxed owing to the state of the times: and this wise director resolved, in spite of the resistance of many of the nuns, to bring back an observance of the rules. This he effected by patience and sweetness: until those who were most opposed to him were forced to confess that *he was a Saint*. By word and example, he never ceased to rouse in their souls a higher esteem for those three columns of the Religious life, Poverty, Chastity and Obedience. "*Virgin Souls*" he would say "*are Sisters of the Angels*", and when speaking to the nuns of the jealous care with which they should guard this jewel, he would mention as an additional inducement, the power which such souls have in converting sinners. On one occasion at the taking of the habit of two choir and two lay sisters, he said: "You must unite the two functions of Mary and Martha, that is, prayer and work. Jesus restored Lazarus to life because He loved both Mary and Martha; and thus the Virgin Spouses of Christ must resuscitate the dead, that is sinners, to a life of grace: our Lord who loves His spouses, will certainly hear their prayers. Even among the Pagan Romans, Virgins were so esteemed that the pain of death to malefactors was remitted at their intercession. O! how much more will a spouse of Christ obtain, who has consecrated to Him her whole life!"

Not less warmly did he recommend obedience. "How easy and sweet it is to obey!" he would often exclaim, "and on the contrary how heavy a burden it is to have to give orders! Obedience puts the sickle to the root and makes every road secure. He who obeys can never err, however much the superior may be mistaken."

He exhorted the Ursulines to *punctual* obedience also, following the example of our Lord who was obedient even unto death. "*Better die than not obey*", he would say. One day he asked: "Who was the best novice?" and as no one answered, he went on: "The best is she who obeys humbly and who is content even to be as a broom with which one sweeps and then puts it into a corner!"

And then he added: "You are not wanted to be perverse but obedient."

F. Clement was very particular as to their observing the Horarium, saying: "That she who observes the Horarium, observes likewise the Will of God."

One day he asked one of the sisters to say an "*Ave Maria*" for the conversion of a sinner: and on her remarking that she would do more, he replied: "Those who have consecrated their will to God by a vow of obedience, pray far more efficaciously than seculars."

He himself was a living example of poverty. "It was enough to see him", said Sister Thaddeus, "to know he loved that virtue. As a priest, who was obliged to observe decency in his appearance, it was not possible to be more poorly dressed. He had only a poor threadbare cloak which he had worn at Warsaw.

He himself mended his own stockings and any other article of dress as long as it would hold together. One day when he had to present himself before the Archduke Maximilian, this pious Prince was greatly edified at seeing his stockings peeping out of the holes in his shoes. During the seven years that he was Director of the Ursulines they never saw him but once in a new Cassock on the occasion of some great Fête and it was such a wonder that they all remarked it. He would often say to the Sisters: "Every thing that a Sister wears is only lent to her. Jesus is her only treasure."

"Poverty," he would add, "is the first Beatitude; the road which our Lord Himself pointed out to us through his whole life, from the Crib to the Cross and from His birth to His deposition in the sepulchre of another."

Another thing which F. Clement insisted on was that each sister should make use of the special gifts she had received from God: and that the superior and mistress of novices should not treat them all alike, but according to the talents, the natural character, the temperament, and the physical and moral force of each, and that which he recommended to others, he practised himself; so that each sister felt as if he were a special Director for herself alone. He was specially careful of the lay sisters and often was more pleased with them than with the choir nuns. He took care that they should not be overworked or overtired, lest they should take a dislike to religious life. He changed a practice which was in use when he first came to the Ursuline Convent, which permitted the choir nuns to go to Communion twice a week and the lay sisters only once. He considered the reasons given for this practice indefensible and obtained a Decree from the Archbishop allowing the lay sisters a like privilege.

F. Clement, who did not know what idleness meant, and who spent every moment in the service of God and of his neighbour, could not endure idleness in others especially in nuns. "*Time should be measured by eternity: and very often the acquisition of Paradise depends on one moment in our lives*", he would exclaim to the Sisters. And the very last sermon he preached before his death was on making a good use of every instant granted to us.

"The time is soon coming when no one can work", he said. "Each moment we may be doing something for God, but the moment that is passed never returns."

What he most disliked among nuns was their habit of complaining of one another, saying: "The worst among them are the most rigorous judges of the faults of their neighbours". When a sister came to him with accusations of that sort, his first object was to make her feel that before finding fault with others she must first correct her own defects. But when he found the accuser was in the right, he would do his best to remedy the evil, but still strive to quiet the complainant lest she should sin against charity.

Sister Thaddeus writes: "When I first came into the monastery I was only 16 and knew nothing of religions life or Christian perfection. But F. Clément with marvellous patience took me in hand and regularly instructed me, giving me also certain counsels which I took care to follow, although I used to be langhed at for doing so. He knew how to temper severity with gentleness. One day, a Sister having said something derogatory of another, he humbled her by depriving her of communion: but seeing that she accepted the humiliation well he gave her leave to go to Holy Communion the following day and in this way got her to moderate her hot temper. He never would let any of us give way to melancholy, which he considered so prejudicial to progress in a soul: but exhorted us all to cheerful acceptance of our crosses and to striving after a willing conformity to the Divine Will. Above all, he would have us practise humility, as being the foundation of all spiritual joy and vigour.

"To love God", he would say, "is so great a thing that it cannot be described in words: but it is even greater to suffer something for His love.... On the cross where our Saviour hangs and by His sacred wounds, let us wish to abide for evermore!"

To the lay-sisters who used to get very tired carrying wood, he would suggest this little prayer: "O! Jesus! give me the grace to bear this cross with Thee."

"Love God and suffer all the little trials of life with resignation", he would say. "Let His love be the motive of all your actions; His holy Will your Law; His honour and glory the end of your being. Do not lose patience in temptation;

but be brave and joyous; and abandon yourself unreservedly to the good pleasure of God. Do not murmur against God, even should you be externally and internally desolate. Only cry out: "Jesus! be my Saviour! Deliver me, for Thy name's sake!" Try and serve God from pure love, and never from any personal advantage. If your will be fully united to His, it will please Him more than any fasting or corporal austerities. Pray to your Angel Guardian that he may teach you this love of Jesus Christ. How can you say with truth that you love God with all your heart, when you are not willing to accept the trials which he sends?"

To an old and infirm nun he suggested the prayer: "My Jesus, I wish to live as long as Thou willest: I wish to suffer as Thou willest: I wish to die when Thou willest."

To Sister Thaddeus he one day said: "In any sickness or tribulation, beware lest you lose patience. Keep yourself in perfect peace, feeling sure that whatever is sent you is according to His will. Every time you pass before the crucifix say reverently." "Father! not my will but Thine be done, in life as in death."

Sister Thaddeus adds that one day she was full of sadness at the delay in her profession, her novitiate having been prolonged for five years. F. Clement said to her: "This sadness is a vapour which comes from hell and therefore weighs so heavily on your mind." And some of the other Sisters having replied: "that her noviceship had lasted too long," F. Clement quickly answered: "All our lives are in reality a novitiate: and it will end only when we shall be permitted to join the communion of Saints in Heaven."

But above all, he was never weary, as we have said, of exhorting the Sisters to humility. His favourite ejaculation was: "*O! my Lord, may I be humbled, and Thou exalted.*" "Humility", he would say with St. Augustine, "is the mother, the nurse, the companion and the consummation of all other virtues. The most splendid works have no merit if unaccompanied by humility. It is the compendium of Christ's doctrine, founded on His own words: "*Learn of me, for I am meek and humble of heart and you shall find rest to your souls.*" But he would have a true and not a false humility. Often he would quote St. Theresa's word's: "*Humility is truth.* To speak and act with humility is an excellent thing *provided it be genuine.*" Some make a pretence of humility whose hearts are full of pride. The true sign of being really humble is to receive humiliations quietly, without bitterness or disturbance of mind, but even with joy." In the same way he defined humility to be "*a firm will to serve others*": "for a soul that has no self-love, does not wish for anything but to be subject in everything, to serve others and to help and exalt them; this is true humility." "With which words", observes F. Frederick Rime, "he, without knowing it, drew an accurate portrait of himself."

"Do be persuaded", he said to another Sister, "*that no one does you injustice:* and then you will accept gladly, for the love of God, any contempt that may be shown to you. And do not do anything contrary to the custom of the convent; act with prudence and under the shield of obedience: and do not fancy that a wish to follow your own inclinations and your own will, is any celestial or wise inspiration. The exercise of humility, the abnegation of yourself, and the mortification of your senses, must be your constant study. Instead of being angry or feeling bitter, you should be grateful to those who misunderstand and persecute you: because in reality they do you a great service."

With such wise and tender yet strong exhortations F. Clement fortified these Sisters to bear the trials inseparable from their state: nor is it to be wondered at that he thus raised the tone of the whole convent and kindled in the minds of the Religious a fervent desire to advance in the paths of perfection. And to show the results of his direction we have only to turn our thoughts for a moment to Sister

Thaddeus Taxböck, to whom we have so often alluded. When she came first to the convent she was a poor and illiterate peasant: but under F. Clement's guidance she became an example to the whole community. At the time of his beatification she was one of the most remarkable witnesses of his sanctity. Her memory was so extraordinary that after 50 years she could repeat word for word both his sermons and his prayers: and her depositions were so clear that they would have done honour even to a profound theologian.

CHAPTER XII.

HIS LOVE AND ZEAL FOR THE SICK.

AS his divine Master spent so much of His public life in consoling and healing the sick, so F. Clement always strove to imitate Him also in this matter: and considered it as important a part of the apostolic life, as preaching and administering the Sacraments.

In the monastery of which he had the direction he was most anxious that sickness should be looked upon as a *precious thing* of which each should profit. He was never weary of visiting and consoling the sick Sisters and exhorting them to bear their sufferings with entire resignation to the will of God. In the infirmary there was one old nun, who, partly from illness and partly from the weakening of her intellectual faculties, was very impatient and capricious and a great burden to the community. F. Clement took to visiting her every day, and passing by the garden, would bring her some fresh flowers or fruit which consoled her for the whole evening. Then he would talk to her on various subjects and by degrees captivated her attention. But what touched her most of all was, that one day Father Clement proposed to her to take a little walk with him in the corridor, making her lean upon him all the while as she walked with difficulty. Such charity and tenderness from so eminent a man had such an effect on the poor old nun, that she changed from that hour and became as patient and cheerful as she had formerly been the reverse. If at any time, she was inclined to be discontented, it was only necessary to remind her of F. Clement and she would be quieted at once.

When death drew near, Father Clement was always indefatigable by the dying bed, praying, giving courage and helping the patient in every possible way. Sister Thaddeus relates that on one occasion, in the school attached to the convent, a child who had made her first Communion and who was called Rosina Göll, became dangerously ill. Feeling that death was near, the poor child was seized with terrible fear and lifting up her hands, cried out: "That black dog is trying to devour me!" Sister Thaddeus ran to fetch F. Clement, who came so quickly that they could not imagine how he had contrived to do so. The instant he came into the room the child cried out: "O! thank God, the dog is gone." F. Clement blessed and tranquillised her, gave her a general absolution and remained with her till she expired with a bright, happy face. Then F. Clement said: "We have now another Angel in Paradise praying for us." The Sisters felt convinced that the cause of the fear of this good child was the visible presence of the demon who had been forced to leave her in peace when F. Clement appeared. The same devoted care of the dying was shown by him in all cases. Often he would sit up to take Holy Communion to them after midnight when they were unable to fast until morning and this not only to the Community under his care, but to the rich and poor, to the hospitals, and in fact, wherever he was summoned to attend a person in danger of death. And this charity of his was so well-known, that on every side he received intreaties to visit the sick especially when they had lost their faith: nor did he ever refuse to go to the most distant suburbs of the town. He would take a little lantern with him to light him in the dark courts and alleys he had to traverse and if the people were poor, he would take with him food and wine and other necessaries for the sick. With his extraordinary sweetness and affability he won their confidence at once and often rescued the most obstinate sinners from the brink of the precipice. Before starting he would get all the prayers he could and all the way along he would say his Rosary. Great was his joy when he could tell the Sisters on his return that "thanks to their prayers" a soul had been saved, or a man had been to confession who had neglected doing so for years and that he had died with sentiments of sincere contrition.

One day he was asked to go see a man who for 22 years had entirely neglected his duties and who would not hear of seeing a priest. When F. Clement came into his room, he burst out into imprecations and ordered him to go away instantly. But F. Clement only answered gently: "Whoever undertakes a long journey provides himself with all that is necessary lest he should faint by the way. And you who are going away, would you refuse that which is so vital to your safety—i. e. the Sacraments of the Church? For the love of God be prudent in this matter."

But as his words seemed useless, F. Clement made believe to go, but lingered at the door, looking lovingly on the sick man, who exclaimed: "What on earth do you want? For heaven's sake, go away and leave me in peace!" "No," replied Father Clement, "I shall not go, for your end is very near and I want to see how a man who is damned is going to die!" These words so startled the dying man that he implored him to come back and .to forgive his abusive language. "I willingly forgive you," replied the Father. "But God, whom I have offended so grievously, will never forgive me!" exclaimed the unhappy man bursting into a torrent of tears. Upon which F. Clement reassured him, saying: "God is infinitely good and merciful. Only make an act of hearty contrition for your past offences, and all will be remitted by Him."

The dying man hastened to make the fullest confession of his sins with the utmost sorrow and penitence and clinging tightly to the Father's hand who was holding the Crucifix, he died a few minutes after in peace and hope, to the inexpressible thankfulness of his wife and mother who had begun to despair of his salvation. The same thing often happened in Warsaw. Once, especially, a soldier who announced himself as a "hater of priests" saw F. Clement coming near his bed when he exclaimed: "Come along, you villain! and I will tear out your eyes." But F. Clement, without heeding his words, walked up quietly to his bedside and there talked to him with such sweetness and charity that the wolf was turned into a lamb and that he was reconciled to God and the Church and made an edifying death.

Canon Veith relates another instance:

"An old gentleman in Vienna was very ill, but would not hear of receiving the Sacraments. If any priest came near him, he would cry out: "Go to the devil!" At least a dozen priests of different communities had tried to get hold of him, but in vain. At last they had recourse to F. Clement, who set off at once, saying the Rosary all the way. He was ushered into a beautiful room where the wife and children of the dying man were sobbing near the door of another apartment where the sick person lay. Simply saying: "You will see, it will soon be all right," F. Clement went straight in and going up to the bed, entered upon the subject unmediately: and to the amazement of every one, the dying man received him gladly, listened to his exhortations with the greatest docility and then and there made his confession."

On another occasion he was sent for by the friends of a young nobleman, who by reading rationalistic books, had lost all faith and who was suddenly seized with a mortal illness. Father Clement went directly to his bedside and without losing time in vain preambles, told him to say the Creed. The young man showed some repugnance at beginning; so F. Clement simply threw some Holy water over him and said: "Now, my child, go on!" And then repeated it with him; after which the youth exclaimed: "Now I should like to make my confession." He afterwards received all the Sacraments of the Church and expired full of contrition and confidence in God's mercy.

Sometimes a single word was enough to induce the sick to receive the Sacraments. Upon this point Father Král wrote. "There was a certain Baron Moser, who had been for a long time ill of consumption, but could not be induced to go to his duties because he could not believe there was any danger in his state, as so many people feel with that flattering disease. His wife called upon F. Clement and implored him to come and persuade her husband to receive the Sacraments. He consented at once and coming into the room said: "Baron, I want you to go to confession for then you will be sure of going to Heaven.

The Baron was so surprised and startled at this speech that he could only answer: "Do you really believe this, Father?" "Certainly I do", was F. Clement's reply. And the Baron at once made a general confession and was full of joy because F. Clement had assured him of salvation. As his illness dragged on for a long time, he would now and then play at cards with his friends, which used to annoy his pious wife, who wanted her husband to give up such amusements. But the Baron answered: "F. Clement never forbid my playing and that is enough for me: for if he had thought it wrong he would certainly not have given me permission to do so." Finally, full of resignation to the Divine will, he slept in peace, full of hope of enjoying celestial joys.

With the same firm confidence in the mercy of God, O! how many persons did he console at the terrible hour of death! The young Countess Lichtenberg who was dying of consumption, sent for F. Clement to prepare her for the great journey to Eternity. When he had left her, she exclaimed, full of joy and confidence: "Certainly I shall go to Heaven. F. Clement has promised it to me!"

It was indeed very rarely that F. Clement assisted at a deathbed without the most consoling results.* But once he was summoned to the great oculist Barth, who was both an atheist and a freemason and who was dying. When F. Clement came in, Barth exclaimed: "O! here comes one with the head of an Apostle!" "And to see one with the head of Socrates," replied F. Clement trying to fall into his humour. Buth though Barth was very much pleased at his visit, it produced little or no fruit: which was not surprising, when we remember that many were not converted who heard the words and witnessed the miracles of our Lord Himself and that Barth was a freemason of the worst sort. The oaths which that sect take to the devil, the excommunication of the Church which weighs on their heads, and their terrible habits, make their conversion when it does take place, very like a miracle, for every impediment is put in the way of Divine grace. Nevertheless in other cases, F. Clement was

---

* We have before mentioned his assisting at the death of Countess Zichy. But we have before us part of a letter written by him on the 23rd of Novbr. to Herr von Schlosser of Frankfort, in which he begs him and his wife to console Frau von Schlegel for the loss of Countess Zichy, and which we here transcribe: "We shall be sure to see her again and that for all eternity where there is no separation; for in the house of our celestial Father, our good Lord has kept a place likewise for each of us. Beloved friends! If we in this land of exile have so much cause to weep, let us turn our eyes towards our true home where all tears shall be dried and where our good God Himself will be our great and exceeding reward. These few moments called Life are given us to sow in: and, like our brothers who have already arrived at their celestial home, we must sow in tears, to be able to gather abundant fruit for all eternity: and thus we also shall rejoice with them for ever. God the Father bless you, as I beg of him for Jesus' sake; and may the Holy Spirit who dwells in your hearts, inspire you to fight valiantly for God and His truth even unto the end."

more successful, not only in Warsaw but in Vienna: and one remarkable instance is recorded of a man in the Imperial household, a member of a secret society, who going by accident into the Ursuline Church heard a sermon of Father Clement's which so greatly touched him that he hastened to make his General Confession and soon after died, assisted by F. Clement, in peace with God and man.

CHAPTER XIII.

HIS PATERNAL SOLLICITUDE FOR THE POOR.

AS a good Father of a family cares for his children so was F. Clement watchful over the needs of the poor. And as he had literally nothing of his own and often deprived himself of necessaries for the sake of others, he could only make himself a beggar for their wants and by degrees enlisted a certain number of rich benefactors who were able and willing to assist him. The Superior of the Salesians sent him every Friday two great loaves for his poor: and two of the Vienna Bakers supplied him regularly and often emptied their purses into his lap when he came to plead for very urgent cases. When he went to hear confessions in a church in a poor quarter, he would hide under his cloak a quantity of food to give to the most needy of his penitents, whom he would go and visit afterwards in their own homes. But his special sympathy was enlished for those who had known better days, "*pauvres honteux*", as the French call them; whom he contrived to assist in all sorts of ingenious ways, so as not to hurt their feelings. For instance, there was a certain painter, whose works were not of much merit, but whom he constantly employed; so as to give him bread without the necessity of begging. In that way he covered his alms with the mantle of mercy and saved the honour of the poor artist. He showed the same delicate charity in a thousand other instances. He maintained two poor students in his own house, one named Srna, who afterwards joined the Congregation, and another who gave himself to the profession of surgery. Many other poor students whom he could not lodge, depended upon him for their daily food. In fact, no poor person ever knocked at his door in vain.

Even at the doors of the Ursuline monastery invalid soldiers used to flock, among whom F. Clement would divide all he had. Very often he would not eat his own dinner to have more to give to his dear poor. And as very often, he was out in the morning visiting the sick or hearing confessions, he would put bread and other things in the sacristy of the church so as to be able to distribute them on his return. Especially in the great famine year of 1817, he redoubled his efforts, so that many hundreds were saved by him from sheer starvation. Canon Greif said truly of him: "Whatever he had, he gave away: and this was his life." And Dr. Veith added: "He employed himself in the service of the poor as a mother does with her children." "So much did he love them," wrote F. Madlener, "that he preferred them infinitely to the rich: and while he was always seeking out the poor and needy the great people complained that he never would come to them, but that they had to seek him out. If he went to pay visits to people of high rank, it was invariably to gain their souls. This was the one object and end of his life." He was also continually on the look-out to help those who were not exactly poor, but who were in want of money for certain reasons at certain particular times. Thus he obtained (probably from the Archduke Maximilian) a hundred sequins for Adam Müller, who was founding an Educational Institute: and once finding Clement Brentano in great straits, he gave him a like sum, as Herr von Stramberg declared he had heard from Brentano's own lips.*

---

* In the Ecclesiastical Dictionary of Friburg it is mentioned that Brentano found himself one day sadly depressed because a play of his had not suc-

As F. Clement had such a love for Religious, he was always striving to help those who had a vocation to enable them to embrace that state. A Salesian nun, Mary Ott, mentions having received this charity at his hands and added: "If I am a religious now, I owe it entirely to him." The Ursuline monastery was alone a luminous example of his charity. During the seven years he was their director, he never would receive anything from them save his poor dwelling and the simple food they sent him. And when, from the reduction of the public debt and other causes, the capital and interest of the convent were greatly diminished, he never rested till he had obtained assistance for them from without. Sister Welschenau relates, that: "One day we were reduced to such straits that the procurator did not know what to do. There was no wood, no food, no medicines even for the sick and in despair she began to cry. One of the Sisters exclaimed: "Ah! now is the time that we want the fish of St. Peter!" But what was our consolation when that very same day F. Clement arrived and smiling playfully said: "I am the fish!" while he gave us a large sum of money which not only provided for all our wants but also paid a large portion of our debts. It happened ever after that our finances prospered, and we never again were in such difficulties.

One day he brought us a lamb under his cloak and another day a heavy packet of wax candles: and he was always begging for us from rich people so that we might not be in want. In the same way he thought of the needs of each one of us, whether spiritual or temporal. I can say so from my

---

ceeded on the stage. F. Clement went to see him and with extreme tenderness condoled with the young poet; but talked to him of the abuse he was making of his talents, of the uselessness of the life he was leading and of the rigorous account he would have to give to his eternal judge. Thus he saved him both body and soul. Probably he had a presentiment of the wonderful position reserved for him by Providence with Catherine Emmerich. Brentano was well known to him and held in great affection by the Redemptorist Congregation.

own experience, for he took as much trouble about me as if I had been the only one in the monastery and to him alone, after God, I am indebted for leave to make my last vows, as the community objected to me on account of my delicate health."

One day the Archduke Rudolph, Cardinal Archbishop of Olmütz, came to visit the monastery and on leaving it turned to F. Clement and said: "Really, Father, the joy of the Holy Spirit seems to rest upon you and upon the countenances of all the Sisters in this holy house." F. Clement answered bowing: "And yet, your Eminence, we are weighed down and well nigh crushed by the burden of our poverty and debts; and unless some aid be speedily obtained, we must dissolve the community." The Cardinal instantly promised to speak to his brother, the Emperor: and the result was, that, in a few days, two gentlemen arrived on behalf of His Majesty, bearing enough money to pay all the debts: so that the Convent was saved and the future position of the nuns was secured.

During this previous time of anxiety and distress, Sister Thaddeus was clothed: but the Superior said to her: "I cannot alas! give you shoes like the rest of the community: but you must wear those you had when you came in here, for I have no money to buy anything." But after meditation was over, F. Clement came in and calling the Sister said: "Here is a pair of shoes such as are worn by the other Sisters. Try them on and if they do not fit, I will change them." The sister adds: "They fitted me beautifully and I used them for 34 years: for, from the great veneration I felt towards F. Clement, I only wore them on great feasts."

In the same way some foreign Fathers were deeply indebted to his charity, as, when they arrived, they knew neither the language, nor the city, nor the money of the country: which, when F. Clement found out, he went and lived with them for three weeks, put them in the way of every thing and was throughout their best friend and counsellor.

CHAPTER XIV.

His Efforts for the Christian Education of Youth.

ANOTHER object which F. Clement had much at heart was the careful training and education of children. It was the frequent subject of his sermons when he would say: "You, Parents! never forget that upon you depends the blessing or curse which falls on the human race: for to you is confided the education of man. If you watch over your children and learn to break, in time, their perverse wills, so that they may become obedient and docile, you will make them good and useful in their generation. That which is sown in the heart of a little child will remain there till it is old: and if you do what in you lies, God Himself will do the rest." Of what F. Clement did in Warsaw for education we have already spoken: and he showed the same anxiety and the same zeal in Vienna. On very many occasions he instructed children himself in the rudiments of the faith and prepared them to receive with fervour their first communion. He had a peculiar gift of winning children and when they came to him, would give them pictures, medals and sweets, of which Cardinal Schwarzenberg himself retained a grateful recollection; having, when he was nine years old, frequently seen F. Clement, who was visiting his sick Tutor, Dr. Greif. Sister Thaddeus relates that when when F. Clement was walking in the streets of the city, children used to come up and kiss his hand and then follow him to whatever house he was going, he entertaining them the while with loving words or little stories. Often they would follow him home, when he had always some little thing to give them, with which they went away rejoicing. One day he said to the son of one of the Aulic Counsellors of Vienna: "My dear little Charles, listen to me. You are now old enough to obey the precepts of the Church and you know it is not allowed to us to eat meat on Fridays. We must offer up this little sacrifice to our Lord Jesus Christ, who on that day offered Himself up on the cross for the love of us." The next Friday, Charles seeing meat as usual on the table and no fish, said bravely: "Papa! To-day I cannot eat meat." "And why not, pray?" answered his father angrily. "Because it is Friday, Papa, when the Church tells us to abstain because our Lord died on the cross on that day." "Who told you that?" replied his father with visible impatience. "F. Clement", replied the child. Then the father in a severe tone ordered him to eat the meat: but the boy intreated him not to force him to do so. His prayer was of no avail and his father, furious at what he called his obstinacy, drove him from the table saying: "Take him out of my sight! he shall have nothing else to-day." Charles ran to his mother, who consoled him and said: "I will get something *maigre* for you." "No, Mama", replied the boy, "because Papa said I was not to have anything else and F. Clement said I must always obey him unless he tells me to do something contrary to the laws of God and the Church. I can do very well without anything to eat to-day!" His mother very much touched at the boy's answer, went to her husband and told him: who, ashamed of his own conduct and admiring his son's obedience, which was in reality a reproof to himself, told him "to eat anything his mother had prepared and that in future he would never ask him to eat meat on Fridays."

Ever after the laws of the Church were obeyed by the Counsellor and his household, and the father conceived such an esteem for F. Clement that he often took his boy to the Ursuline Church that he might serve the Father's mass: so that the wise counsel given to the child influenced the whole family.

Very salutary also was the influence exercised by F. Clement over the young girls who attended the Ursuline Convent or who were received as boarders there. We will here transcribe part of a letter from one of these girls, who afterwards became the wife of General Baron Pongräcz and was a most admirable woman: 20th of Jan. 1877. "My father, who was Captain in a cavalry regiment, placed me in the Ursuline Convent in 1810, where I remained for six years. Here I had the good fortune to be placed under the guidance of F. Clement Hofbauer, whose religious instructions became the rule of my life and have been my support in my old age. My mistress, Sister Louisa, was like a mother to me and when F. Clement came into the house she used to bring me to him to receive his blessing. Even to this day I remember the sorrowful hour when in 1816, my father sent for me to come home and I had to leave the convent where I had been so happy. I knelt at Father Clement's feet crying my heart out: but he, lovingly placing his hand on my head and blessing me, said: "My child, never forget the instructions you have received in this holy house; and then you will succeed in life and live to a good old age." These words seemed to me like a prophecy and they certainly have been fulfilled: for in spite of some little troubles, I have passed many very happy years; and now in my old age, I remember still with deep gratitude the venerable priest who was my first spiritual guide."

On another occasion F. Clement found a boy neglected by his parents and ignorant of the things most necessary to his salvation. He took the child home and to a school in the Parish of St. Ann, begging the master to give him some instruction. At that moment the *Angelus* rang, it being midday, and the master said laughingly: "There's the bell for dinner!" These words displeased F. Clement, who replied quietly: "What do you mean? You, who are a schoolmaster and have to teach children their religion, you do not know the meaning of that bell?" And then and there explained to him how the Church thus kept up the memory of the Incarnation. The schoolmaster was so impressed by his words that not very long after, he gave up his place and went into a monastery.

The greatest sorrow of F. Clement's life was the way in which infidel teachers endeavoured to instil their anti-Christian maxims into the hearts of the young. In Vienna there was literally no purely Catholic College for boys: and F. Clement never rested till he had persuaded the Aulic Counsellor, Adam Müller, to start one for the higher classes, promising the aid of his Fathers as Professors. Müller's College was accordingly opened and succeeded admirably, F. Clement visiting it himself continually. But unhappily, the Government refused to give it any official recognition and the institution had to be given up.

Not discouraged, however, F. Clement went to another friend of his, Frederick von Klinkowström, and passing with him by a certain house suddenly stopped and said: "Look at this house: it would be very well suited for a school. Do buy it!" "That's all very well", replied Frederick laughing. "But where is the money to come from? You know I have got none." F. Clement replied: "Never mind: buy it all the same. I will get the money." Full of confidence in F. Clement's words Frederick did as he was bid and a Protestant, Baron Geusau, lent the money on very favourable conditions and sent his three sons to be educated there, their mother being a Catholic. The great thing now was to obtain the Government sanction, which was all the more difficult from the said permission having been refused to Adam Müller's Institution. At F. Clement's intreaty, however, the Archduke Maximilian d'Este undertook it: and to obtain divine assistance in the matter, he resolved to impose upon himself a special mortification for the rest of his life, and that was, never again to drink sugar in his coffee. The Imperial approbation was obtained in 1818, and the Archduke kept religiously to his promise, though he only revealed the reason of his abstention to his confessor a short time before his death.

The institution thus started by F. Clement was singularly blessed by God: and as it met a want which was very generally felt, it obtained support from all quarters; and not only in Vienna but from Naples, Constantinople, Bucharest, Russia, France, Bavaria and many other countries, pupils flocked to this college which under Klinkowström's able guidance, became an unmixed success. Its students afterwards became remarkable as statesmen, as officers in the army, as ecclesiastics and in the diplomatic service: among whom we may mention Count Crivelli, Baron Hübner (both Ambassadors to the Holy See); the Envoy and afterwards minister, Baron Brenner; Baron Stillfried, so well known for his defence of the Catholic faith, and many others. And all preserved to the last those patriotic and Christian principles with which they had been imbued in this truly Catholic Institution.

CHAPTER XV.

Father Clement converts many Jews and Protestants.

FIRMLY convinced that outside the pale of the Catholic Church there is no salvation and filled with love and charity to his neighbour, it may easily be imagined that F. Clement had greatly at heart the conversion of heretics. "Who will grant me the grace to rescue all these poor infidel souls!" he would exclaim. "O! if I could, how gladly would I bear them in my arms into the bosom of the Catholic Church!" And another time, in the pulpit, he burst out with the following prayer: "Jesus! my Lord! turn Thy gracious eyes towards us from the throne of Thy mercy. Thou, for our salvation, hast shed all Thy precious Blood on the accursed tree to redeem us and obtain for us eternal life. Thy Father in Heaven is ours also, for Thou art our Brother in the flesh. Wilt Thou allow so many beings whom Thou hast created to perish eternally? Lord! If thon wilt, Thou canst save them. Look upon the tears of the Church, Thy spouse. Draw towards her her children who are afar off, so that they too may be gathered into her fold. Diffuse over the erring the light of faith, which alone can save us and make us Saints. And if the groans of my love do not deserve to be heard by Thee, for I am but a miserable sinner, I turn to Thee, O! powerful Virgin, mother of mercy, and implore Thee to pray for us. Then all heretics will be converted and all will praise and glorify Thy Holy Name for ever and for ever and for ever!"

But there was no doubt that the zeal and love of this holy man were largely rewarded by God. In Warsaw as in Vienna the conversions that he made were extraordinary. Sister Thaddeus states, "that it was very rarely that a week passed without some Protestants making their abjuration and some Jews being baptised," but we will mention a few eminent cases.

Dorothea, daughter of the Philosopher, Moses Mendelssohn, married first Simon Veit, a banker in Berlin, by whom she had two children. But in the year 1802, she was separated from him and married the Philosopher, Frederick von Schlegel, when, to the astonishment of every one she became a Christian (having been a Jewess) and was baptised in the Swedish Protestant Church at Paris. Schlegel in 1808 published a wonderful book on the language and literature of the Indians: but what astonished the world far more was, that on the 16th of April of that year he and his wife became Catholics and proceeded to Vienna, where Prince Metternich made him Secretary to the Chancellor of State. In this capacity, he accompanied the Archduke Charles to the battlefield and wrote the Austrian proclamations against Napoleon. When peace was declared, he devoted himself to literature in which he made a great and deserved reputation. From 1815 to 1818 he was Counsellor of Legation at Frankfort, after which he went for a time with his family to Rome, and then returned to Vienna. Here F. Clement became his intimate friend and the Director and guide of the whole family. The two sons of Mme. von Schlegel by her first marriage, John and Philip Veit, following the example of their mother, were baptised and instructed by F. Clement. Philip, who died in 1878, Director of the Pinacotheke at Mayence and who was himself a great painter, writes of his conversion as follows: "Although I had received some instruction in the Catholic Religion in Cologne, it was F. Clement, that holy and great servant of God, whom I can never forget, who really prepared myself and my brother for the reception of Baptism. It is impossible for me to describe the untiring zeal and tender love he showed us on this occasion and I would to God we had profited by it and been as grateful as his wonderful charity deserved! It was only later and by degrees, that we realised how greatly we were his debtors and how often I must have disgusted him and tried his patience by my carelessness and indifference. We were baptised on the 9th of June 1810, being the Eve of Pentecost, in the Chapel of the Nunzio, by the hands of Cardinal Severoli assisted by Father Clement and in the presence of the Marchioness Rangoni, Baron Penkler and many others. He took us also on a little Pilgrimage to Maria Zell, an expedition which made a very deep impression upon me and when I had the pleasure of serving his mass in that holy Chapel..... Father Clement was an intimate friend of Frederick von Schlegel's: he was constantly with us and exercised the best possible influence both over him and over our holy and good mother, who had the greatest esteem and veneration for him. I recollect once going

into the Sacristy with him, where we found F. Werner in
an agony about a sermon he was about to preach and which
he was afraid of forgetting. F. Clement encouraged him:
but F. Werner replied: "It's all very well for you, who, without any preparation, have such a flow of beautiful words
and thoughts!! but a poor fellow like me ....!"

At this time and especially during the Congress of Vienna,
our house was frequented by persons of the highest rank
both Protestant and Catholic. Every one who met F. Clement was delighted and struck with him; and all showed
the greatest respect for his opinion, though, as a fervent
priest, he often threw out little words, such as: "Well when
are you going to Rome?" or the like. In all these occasions,
however, he never forgot his dignity and reserve as a priest
and his noble bearing made a great impression on all."

Schlegel himself was as devoted and obedient to him as
his step-sons. He used to bring him his writings so as to
have his approbation before publishing them. One day when
he had read to him a very brilliant article, F. Clement embraced him and exclaimed: "Well done! my dear Frederick!
but remember only that it is better still to love Our Lord
Jesus Christ with all your heart."

When Schlegel and his wife went to Frankfort and afterwards to Rome, they kept up a constant correspondance
with F. Clement and one of these letters from Dorothea
written on the 28th of June 1817 from Frankfort will show
our readers how great was the influence he exercised over
her sons.

"Very Revd. and dear Father!" she writes. "To-day being
the vigil of the great Feast of St. Peter and St. Paul, I cannot do less than talk to you a little, for no great Feast passes
without my longing to find myself kneeling at your feet and
listening to your wise counsels. You have written about my
dear Philip according to our fondest wishes and hopes. I
bless him for yielding himself with such docility into your

hands: for no one knows so well how to lead him to God and to teach him to submit in all things to the Divine will. We pray to our Lord with all our hearts that you may continue to guide and direct him, so that you, who know so well all his little faults and weaknesses, may strengthen him with your holy counsels and advice, even unto the end.... Finally, beloved and revered Father, help us all with your holy prayers in which we have such confidence, that we may receive the light of the Holy Spirit of God and walk circumspectly in the midst of the snares and pitfalls of this weary world."

John Veit, the eldest son, established himself in Rome, where he painted nothing but Madonnas. He died in 1854, and his wife, who was also a convert from Protestantism and very holy, died eight years later, leaving all her money to good works.

But we must and speak now of another family whom F. Clement converted and who became his intimate friends. Frederick von Klinkowström, son of a Swedish Lieutenant Colonel, was born in Pomerania on the 31st of Aug. 1778. He served first in the army and then gave it up to devote himself to painting. In 1810, being at Paris, he made acquaintance with Antony von Pilat, Counsellor of the Austrian Government, and soon after, becoming intimate with the family, married his cousin, Louisa von Mengershausen of Hanover.

Before going to Vienna, Frederick had experienced in a most extraordinary manner, the salutary influence of the man who was destined by God to be the main instrument of his salvation. He was one day in Hamburgh, when, after spending a night with some young men of loose morals, a woman of bad character was introduced into the room. But as she came in, Frederick, who was leaning against the window, suddenly saw a venerable priest dressed in a cope, who was walking behind her and who cast a look of such indignation at Frederick, that he, startled and ashamed, made an excuse to leave the room at once and ran home, making a note at the time of the event and the appearance of the priest.

Many years after, being at Vienna and having made friends with Schlegel, the latter took him one day to the Italian Church, where F. Clement gave the Benediction of the Blessed Sacrament. He fixed his eyes on the priest and to his amazement recognised the very man who in Hamburgh had kept him from sin. There was no doubt about it. It was the same face, the same dress, the same in everything which he had seen in that mysterious vision and never before or since!

It may easily be understood that after this, Frederick could not resist asking to be introduced to F. Clement and going to see him: and very soon he won his entire confidence and persuaded him to recognise that the Catholic Church was the only ark of salvation. If he abstained then and there from making his abjuration, it was only for love of his wife, who was a strong Protestant and whom he did not wish to pain. But she began to suspect his intentions, seeing that he no longer went to the Protestant Church but to that of the Servites, although he tried to deceive her by saying "that he went there because he preferred the music."

The war, however, absorbed every one's thoughts at that time and very soon Klinkowström had to join the Austrian Head-Quarters: while von Pilat was summoned to Paris: so that their two wives, Louisa and Elisabeth were left alone at home to console one another.

F. Clement frequently visited them: and one day, on Holy Thursday, he found both Ladies very sad and silent, though they had both on that day according to the custom of the Protestant Church, gone to the Lord's supper. F. Clement asked them "what was the matter?" and they confessed to the unsatisfactoriness of the service at which they had just assisted and their wish to study the doctrines of the Catholic Church "to which we should have come long ago" one of them said "if it had not been for confession!" "O! as to that," replied F. Clement, "leave it to me."

F. Clement then began with great prudence to ask them, one by one, certain questions as to their past lives and so won their confidence that they gladly opened their whole hearts to him: so that after a time F. Clement said cheerfully: "Well this formidable thing is nearly over. You have both made your confession to me and very little remains to do!" and then teaching them how to make an act of contrition and a resolution to amend their lives, he gave them absolution and after a little more instruction received them both into the Church in the presence of Schlegel and his wife.

When Klinkowström heard this, he was greatly rejoiced; and returning to Vienna, was himself admitted on the 13th of September and made his profession of faith to F. Clement.

There remained only the 3rd sister, Augusta von Mengerhausen: but the great patience and charity of F. Clement triumphed over all opposition and she not only became a Catholic but a Salesian in the monastery of Gleink, where she gave the highest edification and died a saintly death. When Anthony von Pilat came home in 1814, he found indeed a change in his household. Both his wife and sister-in-law were become fervent Catholics, as well as Klinkowström: and a like grace soon touched his own heart; to that within a few weeks he too made his general confession to Father Clement and embraced the Catholic Faith. As long as Father Clement lived, he continued the intimate friend and guide of both families: and von Pilat's conversion was the more remarkable and important, because he had been a Free-mason and was Secretary to Prince Metternich, in which capacity he could have done much harm:*

---

* Father Kral, his confessor, relates the following anecdote in proof of his honour and probity. To go to his office, Pilat had to pass before the

whereas, as a fervent Catholic and a weekly Communicant, his whole influence was for good and he continued till the end of his life of 82 years in active service both for God and his country. He was much esteemed at the Congress of Vienna and decorated by all the Sovereign Heads. In another and a humbler way, that is, as Editor of "*The Austrian Observer*" he was also able to do good service to the Church: while his honourable integrity won the esteem and respect of all classes of persons.*

Another remarkable conversion of F. Clement's was that of Frederick Schlosser, of whom Rosenthal speaks: "That in all Germany there was not a more pure and noble soul. Adorned with every gift of heart and mind, a wonderful linguist and poet, always at hand to assist the poor and suffering, he was looked upon by all his fellow citizens as an example of a true patriot and a fervent Christian and as such deserving a monument in the hearts of all."

He was born of a noble family in Frankfort in 1780 and in 1815 was sent on important affairs to the Congress of Vienna, where he became acquainted with F. Clement and was by him received into the Church. His wife, Sophia du Fay, writes of this event on the 20th of June 1864 as follows: "It is impossible to say the impression made by this holy man upon my husband, for truly the key-note of his character was love of God and of His Church and a burning desire to lead all Souls to the feet of our Lord. This appeared in his whole person, in his words, in his works, in his

Exchange: and one day a speculator came up to him and offered him a large sum of money if he would only say a word to him in his ear the next morning, even if it were only "good morning!" Pilat saw directly how the man would make capital out of this imaginary conversation with Prince Metternich's confidential Secretary and indignantly rejected the temptation.

* Klinkowström died on the 4th of April 1835 and his wife Louisa, (of whose faith F. Clement spoke as "founded on a rock") on the 7th of March 1821 in the prime of life, amidst the tears and lamentations of the poor to whom she had ever been as a tender mother.

preaching, everything about him, in fact, though perfectly simple, produced a most extraordinary impression. When he spoke of the magnificence of the Catholic Church and said these words: 'Only those who have the good fortune to be within her fold and among her members, can *know* what she is', every one was filled with an ardent wish to become a child of this Church; so much so, that I insisted upon being received even when I knew very little about it. F. Clement received us both on the 17th of Dec. 1815, and never ceased to be a real Father to us. I have never passed happier hours in my life than those we used to spend with him, when, after mass, he would ask us to breakfast and show himself the tenderest, brightest and most paternal of friends."

"I have been asked," she continues, "for this cause of his beatification, to give my opinion of his holiness. But how can I do so? or judge a man, who, to my thinking, never had an equal in this world? whoever knew him must have felt that in his soul, not only was there no guile, nor even an imperfection, but that he was entirely filled with the love and with the spirit of God, and with a burning charity towards all men, so that those were indeed fortunate who could claim an intimacy with such a Saint!"

Schlosser died on the 7th of Jan. 1851 at Frankfort at 70 years of age and his wife, in the Castle of Neuburg in 1865.

We will only speak of one more remarkable conversion of F. Clement's and that was of the two sons of a certain Baron Rieger. He was a Calvinist and brought up his sons in that Faith, but soon after died. The youngest son, Adolphus, was taken dangerously ill in Vienna and his Tutor, John Madlener, who was a devoted follower of F. Clement's, ran to tell him of his danger and to ask his advice. F. Clement replied: "Tell the sick youth that he will die; if not, you will have to render an account of his soul." Madlener went back to his charge, but had not the courage to tell the whole truth and only said: "that a friend of his, F. Clement, wished to come and see him." "Thank him from me," replied Adolphus: "and tell him, when I am cured, I will go and see him." "But, you are dangerously ill!" rejoined Madlener. "Never mind, go away now and pray for me," replied the sick youth. Madlener hurried back to F. Clement, imploring him to come himself. F. Clement at once assented and started off, saying the Rosary all the way. When he came to the young Baron, he spoke to him very tenderly and asked him "how he felt?" "Very ill," he replied, and his manner so pleased the Father that he asked those around the bed to retire and leave him alone with the sick man. After a little time, he came out and saying quietly to the astonished nurses: "The young Baron is now a Catholic. I am going to get the Holy Viaticum. And you, Madlener, go to him and assist him to prepare to receive our Lord worthily," he went out and presently returned with that supreme consolation of the dying. Adolphus received It with indescribable faith and joy and resigning himself entirely to the Will of God, expired soon after in perfect peace.

A few days later, his brother Charles arrived unexpectedly in Vienna, after a long journey, and hearing what had occurred went to thank F. Clement for his kindness and charity towards his brother. F. Clement entered into conversation with him, and the result was, that after a long talk, he too decided to become a Catholic. Later on, he chose the ecclesiastical state, and died at Vienna as an excellent priest in 1863.

Out of gratitude, the sister of the two converts who was herself a Catholic, having been brought up in her mother's Faith, addressed a petition to the Holy Father Pius IX. imploring him to deign to initiate the cause of F. Clement's beatification and cannonisation.

CHAPTER XVI.
MEETINGS AND EVENING CONFERENCES IN F. CLEMENT'S HOUSE.

AFTER the heavy fatigues of the day, some hours of rest were surely necessary to F. Clement in the evening: but after he became known in Vienna, this was impossible. And whenever he came back from his labours in the church, or his late visits to the sick and dying, he always found his house full of people, mostly young men, all anxions to see and hear him.

And this, so far from displeasing F. Clement, was really his delight: for he knew no other rest than to work for the honour and glory of his Lord and the salvation of souls.

His house was open to all and when he came back, often wet through and chilled to the bone, he would never think of himself for a moment, but coming in and finding 20 or 30 young men waiting for him, would playfully welcome them, saying: "O! you young rogues! what do you want?" and then enter into conversation with them one after the other, each feeling that they had found a Father. They were of every class; students in theology and in medicine, lawyers, government officials, tradesmen, some bringing a friend whom they hoped to convert, others wishing to go to confession after some passage in a sermon of his which had struck them, and so on. To all he showed himself as he was, simple, straightforward and just: and it was those qualities which gave him such a hold over these young men. He never flattered any one and knew how to put down vanity and pride or false ambition: while he encouraged the shy and timid ones by a few paternal words.

Often at mid-day, he would have some poor students to dine with him, making them first make a little examination of conscience, and recite the Litany of our Lady and then sit down to table, he walking up and down and helping everybody, eating only a little scrap himself. And when they used to implore him to sit down and have his meal comfortably, he would say laughing: "What does it matter to you if I am satisfied?"

In the same way, he used to make his guests sup with him and they were so numerous that very often there was not room for them at the long table. After supper, he would lead them to talk on some spiritual subject, or read to them from some instructive book, mingling his own annotations as he went on. "I have often seen him," writes Cardinal Rauscher, "sitting in the midst of these young men, his eyes almost closed, but listening attentively to whatever was being said or read tending to edification; while from time to time, he would put in a word to prevent the little conference from becoming formal or wearisome."

One evening, during the conversation, a violent thunderstorm came on, the lightening almost blinding their eyes and the thunder making every one tremble. F. Clement began explaining that passages in the Gospel: *For as the lightening that ligtheneth from under Heaven, shineth unto the parts that are under Heaven, so shall the coming of the Son of Man be in his day*". St. Luke. XVII. Chap. 24. V.

"And so," added Father Clement, "it will be at the moment of our death. Then, with the clearness of a flash of lightening, will all our past life appear to our souls, only with a far different light from that with which we think of it and see it now, for it will be in the light of Eternity." "These words," wrote Father Rinn, who was present, "struck his young auditors so much that many of them asked at once if he would hear their confessions?"

As these young men were at an age when the strongest temptations are felt, F. Clement was perpetually on the watch to defend them as it were, from themselves and by keeping them occupied and amused during these perilous hours of the night to preserve them from dangerous occasions and bad company. He would intreat them not to feed their imaginations with love stories and exciting novels and to frequent the Sacraments as being the best safeguards of chastity. Above all, he hated idleness especially for young priests and would say to them: "That if one thus consecrated to God did not spend every moment in His service, he would undoubtedly end badly."

He used to encourage his young men to talk and give their opinions upon different subjects and ventilate their doubts and difficulties. If any dispute arose, he would instantly calm it with a few wise words. He hated detraction more than the plague and one of the things which pleased him most was when any one took up the defence of the absent. Wonderful also was the patience with which he bore with the defects and faults of his disciples, always contenting himself with their good will and leaving the rest to time. The only thing he could not bear was anything like fraud or double-dealing, especially if cloaked by a pretended veil of piety. Not that he ever was himself deceived, for Werner used to say of him: "I really believe he could see through a deal table!" Sometimes, among those who came to him, were one or two whose interior did not correspond with their exterior appearance. One day a Sister remarked one of these strangers who prayed and sang more fervently, apparently, than all the rest and she congratulated F. Clement on the piety of this new disciple. But he answered. "I am not satisfied about him: look at him and you will see that his soul is not at peace."

The same observation was made by him with alas! too much reason, about Dr. Wolf, who at one time was a devout Cantor in the Ursuline Church. As the great Bishop and Doctor, St. Gregory, discovered in Julian the serpent who was afterwards to pervert the Roman Purple, so F. Clement detected in this youth, who seemed so pious, the future apostate and adventurer.

Joseph Wolf was born in Bavaria in 1795 of Jewish parents. In 1812, he was baptised at Prague and then went to study for two years in Vienna where he made acquaintance with F. Clement, who, however, distrusted him and would not admit him among his disciples. In 1816, he went to Rome and managed to get into the College of Propaganda, but after a few months was expelled for keeping up a secret correspondence with Protestants, defending heretical propositions, and turning everything and every body in Rome into ridicule. Notwithstanding this, Cardinal Litta, then Prefect of Propaganda, treated him kindly and gave him letters to the Nunzio at Vienna, Mong^r. Leardi. At the Nunzio's request, F. Clement saw him and pointed out to him his errors, but in vain. After that, Wolf associated himself with some English Protestants, travelled in America and other countries, and finally became Rector of an English Protestant Church! so that F. Clement's distrust was fully justified. It is fair to say, however, that, before he died, he paid a visit to the Provincial of the Redemptorists in London, enquired after his old friends and asked for their prayers, dying in 1862 on the 2nd of May. These constant meetings at F. Clement's house, however, gave umbrage to the Police, who began to suspect him, as usual, of conspiring against the state. Under this pretext, they sent one or two of their agents, who, under pretence of being students, came in the evening with the rest. One of these men pretended to have been a great traveller and to have made the acquaintance of many illustrious people: but F. Clement detected them at once and warned his disciples of their presence. He spoke, however, as usual, on general subjects, but with increased prudence. And afterwards finding that these domiciliary visits continued, he used to take his young men out walking with him, especially in summer; and often on the bastions of the city which were much frequented. Sometimes the Viennese used to gather round him to listen to the instructive stories he would tell to his disciples; and when the "*Angelus*" sounded, all of them would lift their caps and repeat the "*Ave Maria*", to the astonishment of the bystanders, but likewise to their admiration, as they saw that they said it so simply and without any human respect. Then he would dismiss them to their homes, where they returned, strengthened in all their good resolutions and full of respectful love for their father and guide.

It is impossible to express the good he did by these familiar conferences and the way he thus contributed to revive the faith of the Viennese. Many of these young men who had never before thought seriously, embraced the Religious state and others became excellent public servants and did honour to their holy teacher.

But besides all these, many persons of a higher rank used to seek out F. Clement and consult him in all matters of importance. Among these was Prince Alexander Hohenlohe and many others, even non-Catholics, like the famous Protestant Librarian, Perthes, who was so edified by a visit he paid to him in 1816, that he has written an account of it, describing the poor dwelling of F. Clement, and the way "his face beamed with a celestial light such as he had never seen on any other man." We need only conclude this chapter with the words of Cardinal Rauscher: "That F. Clement was held in the highest esteem by all, noble and simple, learned and unlearned, and that even the most bitter Protestants looked upon him with respect and even with veneration."

CHAPTER XVII.
HIS ANXIETY FOR THE WELFARE OF THE UNIVERSAL CHURCH, AND ESPECIALLY AT THE TIME OF THE CONGRESS OF VIENNA.

THERE is no doubt that Father Clement exercised a very important influence in the affairs of the Church at certain critical times: and if her preponderance in Austria and Germany were not utterly destroyed by the cleverness and cunning of her enemies, it was mainly due to the anxious sollicitude of this great servant of God. Many times did he warn the Holy See of grave impending dangers and the Apostolic Nunzios both in Warsaw and Vienna never failed to consult him on all important occasions. "One day", reports Cecilia Choloniewska, "finding myself with the Nunzio, Monsignor Severoli, he pointed out Father Clement to me, saying in a low voice so that he might not hear: "Do you see that venerable Religious? Simple and unpretending as he appears exteriorly, there is no one who is so good a judge of important affairs. Very often the most difficult and complicated questions come before us, which appear almost impossible of solution. In consequence, I constantly send for that good Father and never have I had occasion to regret having done so: for what with the sanctity of his person, the clearness of his judgment, the force of his reasoning and the simplicity of his explanations of his views, he persuades the most perverse and hostile of our opponents and we consequently obtain what, at first, seemed simply impossible."

Cardinal Consalvi, who represented the Pope at the Congress of Vienna, gives a similar testimony: and affirmed that he never acted without consulting him. And it was just in this Congress that F. Clement was able to render such important services to the Church, thus proving the end proposed by Divine Providence in leading him to Vienna.

It was expected that the Congress, among other things, should reorganise the Ecclesiastical affairs of Germany, which were in the most lamentable confusion. But what was needed for this, was a man with an accurate knowledge of the actual position of affairs and one who was prepared to act with a zeal proportioned to the need. Where was such a man to be found? Consalvi and Severoli had not enough knowledge of the state of things: Dalberg, Primate of Germany had betrayed the most sacred interests of the Church and found no better representative at the Congress than that Baron Wessenberg whom we have before mentioned, a member of the sect called "The Illuminated", and who was his Vicar General at Constance. This man was related to a great number of the aristocracy: and his brother, who was Autrian Minister of State and one of the delegates at the Congress, was in great favour with those in the highest circles; while his principles alternated between Josephism and Protestantism. The Congress opened its sittings on the 1st of Novbr. 1814 and by the 27th of that month, Wessenberg presented a memorial on the reform of the Church in Germany. He proposed to constitute a National German Church, directed by a Primate under whose control all ecclesiastical affairs should be placed. The centre of all ecclesiastical administration was to be a national, provincial and diocesan synod. The organisation of this new Church was to be established by a uniform agreement of all the Confederate States; and then form an essential part of the Constitution of the German Empire.

In this satanic work, which was subversive of the very essence of the Catholic Church, Wessenberg was supported by the Ambassadors of Prussia, Hanover and Bavaria, by Count Spiegel (then Deacon of the Münster Chapter and afterwards Archbishop of Cologne), and by many others. The defence of Catholic interests rested solely in the weak hands of a Prebendary of the Chapter of Spires, Helferich, and in the Baron von Wamboldt, Dean of the Chapter of Worms. These two had been chosen by Cardinal Consalvi to defend the Catholic cause and it is fair to say that they showed great zeal in the matter. But he who sustained them in this difficult undertaking was no other than F. Clement, who by his continual labours, counsels and exhortations supplied what was wanting in their knowledge and gave them the strength and courage necessary for the struggle with these powerful schismatics.

F. Srna, who then lived with F. Clement, narrates that Helferich came every day to consult him and that the different memorandum presented to Congress were all drawn up by F. Clement, while F. Sabelli spent many hours each night in making copies of them. If therefore the schismatic devices of Wessenberg were completely defeated, the person to whom the victory was mainly due was F. Clement.

Beck, Wessenberg's panegyrist, never could sufficiently deplore the failure of his scheme and attributes it mainly to the influence of the Schlegels, Schlosser, Werner and Pilat: but he omits Müller, by whose writings and influence with certain eminent diplomatists much good was effected, and totally ignores F. Clement who was, in reality, the master and director of the whole Catholic movement. Cardinal Reisach speaking of this says: "At the time of the Congress, Father Clement was the centre round which all earnest and learned Catholics were gathered; and by his aid they were able to defeat the schismatics, who strove to form a new National German Church independent of the Pope." Beck laments also the defection of Bavaria in this matter, which was the more wonderful as the real Governor of Bavaria at that moment was the powerful Minister Montgelas, who was most bitter against the Church; and Count Rechberg was the Ambassador at the Congress, who certainly could not boast of any Catholic principles. But the real reason was, that the hereditary Prince Louis of Bavaria, who had great influence over his Father King Maximilan I, was an intimate friend of F. Clement's and took his advice on every occasion, visiting him constantly in his poor dwelling and often staying, as we have already mentioned, half the night with him.*

* One of the fruits of these visits was, the dismissal of Montgelas, and very soon after the Congress, negotiations were set on foot in Bavaria for the establishment of a Concordat with the Holy See, which was finally signed in the year 1817.

Whilst Father Clement was thus fighting assiduously the enemies of the Church, he did not forget by earnest prayer to beseech of God the salvation of their souls. And these is reason to believe that for Dalberg, at any rate, these prayers were granted; as during his last years he became an intimate friend of Dr. Wittmann, the Rector of the Ratisbon Seminary. And after the Congress of Vienna, Dalberg gave up Wessenberg and his proceedings and led ever after a simple, penitent life, dying as a good Catholic on the 10th of Febr. 1817. That very year Wessenberg was elected by the Canons of Constance Administrator of the Diocese: an election the Pope refused to sanction. Wessenberg upon this, started for Rome to defend himself: but Pius VII would not admit him to his presence until he had promised to resign his post of Administrator and expressed penitence for his past conduct. But Wessenberg's pride would not brook this submission and so great was the annoyance caused by his intrigues at Rome, that Cardinal Consalvi desired F. Clement to forward to the Pope certain writings of his which abundantly justified the Pope's conduct in the matter. Wessenberg, furious at being thus unmasked, left Rome and went to Carlsruhe to give an account of his failure to the Grand Duke of Baden and continued to administer the Diocese against the Pontifical Decrees, becoming at last a declared schismatic. The sorrow felt by F. Clement at this proceeding may be judged by a letter he wrote at that time to Pius VII. in which he said: "That Germany ran a greater risk at that moment than when she was the seat of the late disastrous wars; for that he foresaw a rupture of that country from Rome, which could only be averted by the intercession of the Saints."

Finally Wessenberg died impenitent, on the 9th of Aug. 1860, having made, before he expired, the impious declaration that he died faithful to his heresy: and the Freemasons of Constance, to honour his memory, called their lodge after him!

Ten days after the death of Archbishop Dalberg, F. Clement by desire of the Nunzio, Severoli, wrote a letter to Cardinal Litta in Rome to urge strongly the appointment of Baron Francis von Wamboldt, Dean of the Chapter of Worms, as Dalberg's Successor: F. Clement having known him intimately at Vienna during the Congress. "It has pleased our Lord," he writes, "to call to Himself the man under whose authority the clergy have been guilty of such great disorders. But it is most important that a man should be appointed as his successor who should be able to remedy this state of things and also be of sufficiently high rank to disarm the opposition of the nobility. Baron von Wamboldt is of most ancient family, brother-in-law of Count Stadion and related to Count Coudenhove, Prince Metternich and almost all the highest aristocracy of the Empire. More than once a Wamboldt has been chosen so fill the electoral Throne of Mayence: he is also well thought of in Bavaria. Another thing is that he does not seek for the Episcopate and would only accept it if insisted on by the Holy Father. All the good earnestly desire him; for he is devoted to the Holy See and knows how to conciliate all parties. He would he an excellent counterpoise also to the machinations of Sailer and Wessenberg. These two men, under a pretence of devotion, are continually trying to bring about a schism with Rome and the establishment of a new national German Church. It is true that Wambold is not a man of deep learning, but he has a real Catholic heart; and it is easy to give him subordinates who could supply his needs in other respects. I do not think I deceive myself when I assert that in this matter I only seek the greater honour and glory of God. I intreat your Eminence to do your utmost to come to the assistance of this poor distracted Church in Germany: because although it is true that her chief enemy is no more, still we are not yet by any means out of danger."

In a postscript to this letter, which is attested by Cardinal

Reisach, F. Clement mentions having also written in the same sense to the Hereditary Prince of Bavaria.

CHAPTER XVIII.

HIS ZEAL FOR THE PURITY OF THE FAITH. HIS JUDGMENT ON SAILER AND BOLZANO.

IN the year 1816, the Bavarian Government proposed Sailer to fill the vacant See of Augsburg. The Nunzio at Vienna, Cardinal Severoli, asked Father Clement's opinion, who answered according to his conscience: "That Sailer was famous not only in Germany and in Hungary, but also throughout Europe: that it was true that at the University where he was Professor, while others declared themselves against Christ, he alone spoke of Him, and that he had many pious men among his followers. But at the same time, his opinions and doctrines were not always in accordance with the teaching of the Church. He was much given to mysticism and was looked upon as the head of that sect: and therefore he did not think his appointment to the Bishopric would be a wise one."

At that time the Concordat was being established between Bavaria and Rome: and the Bavarian Government accordingly addressed a similar question as to Sailer to the Nunzio at Munich. The latter answered in the negative: upon which the Hereditary Prince Louis, who had a particular affection for Sailer, he having been his Tutor in old times, applied to Cardinal Convalsi to complain of the Nunzio's decision.

The Cardinal replied:

"We are not ignorant in Rome of the talents of Mong^r. Sailer, nor of the books he has written, nor of the influence he exercises over many persons: but we have also many things against him. He has intimate relations with persons holding very suspicious views and his conduct at Döllingen did not meet with the approbation of the ordinary: while at

Coire the Bishop has prohibited the reading of his theological works by his students .... your Royal Highness who so justly esteems the great virtues and sound doctrine of the venerable F. Hofbauer lately dead, will not be offended if I tell you the idea he entertained of Sailer by sending you a private note which he wrote upon the subject at the request of Cardinal Severoli, then Nunzio at Vienna: and I beg your R. Highness to read the concluding paragraph: "If Sailer be created Bishop of Augsburg, or any other important See, few ecclesiastics will like to be placed under his jurisdiction: for they think him more dangerous than Luther, who tried openly to destroy the Church of God, while Sailer does so secretly." ....

The high esteem in which your Royal Highness holds Sailer and the protection with which you honour him, have, however, so much weight with the Holy See, that if Sailer will draw up a public declaration, in clear and simple terms, of his obedience to the Catholic Faith, his condemnation of the principles and maxims of the schismatics and his anxiety to submit himself to the judgment of the Sovereign Pontiff as regards his writings and opinions, His Holiness will have no objection to promote him to the dignity of Bishop. .... If Mong^r. Sailer be really animated by the sentiments ascribed to him by your Royal Highness, he can have no objection to taking this step which will only redound to his honour ....

.... Cardinal Consalvi.
26. July 1820.

This letter was communicated to Sailer by the Prince, who, thereupon published a declaration of fidelity to the Catholic Church and a condemnation of any doctrines or opinions he may have held contrary to the Truth, submitting himself to the judgment of the Holy See.

In consequence, after some years, Sailer was appointed Coadjutor to the Bishop of Ratisbon, Mong^r. Wolf, and after his death, became his successor in the diocese: but he happily only lived to administer it for four years, dying on the 20th of May 1833.

Of Bernard Bolzano, Professor of Religion in Prague, we will only say a few words. In the later years of his life F. Clement heard from several Prague students the way in which Bolzano taught pure rationalistic doctrines: and alarmed and grieved at the probable consequences, F. Clement went to the Parish priest of the Court, the Theologian Frint (afterwards Bishop) begging him to warn the Emperor Francis of the fact. The Emperor desired a certain Professor of dogmatic Theology to give him a report in writing of Bolzano's teaching: but this man excused himself after a year's delay, saying, "it was difficult to give an opinion". The Emperor, much irritated at this answer exclaimed: "I am not a Theologian: but I know that such doctrines are not Catholic!" And he insisted on Bolzano being sent away from the Chair of the University, while his lectures to the young Academicians, being examined by the Holy See, were at once put on the Index. Thus was the wise judgment of F. Clement approved by the highest authority.

CHAPTER XIX.

FATHER CLEMENT DESERVES WELL OF CATHOLIC LITERATURE.

AT the time when F. Clement came to Vienna, Catholic literature in that City was at its lowest ebb. No Catholic books were published either by Clergy or Seculars: and even preachers had recourse to Protestant authors, who were quoted by all as models of eloquence and purity of language. While the Catholic were so inert, the Jansenists, Protestants and so-called "Illuminated" of all sorts, published an immense quantity of books in order to diffuse their pernicious doctrines and draw away the people from the

Church. It was not even possible to obtain a common Catholic Prayer-book and the people were obliged to make use of a little heretical book called "God is pure Love", which might have done for freemasons better than for good Catholics.

F. Clement was in despair at this state of things and exclaimed: "Look at the heretics, who labour day and night to diffuse their bad publications, men who would banish our Lord from the whole of Europe: and yet they spare neither time nor money to propagate their errors! If only Catholics would show one half of their zeal for Religion! But although these poor Germans would gladly read, I do not know any books I could place in their hands!" We may easily guess that F. Clemend did not content himself with vain lamentations. Although he had not himself time to write, he had many disciples and friends eminent in the literary world and he at once determined to set them to work, each according to his power and ability. He pointed out to them how the power of writing was a gift from God, to be used in His service and for the advantage of their neighbours; and thus he was morally if not actually the cause of the revival of Catholic literature in Vienna. He first started a little Periodical entitled "*The Olive Branch*" which appeared from 1819 to 1823, under the editorship of one of his disciples George Passy, and which contained a number of excellent articles on religion, literature and poetry. Madlener, Veith, Silbert, Antony Passy and many others contributed to this weekly paper, which was widely circulated both in Austria and throughout Germany, and the celebrated Joseph Görres, well knowing the lack of good books, had the happy thought of presenting the Redemptorists with a house in which they might establish a printing press.

Even over celebrated writers, like Schlegel, Müller, Buchholz etc., F. Clement exercised a great influence, for these authors had such an opinion of his judgment that they rarely published anything without submitting first their M. S. to him, when he corrected them, if necessary; and they were always ready to make the alterations he wished. Another valuable publication at that time was the "*Austrian Observer*" under the editorship of F. Clement's great friend, von Pilat. Following the inspirations of his beloved master, no article was ever admitted into this paper contrary to Catholic Doctrine: and as at that moment it was the only political and official Journal, the importance and advantage to the public of having it in good hands were incontestable.

Finally, we must mention one more work inspired by F. Clement which was the "*Little book of the Missions*", edited by F. Madlener and written by different disciples of F. Clement, which was intended in some way to take the place of the public missions and retreats which at that time could not be given. It contained, in clear but simple language, a compendium of moral and Catholic Doctrines, an instruction on the Sacraments of Penance and of the Blessed Eucharist, various meditations on the great maxims, a rule of life and a collection of simple litanies, indulgenced prayers and other devotions. This book had such an immense circulation that it is difficult to say how many editions it went through; and it produced incalculable good in Germany and Switzerland as well as in Austria; and likewise brought about innumerable conversions. The result of all these efforts was, that before F. Clement's death, Catholic literature recovered its old vigour, while his zeal inflamed the most able men to give their time to its promotion. Catholics were roused from their lethargy and the science of Religion and morals, which the Josephism of the previous years had well nigh destroyed, began again to flourish and bear fruit to the salvation of innumerable souls.*

* Much good was also done by a circulating library founded at F. Clement's instigation by his friend Baron Penkler. This good man was likewise President of the Society for the diffusion of good books founded by

CHAPTER XX.

THE VICISSITUDES OF THE CONGREGATION IN SWITZERLAND. F. CLEMENT SENDS MISSIONARIES INTO WALLACHIA. WHO WAS FATHER LIBOTZKY.

THE great fatigues endured by Father Clement in Vienna did not prevent his watching over the spread of his beloved Congregation. We may remember that a small number of Redemptorists under the care of F. Passerat, had established themselves at Vissach in the Vallais. They remained there from December 1807 to August 1811, during which time, the Parish priest, Adrian von Curten, never ceased showing them the greatest affection. Father Sabelli joined them from Vienna; and had the instruction of a youth of noble family, Peter Joseph de Preux, who afterwards became Bishop of Sion, and was much distinguished for his piety and ability.

When the Vallais Canton was annexed to France (in 1810) it was felt impossible for the Fathers to remain there: and the indefatigable Father Passerat tried to find a refuge for them at Würzburg.

The good Archduke Ferdinand would gladly have given them a house; but was afraid of offending Napoleon, who was the Protector of the Rhenish Confederation. The only thing he could do, therefore, to show his sympathy, was to send Father Passerat a large sum of money for his journey.

F. Passerat then went off to Vienna to consult the Vicar

F. Diesbach under the title of *"Christian Friendship"* and which still exists in Austria. When the Redemptorist Congregation was founded in *Sta. Maria della Scala* in Vienna, F. George Passy established a circulating litrary in connection with the house, which at present exists everywhere in the monasteries of the order. At Friburg in Switzerland, on Feast-days and holidays, a number of young workmen meet in this Library and after a few serious words, amuse themselves in that way with instructive and interesting reading. Great good arises from these meetings and of these youths, some have joined the Congregation and others have become good fathers of families.

General, F. Clement. But as no refuge could be found for them at that moment, in Austria, he returned to Switzerland and went to Friburg, where the holy Bishop of Lausanne, Maximus Guisolan, of the Capuchin order, received them with every demonstration of affection and obtained leave from the Council of State for them to live together, if not as a Community, at any rate, as individuals and private citizens. F. Passerat joyfully summoned his students from the Vallais to the new house in Friburg: where, under the guidance of a Prefect of studies, they lived in obedience to the rule and continued their philosophical and theological course at the College of St. Michael. In the year 1815 F. Passerat asked permission of the Government to live in community: but for two years this permission was withheld. Finally in 1817 the Prefect of Gruyères, John de Odet, announced to F. Passerat that in his Province there was a monastery which had formerly belonged to the Cistercians and then to the Trappists and was now in the possession of the Government. F. Passerat went to see it, liked it and at once applied for leave to establish his Community there. This affair was discussed by the Grand Council in 1818 at three successive sittings; and in spite of a very violent opposition, the petition was voted by a large majority. The friends of the Congregation took care to point out the heroic conduct of the Redemptorist Fathers when the typhus fever broke out in the camp at the time of the war; on which occasion those Fathers offered themselves for the work of the hospitals both in Friburg and Berne. F. Czech and two Polish priests, Biedrzyki and Schulski, had specially devoted themselves to those poor soldiers who knew no other language: and all caught the fever during their charitable work; though happily they recovered.

No sooner was the leave obtained, than F. Passerat hastened to take possession of this new Convent of Valsanta. It was a day of great rejoicing, Fathers and Brothers going in procession from the Parish Church to the new monastery and joyfully intoning the *Te Deum*. At last they had found a refuge where they could serve God together in peace and with regular observance of their rule, which for so many years had been impossible. So great was their satisfaction that they seemed to forget the lack of all necessary things and even the hunger which they suffered the first few days. Very soon after, they were able to begin giving missions; and that not only in the Canton itself, but also in Alsace.

About this time another foundation was proposed to the Congregation in Wallachia: which did not prevent F. Clement from clinging to the hope of soon sending his missioners to America: as may be seen by the following letter which he addressed to F. Blasucci the Father General in Naples on the 25th of September 1815.

"I receive constant letters from F. Passerat, in which he tells me that with the help of God, they enjoy perfect peace, that they labour without intermission, and that they are greatly esteemed by the people to whom they give spiritual aid. They have begun to give missions everywhere with extraordinary fruit. F. Passerat is indeed a most excellent superior: he is gifted with wonderful prudence and personal holiness; he is exact in the observance of our rules and seems to me to be patience personified. He is burning with zeal for the salvation of souls and seems to care nothing for fatigues or dangers. He has travelled on foot upwards of a thousand Italian miles, and twice he has been in this way to see and consult me at Vienna, actuated solely by the love of God and the interests of the Congregation. In a word, the Congregation possesses in F. Passerat a mirror of all virtues: and I therefore venture to beg your Reverence, that in the event of my death he may be my successor. He has the greatest desire to be sent with some of our Fathers to America and wrote to me not long ago hoping that this, his earnest wish, might ere long be accomplished.

Nothing would give me greater pleasure and I have done all I can to obtain the necessary passports for which I only await the answer."

Whilst F. Clement was preparing everything in this way for the foundation of a house in another hemisphere, Father F. Ercolani, a Passionist, had been just consecrated Vicar Apostolic of Wallachia by the Nunzio Mongr. Severoli; and hearing that F. Clement was just going to send some Fathers to America, implored him instead, to found a house first in Wallachia, where the needs, he declared, were even greater. F. Clement yielded and at once notified the fact to the Procurator General in Rome. He writes on the 4th of Oct.: "That his missioners were starting the following day with Mongr. Ercolani and that if he had consented, it was from the urgent intreaties of that Bishop, who had assured him that he had literally no good priests in his new diocese: that, in consequence, the Catholics were all relapsing into schism or becoming Mahometans: that there were thousands of German Catholics in Bucharest who could not find a single priest to hear their confessions or preach to them in their own language, so that they attended the Calvinist services to the great injury of their Faith."

F. Clement provided his missioners with money, church ornaments, a little library and all he could think of as necessary for the new foundation: appointing F. Joseph Forthuber as Superior and with him, the Cleric, Hätscher the lay-brother, Matthew Widhalm and the student, Joseph Libotzky, of whom we will say a few words.*

---

* F. Clement was always deeply interested in this Wallachian mission. In a letter to F. von Schlosser on the 23rd of Oct. 1816 he calls Bucharest "A *cloaca maxima* of every nation". "Many youths of 18, 'he adds,' have had no religious instruction whatever and do not know which faith to belong to. There are no schools nor any kind of education." He says also

He was born in Prague on the 17th of Febr. 1789, but his parents afterwards removed to Trieste, where they directed a mercantile house. His father died in 1808, and to help his mother, the young Joseph came to Vienna, where he obtained a good appointment. His first thought was to find a good Confessor, and the Count secretary, Herr Cavallar, took him to F. Clement. Josoph took great care of his little brothers and sisters and when his mother insisted on his taking them to the play, he yielded; but contrived by going too soon, to weary and disgust them with it.

On the other hand he would do anything to amuse them in other ways, while he introduced them to F. Clement, taught them to say the Rosary and told them endless stories of saints. When his mother went back to Prague in 1813 as nurse and governess in the household of the Duchess d'Arenberg, F. Clement took Joseph into his own house and finding him anxious to embrace the religious state gave him the habit secretly on the 24th of Septbr. 1814, and the following year admitted him to the religious profession. He was the only student whom F. Clement professed in Vienna, but was not, of course, allowed to wear his habit in public. Finally, on the 5th of Oct., with a passport which pretended that he was the servant of the Bishop, he started for Bucharest. On the 5th of Dec., Häscher made his religious profession in the hands of F. Forthuber and on the 23rd he and Libotzki were ordained priests. Henceforth all three shared in the apostolic labours of this arduous mission, first in a miserable house occupied by the Bishop at Ciopole: and afterwards at Bucharest. Of the labours of these missioners, F. Clement writes on the 23rd of Nov. 1816 to F. von Schlosser in these terms: "Our good Father Joseph is doing wonders in that savage mission, preaching in German and hearing

"that if he could only get help from Propaganda, he would found a large house there, from whence this vast field could be cultivated and a plentiful harvest gathered in."

confessions both in German and Wallachian: he has also established a school which was more needed than anything else. That huge city is like a forest full of wild beasts: there is an utter ignorance of every kind of Christianity: men seem to live without any thought of the future, only caring for spending the money they have earned in every kind of vicious amusement and excess. Parents bring up their children only to work: they don't seem even to understand they have souls. Fancy what a field of work there is for our good F. Joseph! In the simplicity of his heart, as the Bishop writes, he has already done great good and brought about a sensible change in the habits of the people. He and his companious bear every trial and privation with wonderful courage and patience, provided they can only succeed in bringing back these poor Wallachian sheep into the fold."

Nor did they confine their labours to Bucharest, but gave missions all round the country, as at Kimnik, Pitesty, Tergowest, Ploiesti, Campolongo and other places, but especially to the Bulgarians living on the left side of the Danube. Everywhere the people received them with open arms, for their spiritual wants were indescribable and for want of Catholic teachers, two entire counties had become Mahometan!

When the Fathers arrived in any of these places they went to the Inn, which was always a clay hut open alike to man and beast, and began at once to hear the men's confessions. The following morning the cattle were led out, the place made as clean as possible and then they heard the women's confessions: after which Holy mass was celebrated on a portable altar, Holy Communion given and then a very simple explanation of the first doctrines of the Catholic faith. After that, the Fathers went to visit the sick, settle lawsuits and disputes, for the priest in those countries is looked upon as judge, and then went away, blessing their poor and faithful penitents in the name of the Lord.

But the fatigues entailed upon the missioners were more than human nature could stand and greatly distressed F. Clement, who, if careless of his own health, was extremely careful of that of his sons. The Prince of Wallachia was very well disposed towards the Fathers: but the schismatics did all they could to embiter their lives: and the Bishop, who had been so extremely anxious to induce F. Clement to send them, did so little for them that they could only find a miserable little hired house in which to live. Finally, in 1819, F. Libotzky fell ill with a dangerous fever at Bucharest in consequence of the hardships and privations to which they were exposed. And soon after, the Congregation being established in Vienna, he and the other Fathers were recalled to the Austrian Capital. F. Libotzky had the happiness of seeing his two sisters on his return and finding them faithful to his early teaching. In 1826, he was made Rector at Vienna and was most watchful over the establishment of regular discipline in the new house. He was too weak and ill to preach, but was indefatigable in the confessional and often could not say his mass till 10 or 11 o'clock owing to the great number of his penitents. To his mother, who implored him to take more care of his health, he replied: "Everything happens to me as I wish." And on her looking astonished at this answer he added: "I only wish that which God wishes, and so I am always contented."

He visited his mother frequently during her last illness and brought her holy viaticum. She died on the 2nd of July 1833 as her son was saying mass for her.

In the terribly severe winter of 1840—41 F. Libotzky went early to say mass in the Church of the Redemptorists in Vienna, then went to see the Salesians and came back with a violent chill. His fever returned and on the 13th day of his illness he slept in the Lord. This was on the 26th of Jan. 1841. His death was most edifying; and in the paroxysm of his agony he was always speaking of and praying for his "dear Bulgarians."

CHAPTER XXI.

THE ANXIETY FELT BY F. CLEMENT FOR THE REESTABLISHMENT OF HIS CONGREGATION IN POLAND. A FURTHER NOTICE OF THE LIFE AND DEATH OF F. PODGORSKI.

FATHER Clement, as we have seen, had to give up Poland at the very moment when the harvest was the most abundant and the fields he had cultivated for 20 years promised the most abundant fruits. We may remember that when the Fathers left the Fortress of Küstrin, they were dispersed in different directions. F. Podgorski, with F. Clement's permission returned to Warsaw, where he lived near the Church of the Holy Cross, hoping by degrees to collect one or two of the Fathers with him. In the mean time, he gave missions, with the Lazarists, in the Dioceses of Warsaw, Plock and Sandomir: and though, of course, he was at the head of them all, he never would be made Superior for fear of drawing upon himself the attention of the Government. There was one mission in particular given in the church of the Oratorians at Studiana, at which the number of Communicants was above sixty thousand: which showed not only the happy result of the labours of the missionaries, but also the enormous fatigues they underwent. F. Podgorski, though so suffering, preached four times a day and from the pulpit went straight into the confessional.

F. Clement writing on the 22nd of Sept. 1815 to the Procurator General in Rome says: "One of the Fathers whom I left behind me in Poland, is now acting as Parish Priest in the Church of St. Nicolas, in the Diocese of Lublin. This church is under the patronage of a certain noble lady, who is very favorable to us and she has contrived to have another

Father settled close by. For this reason, I beg of your Reverence to obtain for this church the same indulgences as are attached to that of our Congregation in Rome. When order shall have been reestablished in Poland, I trust that this church may become, in time, the new centre of our Congregation. Hence these indulgences would be most useful to the people and of great advantage to ourselves."

Count Choloniewsky, who, in 1816—1817 had made acquaintance with F. Clement in Vienna, was most anxious for the foundation of a House of the Congregation in Podolia, where he had a large property. And Zacchary Werner was consequently sent by Father Clement and lived for a year on a farm of the Count's; during which time he was nominated Canon of Kaminiek. On this subject, Countess Mary Cecilia Choloniewska (afterwards a Salesian Sister) writes as follows:

"In the years 1818 and 1819 certain members of my family had agreed with Father Clement to found a House of the Congregation in Podolia. This proposal was so dear to F. Clement's heart that he resolved to come in person to see the place and obtain the desired foundation. All, at first, went well: when quite unexpectedly, the Russian Government raised some difficulties, which ended by becoming insurmountable. A 1000 pretexts were found to prevent Father Clement's journey; and letters backwards and forwards took up much precious time and advanced nothing. All this time, however, F. Clement was imploring us to persevere and not to despair, declaring he would be ready at any moment to undertake the journey. But God destined him to take a far longer one: for his death happened soon after and with him all hope of a successful result to the negotiations vanished. There must be many letters of Father Clement's in Podolia: but no one can tell where they are to be found. The barbarous fury with which we were driven from our monastery at Kaminiek prevented our being able to take any single-thing away with us. We were obliged to go away on our two feet and to leave every article behind us, with the prohibition of ever returning again to Russia."

The wise and pious Bulinski, Bishop of the Cathedral of Sandomir and author of a famous Ecclesiastical History, relates that a little later (possibly in 1820) a certain Count Tarnowski had obtained faculties to open a house of the Congregation at Piotzkowice, one of his properties in the neighbourhood of Kielce. Father Podgorski was named Superior with the permission to accept novices, several of whom came and were afterwards sent to finish their studies with the Lazarists at Warsaw. The Redemptorists hastened to restore the church, to enlarge the house and to establish a school; hoping the Congregation was now again firmly rooted in Poland. The Bishop of Cracow, Woronicz, was, in truth, a devoted friend of the Redemptorists. But the enemies of the Church were their enemies also: and at last obtained from the Grand Duke Constantine, Viceroy of Poland, a new decree suppressing the Community. Once more were the poor Fathers compelled to disperse, while many of their students entered the Seminary at Kielce and were ordained priests. In the year 1876, two of these men were still living.

F. Podgorski was recalled to Vienna and there lived many years in the new house of the Congregation at Sta. Maria della Scala. After a time, however, filled with fresh hope and having always, like Father Clement, the welfare of Poland at heart, he obtained leave from F. Passerat, then Vicar General, to return to that unhappy country. The new and zealous Bishop of Cracow, Monsg. Skorkowski, had set his heart on giving the Redemptorists a house in Cracow or in its vicinity: but the enemies of the Church were again on the alert and prevented the execution of his plan. However, to get as much advantage as possible out of F. Podgorski's apostolic zeal, the Bishop took him with him in all his pastoral visits; and the good Father thus preached everywhere with incredible success.

Between the years 1833 and 1839, he gave continual missions; especially one in a church of the Cistercians in Mogita, where more than 25 priests went to confession and upwards of eighteen thousand persons received Holy Communion: and another in the church of the Premonstratensians in Zwierzynice, where Gregory XVI. having sanctioned the beatification of the Sister of St. Hyacinth (Bronislava, Premonstratensian) a great function was held in the church attended by an extraordinary number of people from Gallicia, Russian Poland, Hungary and Silesia. It is needless to say that F. Podgorski was as indefatigable on that occasion in the pulpit as in the confessional.

When in 1844, the last Premonstratensian died who had administered a parish of 6000 souls in addition to the care of the monastery, the nuns gave Father Podgorski no peace till he had accepted the vacant cure. But the good Father's course was nearly run. Weakened by his tremendous fatigues and incessant toils he expired in March 1847 and was buried in that church. For over 50 years he had laboured incessantly for souls and not until the day of judgment will be known the number of those he saved! He lived in great poverty with one lay-brother and spent all his money in the relief of the poor and the adornment of his church, in which he would spend whole nights in prayer. He had an extraordinary gift of preaching and even when he was almost dying, he would go into the pulpit, where he seemed to acquire a new life. His style was simple and popular; he was intimately acquainted with the Polish language and was wonderfully clear in his explanations of the Catechism. May it please God to raise up for Poland men like unto him and his great master F. Clement, so that Religion may once more flourish in that unhappy land! At this moment there is but one Polish Father of the Congregation in Cracow, from whom we have had most of the details given above.

CHAPTER XXII.

A NEW PERSECUTION IS STARTED AT VIENNA AGAINST FATHER CLEMENT. FRANCIS I. SHOWS HIMSELF TO BE FAVOURABLE TO HIS CAUSE.

TO a man like Father Clement, chosen by Divine Providence to revive religion in Vienna and fight against the perverse spirit of the times, persecution could not be wanting. At first, as we have seen, he was placed under the surveillance of the police. And when, later on, his authority increased and his apostolic labours had produced such astounding fruit, his words and actions were continually watched in order if possible to find some shadow of crime in them as regarded the laws of the state. By such persons F. Clement was looked upon as a fanatic; a tool of Rome, who was endeavouring to upset the Imperial rescripts and promote superstition among the people. Josephism in certain quarters was still rampant: and every effort was consequently made to stop the mouth of so inconvenient a preacher. To arrive at this it was necessary, if possible, to add ecclesiastical to civil authority. And so, in 1816, F. Clement was through the machinations of the Police, summoned before the Archepiscopal Tribunal to give an account of his proceedings.

The Archbishop of Vienna, Count Hohenwart, although a personal friend of F. Clement's, was very old and so had not the courage to resist the pressure put upon him and thus authorised this inquisition, although he insisted upon being present himself to protect the servant of God.

The day appointed came: and Father Clement appeared, without knowing the object of the enquiry or in what way he was considered guilty. He was received with such incivility that not even a chair was offered him; and he was treated in fact, as a criminal at the bar, standing before his judges, who asked him insolently: "Who he was?" "Where he came from?" "Where he was born?" "What business he had in Vienna?" and even, "*to what religion he belonged?*"

Father Clement looked at his questioners with amazement, and at last not seeing to what lengths they meant to go, quietly answered: "*It is evidently not a right thing for me to stay here,*" and bowing to his judges, withdrew.

These men, very much amazed at his holy frankness and simplicity, looked at one another not knowing what to do next: but the Archbishop who was delighted at F. Clement's departure, turned to them and said: "F. Clement has acted like the Apostles and shaken the dust off his feet before leaving you!" and so closed the Court. His enemies, however, hoped that what they could not obtain from ecclesiastical authority, they would from a civil one; and so addressed themselves to Count von Saurau, Aulic Chancellor for the Kingdoms of Bohemia and Moravia, to whom they represented Father Clement as a Roman spy, who reported everything to the Vatican and whom it was necessary to exile as being dangerous for the peace of the monarchy. These calumnies had much weight with Count Saurau, who was an ardent Josephist.

But the good sense of the Emperor Francis I. detected the infamous plot and when it was proposed to him to exile F. Clement replied: "This I certainly shall not do: for he is one of my own subjects."

Having again failed in this quarter, Father Clement's enemies resorted to menaces to compel him to abandon his country voluntarily: and a pretext was not wanting. Father Sabelli had obtained permission from his superior to be transferred to Rome. But the Nunzio, Mongr. Leardi, who knew the state of things in Austria, thought that such a step was an imprudent one and wrote to Rome saying that F. Clement was most willing to let him go; but that Rome must consider how great was the distrust of the Holy See felt by the Austrian Government: and that they would only give Italian passports with great difficulty. He therefore advised F. Sabelli's being sent to Switzerland instead. It was consequently settled that F. Sabelli should start for Valsanta and he presented himself accordingly to the Police to obtain his passport. Interrogated by them with malicious astuteness as to the object of his journey, he answered in the sense that he and F. Clement belonged to a Religious Congregation, which was not recognised in Austria; and that they depended on a Foreign Superior.

This was a crime against the Josephin laws and was enough to subject Father Clement to a severe enquiry. Consequently on the 29th of January, a certain ex-friar named Braig, councillor for Ecclesiastical Affairs and Vice-Director of studies, appeared at his house, accompanied by a man named Kaufmann, Professor of Roman Law at the Theresian Academy and by a Secretary and servant. Father Clement was in the church and these men waited till he came back to his house. Then having turned out Professor Madlener and put the chain on the door, they commenced an interrogatory of the holy man, which lasted for three mortal hours: and examined every paper, letter, book, cupboard and trunk in his rooms without, however, being able to find a single thing which could tell against him.

They obtained, however, in another way, what they most desired: for, insisting on an answer to the question: "whether he were a member of the Redemptorist order?" he replied in the affirmative: and also as to "whether he did not obey a Foreign Superior?" And as they then informed him that he must either, renounce his Congregation or leave Austria, he answered frankly that "he had never broken his vows and that he would sooner leave his country". Being then asked "where he would go to?", he replied: "To America, only give me time till the spring and do not compel me to make such a journey in the cold mid-winter". The Commissioners enchanted at what they thought the success of their plot, drew up a paper in which they stated that "F. Clement had declared his wish to go to America and begging the Emperor to give him permission to do so". This paper they forced F. Clement to sign and even to add his seal. Then Braig insolently exclaimed: "Now all is done. We have everything in order."

"No," replied F. Clement quickly, "all is not done." "What is wanting?" angrily answered the ex-Friar. And F. Clement lifting his hands to Heaven said gravely: "*The last judgement.*"

The whole of this affair was nothing but a shameful intrigue, contrary to law and a usurpation of authority worthy of the severest chastisement. For this interrogatory was never authorised by any ecclesiastical authority, nor even by the Police, not a single member of which was present. But F. Clement, at the time, did not perceive the deception which had been practised nor the real nature of the inquisition, God wishing thus to prove the fidelity of His faithful servant; this trial eventually redounding only to his greater honour and glory.

As soon as these impious men had left the house, F. Clement summoned his disciples, as usual, for their examination of conscience. He was pale and evidently much moved; but he did not say a word and served them at dinner as usual. But whatever may have been his secret grief at thus seeing all his hopes destroyed of establishing his Congregation in Austria, he did not allow it to disturb his outward tranquillity or his peace of soul: and one who visited him in his room in the afternoon found him quietly humming a favourite hymn.

From his appearance, therefore, no one knew what had

happened, nor did he ever speak of it; but F. Madlener after his death heard the whole account from Baron Stift, the Emperor's physician.

The first consequence of the interrogatory was the exile of F. Sabelli, who received his passport with an order to leave Vienna immediately and the Empire within three days; so that he started on the 19th of Jan. 1819.

The next thing to be thought of was the expulsion of Father Clement himself, who expected it from day to day, as he owned several times to the Ursulines. In that care, he had made up his mind to go to America with F. Pajalich, for whom he had a great affection.

In the mean time, the paper was taken to the Emperor which pretended to prove that Father Clement desired to go to America and presented a petition to that effect. But the Emperor suspecting the quarter from which it came, replied: "If he really be anxious, of his own free will, to go to America I will not oppose his wishes: but as a subject of my Empire nothing will ever induce me to expel him."

In this way the enemies of F. Clement could not obtain what they wished: for God willed otherwise and Providence so disposed human events that the very means taken to ruin the work of His faithful servant contributed to consolidate and bring it to perfection. The news of the danger to which he was exposed came to the ears of the Archbishop, who was profoundly grieved at it and hasteued to the Emperor to make him understand the real state of the case and to implore him not to deprive the Archdiocese of the best priest they had. The Emperor was on the point of starting for Rome: but he gave orders that no one should dare attempt to molest F. Clement in his absence.

Even such precise orders, however, did not prevent F. Clement's enemies from making another attempt with the Archduke Ranieri, who, in the absence of the Emperor, was Regent of the Kingdom and from whom they tried to obtain an order for the expulsion of Father Clement from Austria. But they had reckoned without their host! for the Archduke indignantly replied: "I would that we had not one but six Father Clements in Vienna to amend the condition of religion in this City."

The Nunzio, Mongr. Leardi, arrived in Rome before the Emperor and speedily informed Pius VII. of the state of ecclesiastical affairs in Vienna and of the persecution to which Father Clement was exposed on the plea of his being a spy of Rome. And although the Holy Father could not treat directly with the Emperor as to the position of the Church in Austria, because he had declared he would not speak of it in person, yet he found means to defend F. Clement and to dispose the Emperor favourably towards him.

The thing happened in this way; one day the Pope was having a familiar conversation with the Emperor, when he said, "with what great pleasure he had heard that there were some really zealous priests in Vienna and especially a man like Father Clement Hofbauer, who was a real apostle and an honour to the Clergy", and added: "F. Clement complains of us at Rome because he says we do not treat the Viennese properly and says that much more might be done with the Germans if we acted differently."

These words sounded like a reproach to F. Clement; but were in reality his defence with the Emperor, who was very much pleased to hear them and felt great annoyance at the way F. Clement had been treated. Directly after his audience, he repeated this conversation to his Confessor, Don Vincent Darnaut, and added: "If any one has dared to give any fresh annoyance to that good Father Clement I shall be seriously displeased. If I only knew how to make up to him for the insults he has already suffered!"

His confessor, who was a great friend of Father Clement's, instantly replied: "All he wishes for is, to see his Congregation legally founded in Austria. If your majesty would only grant this, his great desire, he would be supremely happy and contented." Directly after, that is, on the 26th of April, the Emperor started for Naples, where, in the midst of the Fêtes organised for him, he did not forget F. Clement and wrote to Vienna to desire him to draw up the rules of his Congregation for his approval and also to mention under what conditions it could be introduced into Austria. It was impossible to describe the joy of F. Clement on the receipt of this Imperial order, seeing that the day had at last come for the fulfilment of his earnest desire; and no words could express his gratitude to that Providence who had permitted his late persecution only to draw therefrom so great a good.

Hence he set to work at once and in a carefully-drawn memorandum showed the end and object of the Congregation. And as missions were prohibited in Austria and even the name was held in abhorrence, he merely said that the Congregation occupied itself chiefly in instructing the ignorant and giving spiritual aid to those who needed it most, and so strove to be useful to both Church and State. Thus he described the scope of their missions without ever naming them.

When the Emperor returned from Italy, he sent for F. Clement and received him with marked favour, inviting him to ask him frankly for anything he wished. The holy man, without any hesitation said that the only favour he asked for was, that the Emperor would deign to allow the establishment of the Congregation in his States and grant them the Church of St. Maria della Scala. This church, one of the finest in Vienna, had been used as a warehouse for hay: and although it had lately been cleared out and partially restored, it had not yet been reopened to the public, all its revenues having been seized. F. Clement offered to take it and officiate in it without any payment: and the Emperor who thus saw himself spared from the necessity of making any endowment, granted it to him at once with evident pleasure.

The memorial F. Clement had drawn up on the 29th of Oct. 1819 together with the rule, was sent by the Emperor to the Archbishop of Vienna, to the Parish priest of the Court, James Frint, and to his Physician and Councillor of state, Baron von Stift, so that they might examine it: and this was a fresh and signal grace; because by thus avoiding the ordinary bureaucratic course, it escaped the hostile criticisms of his enemies and insured its ultimate success: for those three persons not only enjoyed the full confidence of the monarch, but were also the intimate personal friends of Father Clement.

Thus that faithful servant of God was permitted at last to see the realisation of his hopes; and it would seem as if he had now nothing to do but to gather the fruit he had sown and laboured for with the sweat of his brow. But God had decreed otherwise. Like Moses, who was destined to lead the people of Israel through the desert to the promised Land, in the very sight of which he slept in the Lord, without having been permitted to put his foot on it, so F. Clement, having led his Congregation through a thousand perils to the spot prepared for it by Providence, was not allowed to see the fruition of his labours, but passed to a better life before the final arrangements were made. And this he knew full well; and entirely resigned to the Divine Will and full of the deepest humility, he said smiling to his intimates: "A great honour awaits me, so that now I shall die willingly." In fact, at the very hour when the much desired edict of approval was issued, God called him to himself.

But before speaking of his blessed death, we must say something of the extraordinary gifts with which God honoured His faithful servant even in this life.

CHAPTER XXIII.

The extraordinary graces and miracles granted to Father Clement in his life-time.

THERE is no doubt that to Father Clement were granted extraordinary powers which marked him out as a privileged soul in the Kingdom of God. The first great gift of this sort which he possessed was the power of reading the secrets of men's hearts and knowing the state of their souls. We mentioned before several instances of this: how, with Matthew Widhalm, who had come to Warsaw to enter the Congregation, F. Clement knew supernaturally the anguish of his soul before he had ever spoken to him, and how this anguish was dispelled by his simple presence. In the same way he detected the struggles or vocations of his penitents and the most hidden throughts of their hearts, without any explanation whatever from themselves or others. Sister Thaddeus, Dr. Veith and many others constantly bore witness to this fact and added that, for that very reason, any thing like insincerity or double-dealing was so insupportable to him: for through this gift of the Holy Spirit, he detected it at once.

But let us mention one or two other facts to prove our assertion.

One summer evening, he was walking with some of his disciples on the banks of a little river called the Vienna which runs through part of that city, when they passed by a man, who looked disturbed and anxious certainly, but who was quite unknown to them all. F. Clement looked at him earnestly and then quickly telling his companions to keep at a distance, he went up to him and with a kind and courteous salutation, offered him a pinch of snuff and asked him, "why he looked so sad on such a lovely evening?" The loving words and manner of F. Clement so amazed this unknown individual, that he suddenly burst into tears and opening his heart, he at once confessed to him that he was going to commit suicide by throwing himself into the river. F. Clement quietly answering, "I knew it," began talking to him gently and persuasively and finally got the idea out of his head and induced him to bear his misfortunes patiently and finally to come to his house and make a general confession.

On another occasion, when walking with F. Clement on the banks of the Danube, his companion was amazed at seeing the good Father suddenly leave him and run with all his might towards a woman who was walking quickly in an opposite direction, but who was unknown to them both. She turned out to be one of the unhappy victims of the reduction of the national debt and had lost upwards of 80,000 florins, which was her whole fortune: so that from opulence, she was thus reduced to misery. She had been educated without any religious principles and so had no strength to resist or bear misfortune and was determined to drown herself in the Danube. She was on the point of accomplishing her purpose when she heard a voice, almost breathless from running, exclaim: "Do not make away with your life! Do not throw away your soul!" It was the voice of F. Clement to whom her intention had been supernaturally revealed, and who came up just in time to stop her. Startled and amazed, the poor lady turned round: and was to touched at his words and manner, that she yielded to his persuasion and came home: soon after which, she retired to the Ursuline Convent and in spite of all the kind proposals of her family determined to remain there, under F. Clement's guidance, whom she considered her best benefactor.

But not only could F. Clement read hearts: he could also foresee with certainty future events. Sister Welschenau relates that during her noviciate, her health was so bad that she feared every day to be sent away. Mentioning this one evening to F. Clement, he replied: "You need not fear, you will be professed, you will get quite well and live far longer than others who now have rosy cheeks." And as the time of her profession drew near and she was worse instead of better, he added:

"I can assure you you will be admitted to profession and when you are 28, you will become quite strong." Soon after, the Community met to decide upon her admission and unanimously resolved that she was too delicate to remain and must be sent away. When this decision was communicated to F. Clement, he replied: "You are all wrong, admit her to profession, for she will live to a good old age and render important service to the monastery."

F. Clement spoke so decidedly that the nuns felt he must have some supernatural light in the matter and so admitted the Sister to profession. Everything happened as he had foretold. At 28, her health was entirely reestablished; and at 76 years old and the 52nd of her religious profession, she related these occurrences exactly as we have written them down.

A lady named Benedicta Rizy, who was governess in Count Gileis' family, had tried in vain to be admitted into various convents. This was a great grief to her and she opened her heart to F. Clement one day, who listened attentively to her story and then said: "Be consoled, after some years you will be admitted into a Convent and your age will not be considered an objection." And so it happened: for when the Redemptorist nuns came to Vienna, she applied to them and was at once accepted: and afterwards became Superior of their monastery at Stein.

The Superior of the Ursulines, mother Ursula, was taken seriously ill and vomited so much blood that every one thought her end was at hand. But F. Clement reassured the Sisters, exhorted them to pray, gave them leave for an extra

Communion and offered up Holy Mass himself for her: after which he said: "The mother Superior will soon be well." In fact, having been for a long time delirious, she suddenly recovered and after a fortinght was able to return to the refectory like the rest. She remained Superior for another 15 years enjoying perfect health; which was the more marvellous as before that time she had always suffered from her lungs.

"One morning", (Dr. Veith relates) "Father Clement went to the house of his friend Klinkowström and found them all in great trouble, because their baby boy, Alphonsus, who was hardly a year old, was lying with his eyes closed and his legs already cold, apparently dying in the arms of his weeping mother. But F. Clement playfully patting the little fellow on the cheek said: "It is nothing: this evening you will see he will be hungry and eat a good supper." And so it happened. The child recovered at once, grew up strong and well and became afterwards an Aulic Councillor."

F. Clement prophesied several things regarding the Congregation and especially with regard to its establishment in Vienna after his death. "He often said", wrote one of his disciples, "that the Congregation would soon be founded in Vienna even when it seemed the least likely thing that could happen." And when we began rejoicing over it, he damped our joy, by adding: "This will not happen during my life; but directly after my death."

"I remember", wrote F. Veith, "that one day when we were speaking of this matter, F. Clement said: "As long as I live, nothing will be done: but after my death many houses will be founded," and so saying, he turned round on one foot as if to pretend he had spoken like a fool, which he often did when he perceived that any one had been struck at what he said; so as to cancel any admiration of his words by doing something which would seem foolish."

One of the Ursulines bore a like testimony. F. Clement

often said to them: "First I must die: and then the Congregation will spread. I shall be able to do more for my sons before God than I can do here," and again: "The admission of the Congregation into the Austrian States will not be signed by His Majesty till after my death when I shall be with God." He frequently prophesied, likewise, as to the entrance of certain men into the Congregation.

Sebastian Kiesel, who was a medical student and had no idea of becoming a priest, and John Madlener are instances of this. The latter, one day, was in great anxiety as to his salvation and F. Clement said to him: "You will become a Redemptorist and your eternal safety will thus be secured," words which filled Madlener with joy and consolation.

Canon Veith also relates the following:

"When I was studying Theology F. Clement said to me one day: 'As a preacher you will have great success: but I fear for your pride.' These words struck me as more than ordinarily true: and proved his really supernatural sagacity."

Among his great gifts F. Clement possessed another which was that of Science. We have already shewn how little he had acquired this from men or from schools. Yet his words carried weight with the most learned among his cotemporaries and no one could resist the wisdom with which he spoke or deny the justice of his decisious. Hence the extraordinary effect produced by his sermons, in which he seemed to be visibly assisted by the Holy Spirit. The kind of halo of light which often surrounded him and lit up his whole countenance was only a reflection of that inward light and knowledge with which his mind was illuminated. One of the witnesses for his beatification deposed on oath: "I saw him one day after his sermon go up to the altar and he seemed to me positively on fire with the love of God. The expression of his face and the light in his eyes were quite supernatural. I could not take my eyes off him; and even now, when I go into that church, I always remember the emotion I felt at that moment."

The painter Philip Veit coming one day accidentally into the Ursuline Church saw F. Clement surrounded with light: and Dr. Emanuel Veith adds: "It was impossible not to be struck with F. Clement's face especially at the altar; a certain light which I never saw on any other countenance beamed from his eyes and lit up his whole face so that one could not help watching it." And the same testimony is given by Louisa Xavier von Pilat on the occasion of a pilgrimage to the Sanctuary of Maria Zell, when he was wrapt in an ecstasy and "an extraordinary light was seen round his head." There is no doubt also that he was favoured with visions of our Lady and the Saints although he would never speak of them. One morning however, a man was kneeling near F. Clement's confessional, when to his astonishment, he saw a long procession of virgins dressed in white and bearing garlands of flowers, who offered them in passing to F. Clement in his confessional, to whom he, bowing his head answered aloud: "*I come! I come!*" The good man was so amazed that he went straight into the confessional and asked him what in the world it meant? F. Clement seemed much troubled at his having seen the vision also and said quickly: "Hold your tongue and do not mention it to any one." This was a very short time before his death and was evidently a celestial vision calling him home.

But we must speak now of his gift of miracles. Sister Louisa, one of the Ursulines, had a cancer in the breast which caused her great anguish. One night not being able to bear the pain, she got up and lent on the shoulder of the infirmarian, Sister Cordelia, and did this for so long that the poor Sister caught the disease and an inflammation set in with intense pain from the shoulder to the chest. After mass, the Infirmarian went to F. Clement and told him what had happened. He consoled and blessed her and told her to go before the Blessed Sacrament and repeat the "*Magnificat*" three times; after which she would be quite cured. And it happened exactly as he had said. Another Ursuline, Sister Catherine, fell down the stairs one day and was taken up without consciousness and carried to the infirmary where F. Clement was sent for and found all the nuns crying and preparing everything for giving her extreme unction, the Doctor thinking there was no hope. But F. Clement, putting his hand on her head, blessed her and said to the Sisters round her: "Do not be unhappy. Very soon she will be perfectly well and will go back to take her place in the Choir." Which happened as he had foretold; so that she celebrated the 50th universary of her religious profession and did not die till 1864.

Many such instances might be given: but we will pass on to another kind of miracle which was common to him: and which was, the multiplication of food.

This excited the amazement of all around him, who, at first, were so perplexed that they could not understand it: although by degrees they became convinced of the reality of the miracle. Thus, John de Passy, having often heard people talk of it who attended those suppers given to the young men of which we have already spoken, determined one day to verify the fact and took a seat next to him. They sat down a very large party and F. Clement took up a loaf weighing about 3 lbs. and divided it into 16 portions, leaving only a small bit for himself. Later on, he asked this one and that "if he would not have some more?" And if the answer were in the affirmative, he would cut another large piece from his own portion, doing it again and again, without the smallest apparent diminution of the loaf in question: and he did this so naturally that unless you watched him you had not an idea of it.

In the same way, John Sibert bore witness that with soup, or any other dish, he would distribute such a quantity as the tureen or plate could not possibly have held. He himself came in late one day and received this supernatural food which he said had a most exquisite taste: but if any one were disposed to make a remark on the subject, F. Clement would begin talking on some very interesting matter so as effectually to divert their attention. Canon Unkhrechtsberg narrates that F. Clement always had something good in his cupboard for unexpected guests, which had been given him by the nuns or other people: and that every time any one came in, he would get up and offer them something from these mysterious stores. When others went to look, the dishes would be found empty: but F. Clement laughingly saying: "O! you don't know where I keep my treasures," would go to the self-same larder and bring out enough for all his guests. But we will mention one more fact, deposed by one of the Sisters, Frances Plaschka, which we will relate in her own words.

"I was still a Protestant when I was sent one Friday to F. Sabelli, who lived with Father Clement, to give him a message. It was their dinner hour: and F. Clement asked me to stay and join them, which astonished me very much as he never had women to dinner. Moreover, I had just come out of the kitchen and I knew that only enough food had been sent up for two persons, or, at most, three. In consequence of this, I thanked him, but excused myself, saying I could not stay. And I had all the more reason to say so when I looked round and perceived there were already six people sitting down to dinner and I felt there would not be half enough food for them all. But he would not listen to my excuses and insisted on my sitting down to the table with the rest. Then F. Sabelli made a sign to me to watch what Father Clement would do. He accordingly, having blessed the food, dispensed equal portions to each of his guests and gave so much to each that they were more than satisfied. In the plate before him were two little fish, which

I knew were all that had been sent from the kitchen: he did not divide them but gave to each person a whole fish. To my utter amazement as I went on looking, I saw him distribute also other *maigre* food from dishes which appeared to me entirely empty and he helped out to each a great deal more than the dishes could possibly hold. These was a bottle of red wine also before F. Clement: he filled every one's glass and when it came to my turn, I begged him not to give me any, but he said I must have a little. When I looked at the bottle it was more than half full, although he had helped us all: and certainly there was only that one bottle on the table."

We should only weary our readers by further details of the like nature and will only conclude this chapter with a letter written by Countess Zichy (in 1865) shortly before her death, to the Holy Father Pius IX. In this letter she first begins by saying "how she and her Sister often went to his house to enquire after him: and on several occasions they saw the distribution of the food to the students from the very small portions sent to him by the Ursulines; and yet every one had more than enough." Sometimes the men would come late and to F. Clement's enquiry as to "whether they had dined?" the answer was invariably: "No". Then F. Clement would simply say to F. Stark: "Give me some more plates," and he would then proceed to fill them with food from dishes which to our human eyes appeared to be perfectly empty. In that way he multiplied the food according to the needs of each; but amazed as we all were, no one dared make a remark to him about it."

CHAPTER XXIV.

He begins to be seriously ill, but still continues his apostolic labours.

[1820.]

ALTHOUGH Father Clement had a strong constitution, yet the incredible fatigues he had undergone and especially the long journies he had made on foot in spite of rain and snow, or under the burning rays of the sun, and often passing the nights in the open air, had seriously told upon his health. Add to this, the long sittings in the confessional, the watchings at night by the bedsides of the sick and dying, and his advanced age, and we shall not be surprised at the exhaustion of his physical powers. For a long time in Vienna he had suffered from rheumatic pains which obliged him to use the Baden waters. He had also constant bad sore throats from his trying his voice too much: and finally he suffered a martyrdom from emeroids, especially 'as Dr. Veith, his Doctor and also his disciple, attests', during the last winter of his life. Twice he had a violent attack of fever his pulse going up to 150: but it was most edifying to hear him even in his delirium quoting passages from Holy Scripture, and from the Fathers, proving how such thoughts were engraved as it were, in his mind, to the exclusion of all others. And when the Doctors to stop these violent attacks of fever gave him very large doses of quinine, he submitted without a word, although he knew that in other ways this remedy was very prejudicial to him.

In spite of all these complicated maladies, Father Clement never relaxed his labours in the pulpit, in the confessional or by the bedside of the sick. In February 1820 the only person who could help him in his work, F. Stark, fell dangerously ill, and F. Clement instantly became his infirmarian and although, when he administered to him the sacraments, he said: "I am more ill than he is": still he continued his devoted services by his sick-bed and would not give up the nursing to any one else. Sister Thaddeus told him one day at that time: "That they were going to make a novena to our Lady of Dolours that F. Stark might recover": and he answered at once: "*Do so, but Stark will recover, and I shall die.*" And when the poor Sister replied: "O! we will pray even more earnestly that your Reverence may have a long life and recover your health," F. Clement added: "*Not our will be done, but the Will of God in Heaven as in earth.*" Sister Thaddeus replied: "The death of your Reverence would be the greatest possible misfortune to us all!" but F. Clement said quickly: "*Sin is the only real misfortune.*"

Up till the day he went to bed, he continued to hear the confessions of the Ursulines, although it was a great fatigue to him. Sister Welschenau seeing this, expressed her sorrow at giving him this trouble. But F. Clement replied: "*You must not think of that. It is only the pain which prevents my sitting.*" But to reassure her, he forced himself to sit for a little time. Then the sister begged him not to detain her long by speaking to her in the confessional: but he would not listen to her request and not only listened with his usual patience to what she had to say, but even kept her longer than usual in order to console her.

On the 4th of March, after having heard the confessions of several of his penitents in his house, he was seized with strong shivering fits and fever: but nevertheless he insisted on the reading going on as usual during dinner and consoled his disciples with his usual interesting conversation afterwards. The freshness of his mind did not seem at all impaired: and he proposed various difficulties and solved them as usual. Among the rest, that evening he asked: "Why, under the old law, fishes were never offered up in sacrifice?" And as no one answered, he replied: Because fishes have no voices wherewith to sing the praises of God." And then he went on to exhort them specially to praise God and to join in the public prayers of the Church, declaring that to him it was the greatest possible consolation to be able to sing with the people in church. But as the evening wore on, his weakness and the evident pain he was suffering were patent to all and his disciples wanted to go away earlier so that he might rest. But this he would not allow exclaiming: "*What does it signify if I go to bed a little sooner or a little later?*"

The next day, that is the 5th of March, being the third Sunday in Lent, F. Clement preached for the last time and spoke of the rigid account which every one would have to render to God of his thoughts, words, and actions, and of the good or bad use he had made of the graces received. And alluding to the account he himself would have to give very soon to our Lord, he exclaimed with the deepest humility: "*O! if in the whole course of my life, I had only corresponded faithfully to the graces I have received, what great good God would have done through my means!*"

It was with these words that F. Clement took leave of his hearers. This truly grand and apostolic man, forgetting all the good he had done, after having finished his course and corresponded so faithfully to the designs of Divine Providence, remembered nothing but the Evangelical Counsel and publickly declared himself *an unprofitable servant!*

In the mean time, his illness went on increasing and the medical men could no longer conceal their anxiety as to the result. Any one else would have considered that it was a duty to rest and obtain some relief from his increasing sufferings by remaining in bed. But instead of that, F. Clement would continue his work on behalf of his neighbours, until the violence of his illness utterly prostrated him. Accordingly very early in the morning, in an intense cold, he dragged himself to the church of the Mechitarists to hear the confessions of his poor: and then returned to hear those of the Ursulines. But the long sitting and the severe season, increased his terrible sufferings. On the 8th of March he said his last mass to those Sisters and then went into his confessional: but after an hour and a half, was forced to leave it from the violence of the pain. Before leaving the church, however, he sent for Sister Thaddeus and said to her: "Pray hard for me, for I feel very, very ill." The poor Sister added: "After these words, he left the monastery never to set foot in it again. I was quite heart-broken with sorrow when he looked at me (as I felt) for the *very last* time.

I cried my heart out, thinking what I should do when I could never see him more.

His words were the last Farewell I had on this earth. At that moment I felt and saw he was sick unto death; and the greater was my sorrow and desolation: although he had told me a month before that he should soon die."

CHAPTER XXV.

The precious Death of Father Clement.

[1820.]

IN spite of the serious nature of his illness and the acuteness of his sufferings, Father Clement insisted on going to the Italian Church on the 9th of March to sing a solemn Requiem mass for the repose of the soul of the Princess Jablonowska who had lately died at Rome. As she had been a great benefactress to the Congregation in Poland, he wished thus to show his gratitude; and all the more because her son, who lived in Vienna, had asked him to do so. He accordingly went there on foot with F. Pajalich: but it was as stormy day and the snow, which was already deep, continued falling. At the beginning of the mass, at which F. Pajalich assisted as Deacon and Madlener as Subdeacon everything went well; but at the commencement of the Canon, he was seized with such a faintness and became so deadly pale that it was feared he would never be able to finish the Holy Sacrifice. But God gave him temporary strength and he succeeded in going on to the end. When he got into the sacristy and was taking off his vestments, he received the young Princess Jablonowska who came to thank him for his great kindness and also to express her sorrow at the suffering it had cost him. In the mean time, Baron Penkler offered him his carriage, which he accepted with thanks, although the motion increased his suffering from the emorroids. The two priests, Pajalich and Madlener, went with him and also Herr Kraus, who accompanied him home.

Whilst Pajalich was helping him to undress he said: "I hope my dream will not come true!" a few days before, he had dreamt that he was crying over the death of F. Clement.

Soon after they had got him into bed Dr. Veith arrived, who instantly saw the danger of his patient: but he did not say a word to any one, so that those around him thought he might recover. They could not believe he would die till everything was settled for the Foundation of the Congregation in Austria, for which his personal presence and influence were, they thought, so necessary to its accomplishment. When they saw, however, how seriously ill he was, they determined to remove F. Stark lest the sight of the sufferings of his beloved Father should bring on a return of his illness: and Count Szechenyi had the kindness to receive him in his palace.

Every medical care was given to F. Clement, who submitted to the treatment with the docility of a child. He was ordered warm baths and obeyed, only begging F. Pajalich to read him a devout book in the mean while. As he had no laybrother in the house nor any skilled infirmarian, he had to be content with the services of his disciples, who, however, vied with one another in their care of the sick man: especially a rich and noble Hungarian, Louis von Grachenfels, who looked upon F. Clement as a real Father and served him with the love of the tenderest son.

We have often compared F. Clement with St. Philip Neri; and if they were alike in their lives, still more were they so on their death-beds. Like the holy Apostle of Rome F. Clement, in the midst of his sufferings, never ceased consoling and instructing his penitents, giving them wise counsels as to the choice of a future Confessor, and hearing their confessions even when he was in his last extremity.

He did not have many visitors during those few last days, partly because people were afraid of disturbing him: partly, because no one expected he would die so soon. During his short illness, F. Clement spoke little and only of edifying things: but continually repeated ejaculatory prayers. Herr Kraus having one day expressed his sorrow at seeing him in such a state, F. Clement answered at once: *"That which God wills, as God wills and when God wills, I will!"*

F. Rinn who often saw him in that last illness attests: "That F. Clement bore the most excruciating pain with the utmost patience and quietness: that he was always praying: and always uniting his will to the will of God." Dr. Veith adds: "That the last two days, he hardly spoke at all: but seemed quite separated from the world and engrossed in contemplation."

To relieve his sufferings the first few days he used to ask to change his position: but F. Madlener having said to him: "My Father, for the love of Jesus, try and be quiet": he answered directly: "Yes, yes," and joining his hands in prayer, remained without scarcely moving till he died.

He would not have even the alleviations to his state permitted by the rule of his Congregation and would die as a poor Religious on a straw mattrass. Even in the height of his sufferings he never thought of himself, but like our Lord on the Cross, only strove to procure some comfort for his faithful disciples.

Two days before his death, having had a letter from F. Petrak, he rose in his bed to try and find a picture of St. Alphonsus and desired it might be sent to him.

On another occasion when Madlener was standing beside his bed, he took his hand and pressing it to his heart said: "*My dear Madlener! Many secrets will be buried with me in my grave. I would tell you some of them; but you do not know how to be silent.*"

In the mean time, great was the anguish of the poor Ursuline nuns at the thought of losing their venerated guide and Confessor. Even when the news sent them on the 12th was a little more favourable, sister Thaddeus did not believe in the good tidings and was always in tears. When asked "why?" she replied: "Because I know he will die very soon, for he told me so himself a few weeks ago."

In fact, on the Monday, the illness increased so rapidly that there was no longer any hope. The Ursulines sent their servant, Marianne, to see how he was and when she perceived death on his face, she only burst out crying. But the holy man hastened to console her. "*Marianne, do not cry!*" he exclaimed. "*I am going home, and very soon you will be with me.*" She was a great strong girl and had no sign of illness about her, but eight days later, she was herself a corpse.

On the evening of Monday, gangrene set in, and Madlener asked him if he would receive his Lord? F. Clement murmured: "*Holy Communion? O! yes! yes.*" They hastened to fetch his Confessor, Dom. Francis Schmidt, who heard his confession and brought him the viaticum, which he received with the most profound devotion, after which they gave him the last Sacraments. During the whole time, he remained with his hands clasped in fervent prayer.

The next morning, Tuesday, his agony began and lasted for more than 24 hours. That very morning, Anna Biringer had gone to F. Clement's house to have news of him and on returning to her home, wanted to tell her nurse about him. But she interrupted her and said: "I know more about him than you can tell me, he is certainly dying. He has been here and told me many things." And she went on to say that that very morning at 6 o'clock F. Clement appeared to her, as usual, kind and gentle; and sitting on a stool near her bed, began talking to her on an affair regarding a pension she was to receive from the Emperor. And she having answered that it was all settled, he had spoken of the sad state of religion and how Faith had disappeared from the hearts of the upper classes and the officials, and then having given her some holy advice, he repeated to her three times: "*I am going into my solitude*", and then disappeared. This vision consoled the poor Lady and tempered the sorrow she had felt at the thought of her Confessor's death. And as she had been a great benefactor to him in life, so she felt that by this apparition he wished to reward her.

To return to our dying saint. Towards mid-day on Wednesday, the 15th of March, many of his friends were gathered together in his room foreseeing his approaching end and wishing to be witnesses of his holy death. Among these, besides his Confessor, were Herr Zängerle, Dr. Veith, Don Madlener, Don Pajalich, John Springer, the servant Marianne and others. All were in admiration at the extraordinary patience with which he bore his sufferings and at his recollection in God.

In the mean time, 12 o'clock struck and those who were gathered round his bed were so intently watching and praying for him that they did not notice the bell for the "Angelus". But the faithful servant of the Mother of God heard it and gathering up all his strength for a last supreme effort said to them: "*Say the 'Angelus!' do you not hear the bell?*" They were his last words. All knelt instantly to say it and when they rose they saw that F. Clement had turned his head on the other side. On looking closer they found that at that very moment he had breathed out his last sigh in the hands of Jesus and Mary. They burst into tears, but could not take their eyes off a face which inspired all beholders with such a feeling of holiness and peace. We believe that it was not by accident that F. Clement's death occurred at that moment but that it was as a reward for his peculiar devotion to the ineffable mystery of the Incarnation: a devotion, which by word and example he was always trying to infuse into others and which he suggested at the very moment he was expiring. In the same way, St. Alphonsus died on a Wednesday while the *Angelus* bell was being rung: another notable instance of Father Clement's resemblance to his Holy Founder.

The Ursulines had just sat down to dinner when they received the sad news. Their grief was such that they could not eat, but all with one accord repaired to the church there to implore of our Sacramental Lord for the eternal repose of the blessed soul of their beloved Father; and likewise to obtain through his intercession, a good and zealous confessor as his successor. A little later, some of F. Clement's disciples came to the monastery to give the poor nuns some more details of the last moments of the venerable departed. The sorrow of the Community was only softened by the thought of the new and powerful Protector they had gained in Heaven: while they thanked God who had granted them for seven years so holy and spiritual a guide.

CHAPTER XXVI.

The Solemn Funeral Obsequies of Father Clement.

NO sooner had the soul of Father Clement passed to a better life, than the body was vested in the habit of the Congregation, with a violet stole on which was embroidered the emblems of the Passion and his sacerdotal beretta on his head; and then placing him in an open coffin he was taken to the house of the Chaplain of the Ursulines which was then empty, and placed in a room on the first floor so as to give easy access to the public who wished to venerate the holy remains.

The room was hung with black and on some tressels in the middle the coffin was placed surrounded with torches and lights. The news of his death spread rapidly, even in the most distant quarters of Vienna; so that from all sides they hastened to look once more on the face of him who had been their father and their friend and to kiss the hand which had distributed so many benefits among them.

Towards evening the crowd round the bier was extraordinary and every one was anxious to touch the revered body with some object which they afterwards kept as a relic. It was indeed edifying to see that weeping, kneeling crowd who instead of praying for were invoking him and saying: "He does not want our prayers: it is we who need his intercession." Every one had some tale to tell of his sanctity and his charity; and all implored for some little scrap of his clothes, of his hair and of anything he had used or worn.

Every one, likewise, was struck with his expression, for he seemed not dead but asleep and with a sweet smile on his face, which was pale, certainly, but with a peculiarly bright glow which made every one exclaim: "Look at our Father, reposing like a Saint!" and Father Rinn declared that "his countenance after death was transfigured." Among those who pressed round the bier was the Countess Szechényi, who was not able to restrain her tears, as she kissed again and again the hands that had so often blessed her. And when some one implored her not to do so for fear of infection, she replied: "O! do not fancy such a thing for a moment. The Saints don't bring harm to any one."

Late at night when the room was at last clear, F. Rinn took a portrait of him, which was very successful and which is the origin of all subsequent pictures of our Saint. Under this picture he wrote those words of Ecclesiasticus (48. 11.): "*Beati qui te viderunt, et in amicitia tua decorati sunt.*"

The following morning the concourse of people was still greater. Every one was asking about the funeral: and all that could be said was that it would be as quiet and humble as possible, as there was no one but F. Stark, who was barely convalescent, to see after it.

But our Lord, Who, if He permitted His faithful servant to be humbled in life did not choose it to be so in death, so arranged matters that his funeral was the most solemn and magnificent one possible. And it would seem as if F. Clement had foreseen it: for when F. Stark had asked him his wishes respecting it, he merely answered: "Do not trouble about it all; God will see to it."

The funeral had been fixed for the 16th of March. Nobody expected a great concourse of people: no invitations had been sent out: and even his intimate friends had not made any special arrangements. But nevertheless, to the amazement of every one, not only all the streets through which the procession was to pass were crammed with people, but also the great Square of St. Stephen's. From all the suburbs came troops of poor, artisans, widows, children, labourers of all trades, each one only anxious to give the last tribute of affectionate veneration to their common Father and benefactor. From the University, both Students and Professors poured out with equal eagerness. Official men, soldiers, men of letters, priests and Religious, men and women of the highest rank, with magnificent equipages, were mingled with the people, only anxious to testify their intense love and veneration for him who was being borne to his last earthly home. But what proved the supernatural character of this manifestation was the way in which the students of the Archiepiscopal Seminary came in a body without any orders from superior authority or any previous intimation of the hour when the funeral would take place. On which subject the Prelate Willim, Dean of the Church of St. Peters in Vienna writes: "I had not the happiness of knowing Father Clement in life; but as a student of St. Stephen's Seminary we were all impelled to attend his magnificent obsequies. When we came into the Cathedral we saw to our astonishment that the great doors were thrown open, called of the 'Giants', which only occurs at royal or Archiepiscopal funerals. No one ever knew who had given orders to have them opened: but certainly such a sight was never seen in Vienna. The curious thing was that when we came home, the Rector asked each one of us "who had given permission for us to attend?" But no one could say anything save "that they felt compelled to go."

At 4 o'clock in the afternoon, the procession left Father Clement's own house for the Ursuline Church. Dom Francis Schmidt his confessor and Dom Zacchary Werner led the way. The bier of this poor and humble Religious was borne by twelve young men of noble family including Edward von Unkhrechtsberg, Frederick von Held and many others. The Ursulines had obtained permission to see it from the window of their monastery and Sister Thaddeus deposed: "That the multitude of people was so great of every class and rank that they could hardly move along . . . . people who met the procession asked with amazement what grand personage could be going to be buried? most of those who followed were weeping bitterly which was some consolation to us who were so heart-broken at losing such a Father. When the bier arrived before the door of our church F. Schmidt made the bearers rest and gave the absolution according to the rite."

The weather was gloomy and rainy and it was nearly dark by the time the procession arrived at the Cathedral. But here a new surprise awaited them. The whole Cathedral was a blaze of light and thousands of lighted wax candles were borne by the crowd, which was the more curious because it is not at all the custom in Vienna to have lighted tapers at funerals, and no one could ever find out who had provided them. In the process of beatification this question was asked: but no one could answer it. This enormous crowd entered by those gigantic gates and filled the whole Cathedral to such an extent that as Dr. Veith wrote "they could scarcely move." Yet there was no disorder and the deep religious silence of the people was only broken by the music. Then F. Werner in a voice broken by emotion, pronounced the absolution over the body, which was then borne to the mortuary chapel, amidst the tears and prayers of the crowd, who then dispersed as quietly as they had come. Truly God would thus bear public testimony to the holiness of His faithful servant!

The next day, the body was taken to the Cemetery of Sta. Maria von Enzersdorf, distant about three hours from Vienna, where Baron von Penkler had prepared a sepulchre for it next to that of his own family.

Many of F. Clement's friends accompanied the hearse to the cemetery, where, in the Parish Church of the Franciscans, Werner celebrated the solemn Requiem Mass; after which the body was placed in the sepulchre, Werner giving the last absolution. A marble cross was raised above the tomb at the foot of which was the following inscription:

Joannes Clemens Maria Hofbauer
Congregationis S.S. Redemptoris Vicarius Generalis
Natus Tassovici in Moravia an. 1751.
Obiit Vindobonae die 15. Martis an. 1820.
Fidelis servus et prudens.

On the octave of his death, that is, on the 23rd of March, a solemn Requiem Mass was sung in the Ursuline Church which his friends had united in decorating in the most beautiful manner. The celebrant was one of his warmest admirers, Professor Ackermann, a regular Canon of Klosterneuburg, near Vienna. So magnificent a funeral for a humble Religious was the talk of all Vienna. The "*Austrian Observer*" published the following notice of his death from the pen of Adam Müller.

"On the 15th instant at midday there expired in this city, at the age of 69, Father Clement Maria Hofbauer, Vicar General of the Congregation of St. Alphonsus de Liguori, called Redemptorists, and the Confessor of the Ursuline Sisters in Vienna. How much good, even in the most disastrous times, one single man can do who is faithful to his Lord, the very walls of St. Bennone in Warsaw would tell, if there were not thousands and thousands of other witnesses who by him were fed and clothed and led back to God and guided in the narrow road of true Christian virtue. When at a sign of the French Emperor, who then had the fate of Poland in his hands, Father Clement was compelled to abandon the magnificent and invaluable foundation he had made in Warsaw, he returned to his own country, and since 1808 lived in Vienna. The incalculable good he has done in our midst and the fruits of his apostolic labours will only be known to our grand-children. Nobles and peasants, learned and unlearned, weep equally the loss of their common father and guide: and those who have only known of him by report, will feel that a grand column of faith, of Religion, and of Patriotism has been cut down in our midst. The sorrow of so great a loss can only be mitigated by the thought of his exceeding happiness and the feeling that he is still living in the incalculable good he has done amongst us."

Even the Emperor was much afflicted at the news and mourned that he had only so lately appreciated him at his just value.

From that hour many and especially his confessor gave him the title of "*Saint*". Canon George Uhl wishing to console the Ursulines, told them: "That the Church had lost, in that admirable priest, a burning and a shining star which would not cease to give light for all eternity." And the Chaplain of the Court and Confessor of the Empress Caroline, Don Sebastian Job, speaking to the Salesians the day after his death, said: "Lift up your hands to Heaven and pray to our Lord that He may send fresh labourers into His vineyard: for yesterday He sent us a terrible blow, when He called to Himself the Apostle of Vienna, the column and example of all this Diocese. Pray to Him that He may in some way make up to us for this irreparable loss: and grant us the grace to imitate the virtues of His faithful servant; so that being united with him, we may one day praise and glorify our Lord for all eternity in Heaven."

Even in Rome, F. Clement's death made a great sensation: and the sorrow was felt by none more than by Cardinal Consalvi, who communicated the sad news to John von Pilat and Baron Bucholz, two of Father Clement's great friends, who where then in the eternal city.

CHAPTER XXVII.

Father Clement's personal appearance and character.

WE think our readers may like to have some idea of Father Clement's personal appearance and we will therefore quote the words of one of his first disciples in Vienna, Josephine Biringer.

"He was of middle height and naturally of a strong constitution, his chest and shoulders were broad, his head round and well formed, and his face rather round than oval. Although he had always a kind of dignified manner yet he was ever amiable and smiling. He generally spoke with his eyes half shut: but when he had to defend some truth or article of faith then a sort of light would shine in them which I can only compare to a lamp. He walked well; only his head was generally a little bent forwards. Though he eat little and was generally overwhelmed with fatigue, yet he could not be said to be either pale or thin. His strength and energy were shown in every action; but he had no symptom of pride about him. He always wore the habit of his Congregation: in the summer a black cloak of thin material with a high collar, which he used to throw over his arm so as not to show the rosary he almost always held in his hand: in the winter he wore a dark blue cloak. He hardly ever wore anything on his head even out of doors but a little black scull-cap. He had black hair which in the last years of his life became grey." A Salesian Sister, Maria Antonia Olt, adds to this description: "In the spring of 1816 I used to stand in the Vienna market to sell butter and eggs and one day I remarked a venerable priest passing by whose appearance struck me so much that I followed him with my eyes till he turned into a side street. I cannot tell you what it was in his manner which made such an impression upon me; but he looked like a picture of our Saviour bearing His Cross. I asked who he was and found out it was Father Clement, who was looked upon by all as a model of goodness and charity. His face positively beamed with sweetness and kindness; but I never saw him laugh."

Dr. Veith writes: "After 44 years he always appears before my eyes as I used so see him in life. He was a man of singular amiability; modest, simple, humble, prudent and whose charity was really engrained in him. He was always burning with love towards God and man, rooted in Faith, beyond measure merciful, and one who never sought his own interests but always those of Jesus Christ. In Faith and charity he was really an Apostle, who made himself all things to all men, and who was full of the grace of God. I do not hesitate to compare him to St. Philip Neri and St. Vincent of Paul; for in the authority he exercised over the hearts of men he certainly was not second to either of those two great Saints." And later on he writes: "I was always persuaded that he practised all Christian virtues in an heroic degree: that is with all the strength of his soul; in the full vigour of his faith; with habitual and remarkable abnegation of himself; with extraordinary purity of intention; with intrepid courage both in his works and in his love of suffering for the glory of God and of the Church; above all, with a charity and a mercifulness which I never saw equalled. And I can positively assert that he practised all these virtues up to the very last moment of his life."

Canon Greif expresses himself in the same manner. "He was a man after God's own heart, full of love and simplicity and a mirror of virtue to all around him. He had the secret of drawing to himself the hearts of men and of treating each according to their different natures and dispositions. This good shepherd never hesitated to go out of his way to seek a sheep that was lost and never wearied till he had brought him home to the fold and put him in the way of salvation. His extraordinary charity disarmed even his bitterest enemies. The only person he never appreciated or took any care of was himself: and he would give away every single thing he had. Such was his life."

Canon Maximilian Hurez adds:

"What I admired so much in F. Clement was not only his acuteness of intelligence and the great clearness of his judgment, but his sobriety of spirit: his continued zeal in prayer; his constancy in the practice of every virtue; his incessant striving after perfection; the sweetness and truly Christian courtesy with which he dealt with every one, noble or simple: his extraordinary prudence in action: his intense gratitude for favours received: his courage amidst the most unjust persecutions; his remarkable modesty in words and works; his gentleness in correcting or teaching: his inexhaustible charity towards the poor; his extraordinary temperance as regarded himself; his great vigilance in guarding purity of heart: his extreme circumspection in the guidance and direction of souls; his warm attachment and devotion to the Holy See: his extreme anxiety for the maintenance of Catholic Doctrines in all their purity: his lively faith: his unshaken hope; his charity both towards God and his neighbour — a charity which was ever ready for every sacrifice; his entire submission to and acceptance of the will of God, whether in moral or physical sufferings; his strength of mind in bearing trials and adversities: and finally his invariable perseverance in the exercise of all these rare virtues until his death."

We will conclude with a few words from Sister von Welschenau and Louisa Xavier von Pilat whom we have often quoted:

"F. Clement was never out of humour or sad: neither was he too gay. On his face there was always the same expression of sweetness and peace and union with God."
"Sometimes there was an extraordinary light on his coun-

tenance, as if it were the reflection of the purity of his soul, and that blessed tranquillity of spirit which is the fruit of holy joy. There was always a quiet brightness and joyousness about him which was never disturbed by any passion." In fact every witness in the process of his beatification spoke in a like manner. Some called him a *Seraphim* burning with Divine Love; others an *Angel* of peace and consolation; a third would speak of him as an *Apostle* in zeal, and as a *Martyr* for the rights and liberties of the Church. All joined in calling him the *Father* of the poor and an *example* of every virtue.

# THE FOURTH BOOK.

CHAPTER I.

ON THE FOUNDATION OF THE CONGREGATION IN VIENNA.

[1820.]

WITH the death of Father Clement all hope of the establishment of the Congregation in Vienna appeared to have vanished. Such a work required a man of talent and energy and with special graces for the purpose: and who could be found to possess them in the same degree?

The only Redemptorist then remaining in Vienna was Father Martin Stark: but he was a stranger in Austria; young and without experience; nor would it have been possible for him to conduct such delicate negotiations or to govern a Religious Community in its birth. F. Clement had said in confidence to his disciple Madlener: "If the Congregation be established in Vienna, I shall send F. Stark into Switzerland; for he is not fit to be Superior."

Hence F. Clement's companions were thrown into the utmost despair by his death: and some of his disciples had almost made up their minds to give [up the idea of forming a Congregation of Redemptorists and to go and join the Oratorians. But such was not the will of God. Don John Madlener, who was the one of F. Clement's disciples who best understood his wishes, who had entered so greatly into his spirit and to whom he had confided most of his plans, began by determining to continue the evening conferences of young men which had done such good and persuaded F. Darnaut, the confessor of the Emperor, to undertake their direction. This from veneration towards F. Clement, he willingly agreed to; and soon proposed that these conferences should be held in his own apartment in the palace, instead of in Madlener's house. The excellent spirit which F. Darnaut discovered in these young men, their pious feelings and the solid principles which F. Clement had instilled into them, pleased him so much that when they came to him one day, in a body, and made known their earnest wish to be admitted into the Redemptorist Congregation as soon as it was legally established in Austria, he decided, by the advice of the Councillor of State, Baron Stifft, to present at once a petition to the Emperor for the fulfilment of his old promise to Father Clement.

Accordingly, the petition was drawn up and signed by 30 of F. Clement's disciples, some of whom wished to enter at once and the rest, as soon as their worldly affairs could be settled. F. Darnaut presented it and it was most favourably received. This was only six weeks after F. Clement's death and already his prophecy was being fulfilled! On the 30th of April the Imperial Decree appeared, approving of the Foundation of the Redemptorist Congregation in Austria, giving them leave to receive novices, and assigning to them, in Vienna, the Church of St. Maria della Scala, with the house adjoining. In addition to this, the Emperor wrote a letter with his own hand to the Archbishop, begging him to arrange with Madlener for the immediate formation of the Community.

Great was the joy and consolation of Father Clement's friends and spiritual sons when this decree was promulgated and every one was filled with admiration at the wonderful leading of God's Providence. Who could have thought it possible that a Congregation so devoted to the Holy See, so contrary to the spirit of the times, could be approved of in a State where Josephism was still rampant and all the men in power were its bitter enemies? Well might Archbishop Hohenwart exclaim to Madlener: "Look at the effect of Father Clément's prayers! God has dealt with him as with Moses, to whom He showed the Promised Land. Now he is praying for you in Heaven and he is more powerful and more useful to you there than he could be on earth."

Madlener being still Chaplain of the Church of St. Augustine could not at once enter the Congregation: but he worked energetically in its formation with F. Stark and the little band who had gathered round him; and obtained himself all the necessary faculties from the ecclesiastical and civil authorities. But they could not at once take possession of St. Maria della Scala, for the repairs of the church were not yet completed and the house was still occupied by certain tenants. However the holy Sons of St. Francis came to the rescue, and in their charity offered F. Stark and his companions part of their convent of "St. Jerome" until their new quarters were ready. They also gave them free entrance to their choir, sacristy and church for all spiritual exercises, and likewise the use of their refectory at certain hours. In this way the little community in Vienna was begun.

The 19th of May, the vigil of Pentecost, was chosen for the giving of the habit to the first novices, who if they were not numerous, were all remarkable men in their different ways and had all been disciples of Father Clement.

It was a source of edification to all to see these young men, mostly of noble birth, carrying their own straw mattrasses through the streets of Vienna to the Franciscan Convent. They were seven: the Priest Pajalich, who had already received from F. Clement the permission to wear the habit of the Congregation except the white collar: Francis

Springer, Edward Cav. von Unkhrechtsberg, Frederick von Held, and Antony Prigl. There was also a certain Nossal, an ex-novice Premonstratensian, and a lay-brother, Fink.

Great was the joy and consolation of the devout followers of F. Clement, when on the Feast of Pentecost, they saw them serve at the altars in the Religious habit which F. Stark had given them the day before. The necessity of the case had created F. Stark Superior and he did his utmost to instruct the novices in the practices of religious life. Frederick von Held who was well known in Vienna and had a good judicial practice, gave incalculable help to F. Stark, and Pajalich was made master of novices. On the 30th of June the young community experienced a heavy loss in the death of the venerable Archbishop Hohenwart, who had always been their greatest friend and protector. On the 2nd of August, the Feast of St. Alphonsus, two fresh novices joined their Congregation, Francis Doll, and Francis Kosmacek, who took on that day the habit of the Congregation, and they were joined a little later by Joseph Puz and Joseph von Ries, so that the little community increased steadily. Father Stark, however, feeling strongly the need of a more experienced Superior, intreated permission of the Emperor to call in a stranger: and the Emperor, without consulting his ministers and listening only to the dictates of his own heart, granted the desired permission: so that on the 20th of October F. Passerat arrived in Vienna, the Father who had succeeded F. Clement in the charge of Vicar General of the houses beyond the Alps, and F. Clement's most intimate friend.

P. Passerat was received by the Vienna novices as an Angel from Heaven, for they knew him well by reputation, having so often heard of him from F. Clement. And his venerable and dignified appearance and edifying life only increased their high esteem for his person and character. He undertook at once the education of the novices and the spiritual direction of the Community, leaving the care of temporalities to F. Stark.

On All Saints' Day he gave the habit of the Congregation to Dr. John Madlener, who had done so much for the foundation and who was the twelfth to receive the habit in the Franciscan Convent.

The restoration of the Church of Sta. Maria della Scala and the repairs of the house, being completed, Christmas Day was chosen to take possession of the new buildings by the Congregation. On Christmas Eve, likewise, F. Passerat gave the habit to three more of F. Clement's disciples, Antony Passy, Count Charles Welsersheimb and John Reymann.

On Sunday the 24th of December the Auxiliary Bishop and Vicar Capitular, Matthew Steindl, solemnly blessed the church, said mass and, in an eloquent sermon, declared it opened anew for public worship. In the mean while, F. Passerat studied in every way to form his novices into perfect Religious and to infuse into them the spirit of St. Alphonsus. He succeeded admirably and on the 2nd of August of the following year nine of them were admitted to their Religions Profession, among whom were Pajalich and Madlener. Father Passerat also recalled the Fathers who had been sent to Wallachia, the work in Vienna increasing daily.

The good lay-brother, Emanuel Kunzmann, who on the suppression of the Congregation in Warsaw had retired to the Cistercian Abbey of the Holy Cross, no sooner heard of the new Vienna foundation, than the hastened to join it; only too happy to end his life with his Religious bretheren.

The Congregation at Sta. Maria della Scala increased so rapidly that the house could not contain them; and the centre of a populous city being unfitted for a noviciate, F. Passerat determined to look for a second house in the country; and in this matter Divine Providence again came to their aid; for Archduke Maximilian d'Este, F. Clement's old friend and benefactor, heard of their need and bought them a house at Weinhaus near Vienna; to which place the noviciate was removed; and remained there till, after some years, it was transferred to Eggenburg, a small town in the diocese of St. Hippolytus, where it still exists.

In course of time, many more of F. Clement's old friends and disciples joined the Congregation including John von Pilat, the Court Architect, the Court Chaplain, Joseph Reymann, and many others. Upwards of 30 of his spiritual sons thus entered the Community and showed themselves by their piety and zeal to be worthy followers of their holy Father and friend.

CHAPTER II.

THE VENERATION SHOWN TO F. CLEMENT'S TOMB IN STA. MARIA DI ENZERSDORF. SOLEMN TRANSLATION OF HIS RELICS TO VIENNA IN 1862.

FROM the earliest days of the Church the tomb of the Saints have been places of pilgrimage and devotion: so that it was no wonder that the Sepulchre of F. Clement at Enzersdorf became at once an object of veneration to the faithful. Francis Fuchs, Councillor of Finance, asserted in the cause of his beatification, "that the crowds who flocked from all parts and of every class to pray at his tomb was extraordinary." The cemetry was some way from the town and ordinarily closed: so that the people would either scale the walls or bribe the porter to open the gates. This man, however, complained bitterly of the way the pilgrims wasted his time and his money; and declared "that they would stay for hours and gather every little flower which grew near his grave and even carry off the earth, from their intense devotion to his relics." Nor was this a barren devotion: for many were the prayers granted through F. Clement's intercession: and a great many of his friends begged to be buried near him; so that if any one now visits that spot, they will find the names of many whom we have mentioned in this biography.* In the year 1846 some of F. Clement's most devoted disciples wished to examine his mortal remains: and accordingly the sepulchre was opened in the presence of the Father Guardian, the Parish Priest of the place, Father Weidlich and other Redemptorists, a surgeon and various other persons. The dress appeared at first to have remained intact: but on exposure to the air it was reduced to dust. Only the violet stole and the berretta were found fresh and entire, although they had been interred for 26 years! And as these two things are the special signs of the Priesthood indicating jurisdiction and the faculty of announcing the Divine Word, so it seemed as if God had permitted this miracle of preservation to glorify His servant, who had been so indefatigable in the administration of the Sacraments and in preaching eternal truths. F. Weidlich carried both off as precious relics and hid them in his own room during the revolution of 1848. In his last illness he frequently impressed on the woman of the house the importance of these relics: so that after his death, when the Congregation was reestablished in Vienna, she brought them back to the house; but they were given to some one who did not know their value and so they were unhappily lost.

The examination of the relics being concluded the bones were enclosed in a new coffin and placed in a sepulchre which had been prepared on purpose with a stone cover, on which was engraved his name. And here they remained till the year 1862.

---

* Among the rest we find the tombs of Werner, of Adam Müller, of Frederick Klinkowström and his wife Louisa, of Baron Paul and Maria Hübner, of Elisabeth and Mary Paul von Pilat. of Francis Bernard von Bucholz, of Baron Penkler, of Münch-Bellinghausen, of Charles Ernest Jarke and many others. awaiting with him the moment of a glorious resurrection.

But the Redemptorist Fathers could not bear to be separated from the body of one, who, after St. Alphonsus, they looked upon as their founder, and so on the 3rd of November 1862 the Rector of Sta. Maria della Scala, F. Joseph Kassewalder, accompanied by other priests, by the doctor of the district of Hietzing, Dr. Effenberger, and the Surgeon Seng, arrived at the convent of the Franciscans at Enzersdorf towards evening. Then, the Redemptorists and the Franciscans went in procession to the cemetery, from whence they carried the precious case of relics and deposited them in an outer coffin of zinc. The next morning it was taken to the church and after the absolution according to the rite, the Redemptorists and Franciscans accompanied it to the limits of the parish, followed by a multitude of the faithful, weeping at the loss of what they considered so great a treasure. The precious case was then put in a coach and when it came to Hietzing, a village near Vienna, all the bells began to toll. It was late when it arrived at Sta. Maria della Scala; but nevertheless not only the church but the Piazza and the adjoining streets were so thronged with people that it was with the utmost difficulty the carriage could draw up to the door of the church. Here the sacred relics were received by a large number of priests to the sound of the ringing of a multitude of bells. All the Superiors of the different Austrian Houses were present with F. Mangold, as the representative of the Archduke Maximilian, F. Antony Miller, Rector of the College of Altötting, and Michael Benger, master of novices, who had come from Bavaria. But among all the Redemptorists none came more joyfully than three of F. Clement's special disciples, F. F. Hätscher, Král and Petrak, the latter of whom had the honour of bearing the cross which ushered in the triumphal entry of their beloved Father into that church. Finally, after the Provincial F. John Jentsch, had received the precious treasure consigned to his care, the office of the dead was sung and the absolution given. Then the coffin being closed and sealed, it was placed in a mausoleum erected at the Gospel side of the High altar. The upper part of this marble tomb represented the recumbent figure of this great servant of God and is the work of the famous sculptor, Gassner.

At this solemn function, the Apostolic Nunzio and the Archbishop of Olmütz (von Fürstenberg, now both Cardinals) were present, together with several other eminent ecclesiastical dignitaries.

God deigned to show by an extraordinary event His approval of the honour done to our Saint. A woman who was infirmarian in the house of the Sisters of Charity at Gratz, was one day violently assaulted by a patient in delirium, who threw her on the ground and stamped on her chest, so that the poor nurse had ever after violent spittings of blood which medical science had tried in vain to cure. She had that day obtained leave to assist at this function in Sta. Maria della Scala, and all of a sudden felt a certainty that F. Clement would heal her. She drew near the relics imploring his intercession and instantly obtained what she desired. This sudden cure was the first of many which it pleased God to grant through the prayers of His servant in that church.

The following day being the 5th of Nov., the Cardinal Archbishop, Rauscher, sang a solemn High mass of Requiem for his beloved Father and Director and F. Staffler pronounced a touching panegyric on this great servant of God, which was published in all the papers.

From that day to this, the concourse of the faithful round F. Clement's tomb has gone on steadily increasing and the fresh wreaths and flowers which are continually placed there are an irrefragable proof that his memory is held in grateful veneration by many faithful hearts.

The place which his remains had occupied in the cemetery at Sta. Maria in Enzersdorff was never given to another, but left as it was and looked upon as a sacred spot: and Canon Unkhrechtsberg adorned it with the following inscription:

Ossa Ven. S. Dei Clementis M. Hofbauer inde Viennam translato,et in Ecclesia B. M. V. ad Litus deposita sunt die 4. Nov. 1862.

CHAPTER III.

His apparition after death. His miracles.

IT was not only by the veneration paid to his tomb that our Lord was pleased to glorify His servant, but by his apparitions and the miracles wrought through his intercession after his death.

We have already mentioned his appearance to F. Pilat to whom he smoothed the way for his admission into the Congregation: we will now relate what happened to F. Werner, which he announced publicly in the pulpit on the 1st Sunday in Advent 1822 in the Ursuline Church.

"I shall not live much longer," Werner began, "for Father Clement has warned me that my end is at hand. I had finished my night prayers and had just laid down on my bed when my room was filled with a bright light which surpassed that of the sun. In the midst of that light I saw F. Clement, my beloved father, master, and friend. He held in his hand a lily, an olive branch and a palm and spoke to me as follows: "Zacchary! come, come, come quickly!" and having said those words he disappeared. This apparition was no imagination on my part. I was neither asleep, nor dreaming: and I am as certain that I saw F. Clement as I am that I am now alive and that I am at this moment in church before Our Lord present in the Holy Eucharist. From that instant, a weakness which I never felt before, has never left me and I am quite sure I shall die very soon."

His death happened, as he had foreseen, only a week or two later.

In the same way F. Clement appeared to one of the Ursuline nuns, Sister Sebastian, who for her piety and simplicity was much esteemed by the Community as well as by Father Clement. One day he jokingly called her "a Saint." She replied. "I? a poor worm! But your Reverence, who converts so many sinners, baptises Jews, instructs such multitudes of people and bears our Lord to the sick and dying, well deserves that title, for those are the acts of a Saint."

F. Clement turning laughingly to the other Sisters replied: "She has paid me in my own coin!" and then added: "I will assist you at the hour of death and send you to Paradise." "That is all right!" exclaimed Sister Sebastian. "Recollect your Reverence has pledged your word: and I shall remind you of your promise." Accordingly many years after F. Clement's death, this good Sister's last hour came; and she, remembering well his words, called upon him for help. She had scarcely invoked him when her whole face lit up with joy and she cried out: "O! Father Hofbauer! Father Hofbauer! he is here!" after which she expired directly and with such calm and peace and joy that the expression remained long after her death. Evidently F. Clement had fulfilled his promise and came to conduct her home.

Another fact of the same nature is related of an American Lady, who had become a Catholic in Rome in 1868, and two years after, fell into a consumption. The thought of death was terrible to her and still more to her husband. In this state she turned to Father Clement with confidence and hope: and made a novena before his picture and a relic she had obtained of him. Towards the end of the Novena he appeared to her, surrounded with light and looking at her with great tenderness pointed with his finger to Heaven and then disappeared. She understood at once that she was to prepare for the last dread passage; but with that vision of

Heaven, her fears were dispelled and she told her husband what she had seen; which gave him also such consolation that both willingly accepted whatever should be the will of God.

We will not weary our readers with the details of all the miracles operated by Father Clement since his death but only mention a few of the principal ones:

Magdalene Kuntz cured of varicose veins which had burst internally and threatened her life—1862.

Baroness Agnes Fiath-disease of the hip joint — 1864.
Maria Hoffman—dangerous tumour—1864.
Anna Berger—paralysis—1864.
Catherine Seidel—lameness and twisted legs—1864.
Vincent Felber—dropsy—1866.
Mary of St. Lucia—obstinate hemorrhage—1865.
Magdalene Sonnleithner—breaking of right arm—1869.
Mary Dunkel—dangerous confinement—1864.
Francis Peschke—a dead arm restored to life—1876.
The Superior of the Franciscans — inflammation of leg —1881.
&c........ &c........

Each and all of these cures were instantaneous, and each case had been given up by the doctors, who have since affirmed that the recovery of their patients in each instance could only be ascribed to miracle.

No less remarkable were the results of the invocation of F. Clement in temporal concerns. People were unexpectedly saved from ruin; fires were suddenly quenched; men desperate from poverty, obtained work; servants found good places; totally unhoped-for aid came from various quarters to the destitute—in fact, under whatever circumstances his intercession was asked for in faith and simplicity, the want was immediately supplied. May the narration of the graces thus obtained by his intercession, increase the faith of our readers in his patronage and may they experience in their own persons the beneficial effects of his power with God.

CHAPTER IV.

THE FULFILMENT OF FATHER CLEMENT'S PROPHECY AS TO THE SPREAD OF THE REDEMPTORIST CONGREGATION.

AT the time of Father Clement's blessed death the Congregation only numbered 43 priests and a few lay-brothers north of the Alps.

Revolutionary storms prevented him from gathering his disciples together in a regular Community and the only existing one was in Switzerland, which after 1828, was transferred to Friburg. He had laboured hard to establish a house in France with F. Passerat and had been able to purchase a little property at Bischenberg in Alsace: but it was not occupied till after his death.

To Bucharest he had sent (as we have seen) three missionaries, who, in the insurrection of 1821 were compelled to fly and return to Vienna.

In fact, in 1820 almost all the Fathers were dispersed in various parts of Poland and Switzerland. From 1793 to 1820, that is for 27 years, F. Clement had borne the burden of Vicar General: which office was afterwards filled by his Successor, F. Passerat, for another 27 years: that is from May 1820 to April 1848: and he had, like Father Clement, his full share of troubles and persecutions. Nevertheless, in the midst of these hostile influences, God permitted the Congregation to spread in an extraordinary manner. Houses were founded in Vienna, Frohnleiten, Mautern, Marburg and Leoben in Styria: also in Innspruck in the Tyrol and at Eggenburg in lower Austria. In 1835, Francis the IV., Duke of Modena, called the Redemptorists into his states and gave them first the Hospital of St. Margaret in Modena; then a house at Finale; and another at Montecchio. There was also a Foundation at Lisbon in 1826, though afterwards suppressed. In 1831 the Redemptorists were called for in Belgium; first at Tournay; then, in 1833, at Liége and St. Trond: and in 1841, at Brussels, where they were given the church called "The Magdalen". In Holland, up to 1836, they occupied an old Capuchin Convent at Wittem. In France, from 1842 to 1847, four houses were founded: namely that of Landser in Alsace; of St. Nicolas du Port, near Nancy; of Teterchen in the Diocese of Metz; and of Contamines-sur-Arve in upper Savoy.

Whilst the Congregation was thus spreading in Europe, other houses were being founded in North America where the first Congregation was begun in 1833. They had great difficulties to overcome and were obliged to content themselves at first with small and scattered missions up to the frontiers of Canada and among the Indians. But from 1836 to 1847 they founded houses at Rochester and Buffalo in the State of New York; at Baltimore in Maryland; at Philadelphia and Pittsburg in Pensylvania; in New York itself; at Detroit in Michigan; and finally at New Orleans in Louisiana.

At the request of the Apostolic Nunzio of Vienna Father Passerat sent some Fathers in 1833 to Bulgaria to provide for the spiritual wants of the neglected ,Catholics in the neighbourhood of Philipopolis.

The Congregation of Propaganda gave the Superior of that mission the title and faculties of Vicar Apostolic and these Fathers laboured there till 1840 when a different arrangement was made by this same Propaganda. During that time many sunk from the plague and fevers to which that country is subject and died victims to their charity.

When in 1839 the Cannonisation of St. Alphonsus was solemnised in the Vatican Basilica, F. Passerat, Vicar General, with several other Fathers repaired to Rome. And it was then that this Transalpine Congregation attracted the benevolent attention of Pope Gregory XVI.; and a change in the administration was considered advisable. Hitherto, the houses north of the Alps had been governed by the Father General in Italy, which did very well when the houses were few. But now that the Congregation was so widely spread and even extended to America, it was necessary to form separate provinces and create Superiors as Provincials, like other Religious orders.

A Pontifical decree was consequently issued on the 2nd of July 1841, whereby the Congregation was divided at first into six provinces, three in Italy, and three beyond. Thus, while the Roman, Neapolitan and Sicilian Provinces depended on the Father General, whose residence was at Nocera de' Pagani, the Austrian, Swiss-French and Belgian were governed by a Vicar, nominated by the F. General, to whom the fullest faculties were given.

In the year 1841, King Louis of Bavaria, who had assisted at the Cannonisation of St. Alphonsus, called the Redemptorists into his Kingdom; and gave them a large house in the vicinity of the famous Sanctuary of Maria di Altötting. Thus the door was opened to them once more in Germany. A few years later they had a second house at Vilsbiburg in the Diocese of Ratisbon.

Such was the progress of the Congregation till 1847, when the revolution broke out furiously against them. In November of that year, they were forcibly expelled from their house at Friburg in Switzerland; and in 1848 their enemies obtained the suppression of the whole Community in Austria, and the Modenese. Even the house of Altötting was condemned by the Governor of Bavaria; but thanks to the intercession of our Lady, the decree was not carried out.

F. Passerat took refuge in Belgium where, from his advanced age and sickness, he resigned the office of Vicar General: but owing to the disturbed state of the times, it was impossible to give him a successor, and on the contrary, the Provincials were given extraordinary faculties during the two following years.*

The Vienna House being closed, two of the Fathers were sent to Norway. They established themselves at Christiana and built a fine church dedicated to the Saint and martyr King Olave, which was the first opened in Norway since the so-called "Reform" of Luther.

When, in 1820, Father Passerat was made Vicar General of the Transalpine Congregation, the number of Fathers was *43*. Twenty years later they numbered *164*, divided among 17 houses, and when he gave up his office in 1848 there were upwards of *300* priests in the northern Congregation.

The revolutionary storm having spent itself and liberty being once more restored to the Church in Austria, the Fathers returned to their respective houses and recommenced their missions among the people, which produced extraordinary fruit. The houses in the Modenese were also reoccupied.

In Belgium a house was opened in Mons in 1848, and in 1849, a second in Brussels, with the Church of St. Joseph.

In America, a new house was founded in 1849, at Cumberland in Maryland: and one in Bavaria at Niederachdorf.

In the mean while, that is, in 1843, some of the Belgian Fathers had gone over to England where they began working in different missions; till, in 1848, they were able to purchase the house at Clapham near London, where they once more could form a regular Community and where they built a fine church along side.

In 1850, with the approbation of the Holy See, the American Houses were formed into a separate Province. Then

---

* Father Passerat expired at Tournay on the 31st of October 1858 at the age of 86, rich in virtue and merits and a worthy son of Father Clement.

the Transalpine Congregation numbered 40 Colleges with 320 priests and 220 clerics and lay-brothers.

On the 1st of July of that same year Father Rudolph de Smetana was named Vicar General.

He was born in Vienna on the 7th of September 1802, where he had made his legal studies with great success and obtained a Government appointment. But after the early and unexpected death of his wife, he resolved to become a priest: entered the Congregation; made his vows on the 5th of Jan. 1831, and was ordained Priest on the 31st of July of that same year. In the first years of his Religious life he devoted himself to philosophical studies and published a book of spiritual exercises which went through a great many editions.

When he was appointed Vicar General, he established himself, with four consulters, at Coblentz in the Rhenish Provinces, and from thence, though always in a very suffering state of health, he visited the houses in France, Belgium, Holland and England, so as to make himself thoroughly acquainted, with the state of the Congregation. In 1853, having visited the Modenese Houses, he was summoned to Rome by Pius IV.; and on the 2nd of July arrived in the eternal city and had the consolation of meeting the Holy Father Himself at the gates and to receive from him (together with his companion, the author of this work) the Apostolic Benediction as a pledge of his success. Very few days after, Cardinal Fornari named him a member of the Commission appointed to prepare the difinition of the immaculate conception, and the Secretary of the Congregation of the Index requested him to pronounce judgment on the doctrines of Günther. Thus Smetana's great learning was at once recognised in Rome, where he rendered important services.

On the 8th of October 1853 a very important decision was arrived at as regards the Congregation. The Holy Father Pius IX. had obtained leave from the court at Naples that the Father General should remove his residence to Rome. But certain difficulties having supervened, a decree was issued by the Sacred Congregation of Bishops and Regulars, that a General Chapter should be held in Rome for the Election of a Father General, who should hereafter reside in the eternal city and on whom all houses should be dependent save those in the Kingdom of the two Sicilies.

It was incumbent, consequently on F. Smetana, in pursuance of the Pontifical decree, to find a house in Rome; and the Villa Caserta was then bought (which belonged to the Dukes of Gaetani), to form the centre and seat of the Superior General; besides being a fitting place wherein to hold the first General Chapter.

During the five years that F. Smetana, as Vicar General, administered the affairs of the Transalpine Congregation, he conferred great and important benefits on the Society.

During this time various new houses were founded. Through the munificence of Archduke Maximilian d'Este and of his niece, the Comtesse de Chambord, the house at Puchheim was opened in Upper Austria and another at Bussolengo near Verona. In France also, there were two fresh ones established, one at Douai, and another at Dunkirk, in the Archdiocese of Cambrai. In North America one was founded at Anapolis in Maryland: and in Germany one at Bornhofen in the Diocese of Limburg, and one at Treves. In Holland two houses were opened: one at Amsterdam and the other at Bois-le-Duc: and finally two more were opened in Great Britain, one at Bishop's Eton near Liverpool and one at Limerick in Ireland.

On the 26th of April 1855, being the Feast of our Lady of good Counsel, the first General Chapter of the Congregation was held in Rome. F. Smetana gave up the office of Vicar General; and on the 2nd of May Father Nicholas Mauron was elected Father General and Superior of the whole Congregation. He was born on the 7th of January 1818 at

St. Silvester near Friburg in Switzerland, where in 1825 the Congregation had a little house containing several Fathers with whom the young Nicholas contracted an intimate friendship. F. Joseph Hofbauer taught the first rudiments of Latin to him and his cotemporary Christopher Cosandey, who was afterwards Rector of the Friburg Seminary and is now Bishop of Lausanne. Mauron took the habit of the Congregation on the 17th of October 1836, and after having laudably gone through his noviciate, was professed on the 18th of October 1837. Ordained priest on the 27th of March 1841, he was at once made Prefect and master of studies, in which double office he showed the most earnest care for his students. Then came the war of the Sonderbund and in Novbr. 1847 Friburg fell into the hands of the Radicals, who instantly suppressed the Redemptorist College and Father Mauron escaped with great difficulty into Savoy, where he remained till March 1848, teaching moral theology to the clerics. Then the Provincial, F. Ottmann, called him to Landser in Alsace, where he laboured hard in the pulpit and the confessional: and the following year, while the Grand Duchy of Baden was occupied by the Prussian troops, he took part in a great mission given at Gengenbach near Offenburgh. On the 8th of Sept. 1849, he was appointed Superior of the house at Landsee: and on the 1st of Jan. 1851 he was made Provincial of Franco-Switzerland by Father Smetana, which post he filled till the General Chapter of 1855.

The universal esteem which F. Mauron had acquired by his prudence, firmness and paternal charity in governing, induced the Chapter to elect him as Father General, although he was but 37 years of age. He has governed the Congregation ever since: and in spite of the grave political troubles of the times, its increase has been steady and continual. In America the number of houses have necessitated their division into two provinces, and the same in Germany. Holland and Great Britain have also been erected into separate provinces: while it is impossible to say how much F. Mauron has done to foster the spirit of St. Alphonsus, to maintain an exact observance of the rule and to defend the rights of the Congregation on all occasions. Hardly was the Chapter over, than the Fathers set to work to build a church in honour of our most holy Redeemer and St. Alphonsus, contiguous to the Father General's house; which in 1866, was enriched by the ancient picture of the B. Virgin so well known under the title of "*Perpetual Succour*". The veneration felt for this celebrated painting spread rapidly throughout the world and many have experienced the benefits of our Lady's intercession through that channel. Pius IX. visited twice the new Church of St. Alphonsus and prayed before this venerable picture, of which he had a copy made for his private chapel in the Vatican. The Holy Father also visited the house and the room of the Father General, all of which gave him great satisfaction. Only a short time before that great Pontiff passed to a better life, he told the Father General how great was the consolation he derived from hearing of the good effected in that church, as well as all over the world, by the sons of St. Alphonsus.

The last catalogue printed in 1867 of the numbers of the Transalpine Congregation were as follows:

Fathers 664, clerical students 145, clerical novices 52, lay-brothers 441: in all 1302, divided into 9 provinces which contained altogether 71 houses. But in the following years, the Congregation greatly increased; and now the Redemptorists number more than a thousand priests and upwards of 600 lay-brothers and students.

We have mentioned that in 1876 the American Province was divided into two: but the Congregation had spread beyond the confines of the United States, both in the North and in the South. In 1858 they had accepted the difficult mission of St. Thomas, a Danish island in the West Indies, where many of the Fathers fell victims to the yellow fever so prevalent in those islands; and they subsequently undertook the no less difficult mission of Paramaribo, in the Dutch Colony of Surinam, where the care of the lepers is both arduous and perilous. At the intreaty of the Excellent President, Garcia Moreno, who died a martyr to the cause of religion, the Congregation also accepted in 1870 the formation of two Colleges in the Republic of Ecuador, namely Cuença and Rio-Bamba; and in 1876 that of Santiago in Chili. In later times two houses were also founded in Canada, one English and the other French. In Spain also, after the political storms of 1868, the Congregation was reestablished and now reckons five houses, all working admirably to the glory of God and the good of souls. In conclusion, from all parts of the world, earnest requests are sent to the Father General for more missioners to found fresh houses: requests which, to his sorrow, he has to refuse for want of sufficient subjects. Was not then F. Clement's prophecy abundantly fulfilled when he said: "After my death, the Congregation will be extended throughout many nations and will found many houses, which will last a long time."

CHAPTER V.

CONCLUSION.

WE will not detain our readers long with the account of the process of Father Clement's Beatification and as we hope, ultimate Canonization: for this process is the same in every case. From the hour of F. Clement's death, his disciples and friends felt confident that he would, in due course, be raised to our altars: but it was not till F. Mauron was elected Father General that the matter was taken seriously in hand. In 1863 he named F. Brixis Quelox postulator of the cause, together with the Austrian Provincial, F. John Jentsch.

This cause went its usual slow but sure course; and out of 30 of the witnesses examined, 29 had known F. Clement personally. The enquiry at Vienna being finished, it was sent to Rome in May 1865. Then Pius IX. appointed Cardinal Reisach zelator of the cause, which was brought before the Congregation of Rites. The Emperor of Austria added his own petition to the Pope in favour of the cause, which was pleaded with equal zeal by all the most eminent Cardinals and Bishops who called F. Clement the *"Liguori of the North"* and *"the Apostle"* of the countries north of the Alps: as well as by the greater portion of the Polish, Austrian and German nobility. Finally Pius IX. on the 14th of Febr. 1867, himself signed the decree for the introduction of the cause: and after nine years of careful enquiry into his acts, virtues, writings and miracles, the final decision was solemnly proclaimed by the Sovereign Pontiff, in presence of the assembled Cardinals, Bishops and Religious, declaring him "*Venerable*". This was on the 14th of May 1876.

In virtue of this decree, the heroic nature of his virtues was likewise recognised and approved and nothing remains but a favourable decision on the miracles operated by God at the intercession of His servant. On the 31st of August 1880 a fresh Congregation was held to this effect called *"antipreparatoria"*.

Hence, we have a well-grounded hope that this matter will have as successful an issue as the last; and that before long we shall have the consolation of assisting at the solemn canonization of a man whom Divine Providence raised up in these calamitous times to encourage us in virtue and fill us with greater courage to fight valiantly the battles of our Lord.

Father Clement may indeed exclaim with the Apostle: "*I have fought a good fight: I have finished my course: I have kept the Faith;*" for to all classes of persons he has left an example for imitation.

To young men in the world and especially to students, he has shown how, in the midst of the corruptions of the age, they can keep themselves pure and live christian lives, avoiding idleness and dangerous occasions, trampling under foot human respect and frequenting the Sacraments as the best safe-guards against temptation.

To Religious he was a model of perfection and of every kind of virtue, in the midst of the most difficult circumstances; and he showed them likewise how they might remain faithful to their vocation even at the cost of great sacrifices.

To missionaries he was a living example of the Apostolic life, being all on fire with the love of God, and with zeal for His honour and glory, and for the salvation of souls.

Finally, to all Catholics he taught this important lesson: i. e. how to preserve purity of faith and veneration and obedience to the Roman Pontiff; while he showed them how in days of struggle and persecution, they should fight bravely for God and the Truth and thus defeat the enemies of the Church.

Ah! let us strive to follow in the holy footsteps of him whose biography we have thus ventured to write and to reproduce his virtues in our daily lives. Then may we hope with confidence to share in his reward and to obtain that crown of glory which God will give to all who have faithfully served him on earth.

TROUBLES

OF THE VENERABLE SERVANT OF GOD

CLEMENT MARIA HOFBAUER

DURING THE PRUSSIAN GOVERNMENT IN WARSAW.

A KULTURKAMPF STORY AT THE BEGINNING
OF THE 19TH CENTURY.

BEING AN APPENDIX TO THE LIFE OF THE
VENERABLE F. HOFBAUER

BY

MICHAEL HARINGER.

PREFACE TO APPENDIX.

AFTER having, two years ago, completed and published the second edition of the Life of Father Clement Hofbauer, that venerable servant of God, we received, to our great and joyful surprise, a number of documents faithfully transcribed by an unknown hand in Warsaw, concerning the life of this brave soldier of Christ. They consist of decrees of the Government inimical to the Church and amongst them are two addressed directly to F. Hofbauer; and the rest to the episcopal officials, with their answers.

We thus have before us, in due form, the account of an important religious strife in Prussia at the beginning of the 19th century: and the only difference between this conflict and the present one, is, that, during the former period, Father Hofbauer fought the battle alone for the rights and liberty of the Church, whose ecclesiastical dignities did little or nothing to help him: whereas now, Bishops, Clergy and Laity hold firmly together and, like a strong wall, repel bravely every hostile attack and by their united action, ensure eventual victory.

As the Life of F. Hofbauer had /already left the Press when we received these unexpected documents, we were, at first, much puzzled to know what to do with them. But as the religious strife in Germany still continues, to the great detriment of the common welfare, in spite of the recent modifications of the May Laws, we resolved to publish this interesting matter as an Appendix, to complete the Biography of this great and holy man, and as an important contribution to the History of the first ten years of this century. For the information of those readers who may not remember certain passages in F. Hofbauer's life, we will repeat a few facts: in other respects we will only add one or two remarks on the documents themselves.

Rome, Nov. 1. 1882.

I.

IT is well known that at the time of the third partition of Poland, a large portion of the country, with its chief town, Warsaw, came into the possession of Prussia who ruled over it for about twelve years, that is, till 1807. At first, the Prussians showed themselves favourable to the Redemptorists. Most of the Priests were German; St. Bennone was the only Church in which sermons were preached in that language; and as the Poles also frequented it, the variance between the two nationalities gradually disappeared; which the new Government were wise enough to know was very much in their own interest. The people saw with great satisfaction that Prussian officials frequented their Church, listened to their sermons and if they were Catholics, received the Sacraments.

The self-sacrificing devotion and zeal with which F. Hofbauer received the poor abandoned children who had been left orphans by the late war, whom he washed and dressed with his own hands and for whom he was not ashamed to beg, was spoken of by every one and won all hearts. We have given an account in his life of the manner in which he founded two orphanages: one for boys and one for girls. He not only provided these poor children with food and clothing, but attended himself to their education, both as regarded religious and secular knowledge. He also opened workshops in which they were taught different trades. To teach the girls, he formed a guild among young ladies of noble families who eagerly came forward to assist him and devoted themselves to the instruction of these poor children: while for the boys, he chose out the most capable of his laybrothers and other young men who sought admission into his order, which gave him an opportunity to test their capabilities.

At first, their efforts were confined to the boys in the home: but after a time, when F. Hofbauer perceived the extreme ignorance of the young lads in the town of whom no one took any heed and for whom there was no school whatever, he felt that something more must be done.: He determined therefore, to open a public Gymnasium in connection with his orphanage and equally under his control, to which he added a Refectory for the most destitute. The need of such an Institution was very great: for since the suppression of the Jesuits, all the Schools and Colleges had been closed: and in the political distractions of the time, all learning had been neglected. There were, in consequence, very few vocations either for the Priesthood or the Religious Orders—a want which F. Hofbauer felt he must do his utmost to supply. It is true that according to the Rule of St. Alphonsus, Seminaries and Schools were not included among Redemptorist works, so that those Fathers might give themselves up more entirely to missions and retreats. But when the Jesuit and other teaching orders were suppressed, Pope Pius VI. enjoined a modification of the Rule in this respect: and F. Hofbauer, on account of the urgent need and necessities of the times, gladly availed himself of this permission. By degrees a large number of external students begged permission to attend the classes, among whom were several who were desirous of embracing the ecclesiastical state. He took care that these should be thoroughly instructed in Latin and Theology, seeking to obtain from them a genuine interest in and understanding of what they learnt rather than a great amount of knowledge.

This College became a great success: the most talented theological candidates came expressly to Warsaw to study at St. Bennone, and among the rest, the former Bishop of Ermeland, Joseph Göritz, who, with many other excellent Priests, spoke most gratefully of the admirable instruction they had received and the noble examples they had had in F. Hofbauer and his monks of a truly apostolic life. Even the Government seemed, at first, to favour the Institution. The previous Russian Governor General had decreeed a considerable sum for the enlargement of the school-buildings: and although this money was not paid owing to the change of Government, the Prussians gave yearly a considerable sum towards the maintenance of the students: and F. Hofbauer wrote to the F. General of his Order at this time as follows: "The Government looks with a favourable eye on those who devote themselves to teaching: and thinks so well of our Institution that they even prefer it to any other."

Such hopes, however, were destined to be speedily overthrown: and F. Hofbauer soon found that the subsidy given was not by any means from good will to the Redemptorists, but rather a clever and well-laid scheme to ruin their work. It was true that during the first few years, the Government could find no suitable Professors, so that they were obliged to delay and conceal their projects. But after a time, they found certain apostate and married Priests, who, in their opinion, were more fit to train and educate the students than the members of a Religious order and then they forthwith made proposals to F. Hofbauer, to which he could not possibly accede. They demanded, in virtue of the authority belonging to the state, the chief superintendence of the schools, the choice of the Professors, and the control of the money granted by the state treasury towards the College. Now it was that poor F. Hofbauer discovered the secret of the generosity of the Government towards the Institution! From being a school where religious influences were everywhere felt, it was, on the ground of the state contributions, to be converted into an atheistical Gymnasium where only secular instruction would be given.

II.

WE will now give the documents which refer to the College and to the admission of theological students.

"Frederick William .... &c. to Our .... &c.

Although we are convinced that the Order confided to your care has carried on the business of education to which it has devoted itself, from the purest zeal for the moral welfare and good conduct of the students, yet, if the state is to enjoy the wished-for fruits of this zeal, the noviciate and the Seminaries administered by the latter, must both undergo a thorough and radical reform.

The state desires, that through its Seminaries and Schools, its future citizens should be brought up, not only to be morally good, but to be made useful for their different callings in life. For this purpose, Professors are required who shall possess the necessary knowledge and the talent for teaching. Hitherto, the preparation which the student has received, in no way answers to his future calling as a schoolmaster.

The education given in the so-called schools of your institution are quite as unsuitable.

The South Prussian Department of our *Directorium Generale* has, therefore, for both these reasons, felt itself compelled to decree:

I. With regard to the reception of students who wish to become members of the order:
   1. That the order may educate young men as future teachers: but that
   2. No one shall be received into the noviciate before he has completed his 24th year: though he may then be allowed to take the "*Voto semplice*".
   3. The consent of our chamber is necessary for the reception of a novice: and this will only be given when the candidate is found fitted for teaching by the Examining Committee; with the exception of those received in the usual way into the cloistered order.

      For this it will be required:
      a. That he should know perfectly both Polish and German.
      b. That he should give proof of a thorough general knowledge of Geography, History and Natural History.
      c. That in all things he should show a natural capacity for further improvement.
   4. During the noviciate, no one may wear the dress of the order and still less before he has been received into it. He may only do so after taking the solemn vow (votum solemne) or if he be really a Professor: and even for that, special permission from our Chamber will be required.

II. During the noviciate, the young men must receive instruction in the following branches of knowledge:

1. Written compositions in the Polish and German languages.
2. In the theory of Arithmetic and the art of imparting it to others.
3. In free-hand Drawing and likewise in Drawing with rule and compass.
4. In Natural History, Physics and Technology, in so far as the knowlege of them may have an influence on practical life.
5. In the art of teaching, theoretically and practically. The novice shall on that account take a class to whom he shall communicate the necessary teaching: and this instruction shall be given under the superintendence of the Professor who has taught him the art and method of imparting knowledge to his pupils.

III. With regard to the education itself which the Order is to give in the different Schools under its superintendence, it is directed that:
1. In general:
   a. Those who undertake the instruction of youth must be entirely free from any of the priestly concerns of the order and shall confine themselves exclusively to the duties of instruction.
   b. Every one of these teachers must be examined and approved by the Examining Committee appointed for that branch in which he is to give instruction.
   c. Every teacher must teach at least 4 hours a day.
   d. The number of hours for study is arranged for six hours a day.
   e. The instruction in the different branches of knowledge must be given from those books which our Chamber will choose for that purpose.

f. These schools shall not be designed for any special confession of faith, but will be open to all, without regard to the religion to which the pupil belongs. Therefore, the instruction in matters of faith for the young people belonging to the Catholic Church, must be given in hours set apart for this purpose; as, of course, only those belonging to the Catholic Church can be enjoined to attend the public worship in the Church of St. Bennone. The non-Catholic pupils must, during the religious instruction of the Catholics, be taught other things and employed in industrial work.
2. With regard to the Boys' Schools:
   a. The Latin classes will be closed in these schools on the 1st of May: because the class of boys who are taught in these schools do not require Latin and could only learn it in a very imperfect manner and at the cost of more necessary branches of knowledge.
   b. The children shall be divided into different classes according to the measure of their capacity and knowledge.
   c. They shall also at certain times be instructed in industrial work.
3. With regard to the Girls' Schools:
   a. Girls may only remain in the schools of your order till their 14th year.
   At the expiration of this time they shall be placed as servants in noble families, if their parents should not be in a position to support them.
   b. Their instruction is to be restricted to reading (both Polish and German, if possible), Arithmetic, writing and needle work.

These are the principles of the plan according to which the reform of the Institution of St. Bennone will be conducted.

In order to carry out this new plan of organisation we impose herewith upon you:

1. To prepare a full and exact specification of your order, that is:
    a. Of the priests.
    b. Of the monks.
    c. Of the novices.
    d. Of the lay-brothers.

To which must be added; the age of each: the period of residence in the monastery: and the birth-place of each. With regard to the monks there must also be added the date when each made his profession (took the vow). And with regard to the novices, it must be stated when the permission was given by our Chamber to enter the noviciate; the date of the aforesaid decree must also be given.

This information, therefore, we require you to give us and to declare:

2. a. Which members of your order up to this time, have occupied themselves with education? and what branches of knowledge they have taught?
    b. Which of your novices have specially qualified themselves for the office of teachers?
    c. To whom is entrusted the administration of the temporalities of the order, in the widest sense of the term?
3. We desire a circumstantial account of the education given, especially that of the boys.
    a. Into how many classes they are divided? What is taught in the different classes? and at what hours? Also, the names and ages of the scholars in each class: the time of their stay in the college: and the

names and occupations of their parents. If the boys be employed in industrial work, this also is to be described, and where the instruction in this work is given? and to what use it is turned?

b. An equally circumstantial account of the Girls' Schools is required, with their names and ages, &c. Their needlework is likewise to be exactly described, with the way in which they are taught. Also, whether the work is ever sold? and how? and what has been received from the sale since the foundation of the school?

4. As we are disposed to leave to you the Cloister buildings of the Carmelites in the Losche suburb or that in the Cracova suburb for the schools under your control, you must examine these buildings with the Provost von Raszmowski and make such arrangements as may be convenient for both parties.

5. Should you, however, have any proposals to make for the improvement of the Industrial School, we desire you to make such immediately and if they be found good, our Chamber will do all that is possible to support them.

To the College of St. Bennone, especially, (if it be remodelled according to the afore-mentioned principles, so as to become a Standard or Model School,) we would allow all the improvements which the funds render possible, according to what is ascertained of its requirements, and that beyond all the other schools.

We are .... &c. .... &c.

Given at Warsaw, Jan. 4. 1801.

      The Royal South Prussian Chambers.

To the Vicar General Hofbauer,
at the College of St. Bennone."

III.

THE carrying-out of this so-called reform, would have been the complete ruin of the order. There were at that time in the monastery of St. Bennone twelve Fathers, including F. Hofbauer. They had all been employed in the schools more or less. Therefore, if, as Professors, they were not to be allowed to perform any functions in the church, Father Hofbauer would be compelled to give up the College altogether. The Fathers would have become nothing but Prussian schoolmasters; and before even being allowed to teach, would have been obliged to pass a strict examination before the Royal Committee upon subjects certainly useful, but not at all adapted to a missionary career. All the Professors were to teach for four hours daily and also must have leisure time to prepare their lectures. All were to know Polish and German perfectly. But the Poles and the French knew very little German, while the Germans knew scarcely any Polish. It was evident then, that the examination was so arranged that few if any of the Fathers could pass it and consequently their College would have to be closed. As it was forbidden also to teach Latin, the idea which Father Hofbauer had at heart to form thoroughly qualified priests and gain able members for his order, was entirely frustrated.

According to this new decree also, the College was to be open to all, without distinction of creed; and instruction in the Catholic religion was only to be given at special hours. No books were to be used save those allowed by the Government, which, to a Catholic priest, would be simply impossible. The real object of the Government was to start a Secular School and so to damage the Catholic Faith, as may be clearly perceived by the decree of the 4th of July which we shall shortly give to our readers. But the Government, not content with ruining the schools, were determined to destroy the order also, if possible. They decreeed, as we have seen, that no one should be allowed to enter the noviciate before his 24th year and even then he might not wear the dress of the order.

The postulant must be exempt from military service, which was almost an impossibility: and he was to undergo an examination before a hostile Protestant Committee (as Father Hofbauer writes) to prove that he was a proficient in the Polish and German Languages and that he possessed a general knowledge of Geography, History and Natural History: also that he showed a good disposition for further improvement. But even when he had fulfilled all these conditions, he must again undergo an examination before the Protestant Committee and receive from them the permission to take the vows. And while the rules of the order of the Holy Redeemer ordain that their novices should be specially trained in the spiritual life and during that time should not give themselves up to much study, the Government demanded that they should devote themselves entirely to it and that they should perfect themselves in Polish and German, in Arithmetic and Drawing, in the study of Physics and Natural History and in the art of Teaching! Where are novices to be found who, at 24 years of age, after having attained to such extensive acquirements as to become able masters in a Gymnasium, would subject themselves like a set of school-boys, to the annoyance of an Examining Committee avowedly hostile to them? And even supposing them to have passed the first examination, they would still have to take care that they were not prevented at the second, from taking their vows! No wonder that it was impossible for Father Hofbauer to accept these conditions.

Besides all this, another examination before a Secular Committee awaited the would-be priest before he could receive ordination: while foreigners could not be ordained priests at all, the Government having forbidden the Bishop to ordain any such. The Redemptorists, in fact, were to be reduced to the position of Secular Schoolmasters and to be made use of to germanise the Poles. Hence all were to undergo an examination to see if they were perfect in those languages and even the poor orphan girls were not to be exempt! Very remarkable is the demand that the Redemptorists were to notify to the Government to whom the administration of the temporalities of the order were confided. The Government hoped in this way to take away from them the last remnant of independence and to become themselves (instead of the Father Superior), the Administrators of the monastery. They wished to have the oversight of the revenues and expenses and might have decreeed in the end what the Fathers might eat and drink, how much yearly was to be given for their clothes, &c.! It is obvious that no Religious Order could brook such interference with their Rules.

IV.

THE Government on the same day (Jan. 4) had demanded of the Episcopal Officials that they should give information regarding the institutions of St. Bennone and as their officials delayed doing so, they received (on the 28th of April 1801) a severe order to send in the required information within one month.

The answer is as follows:

"We have the honour to present to your Majesty according to your Royal Command the accompanying report with regard to the Institution of the Bennonites here and we are, till death, with the deepest reverence, your gracious Majesty's most obedient and humble servants,

The Roman Catholic Consistory."

Warsaw,
June 8. 1801.

The Government was not at all satisfied, however, with this answer, as appears from the following decree:

"Frederick William. By Gods Grace King of Prussia, &c. &c.

Most reverend and trusty servants! we send you our gracious salutation and greeting. You were commanded according to the rescript of the 28th of April, to give us circumstantial information as to which members of the *Ordo Clericorum ad St. Redemptorem* (Bennonem) the offices of preaching and of the administration of the Sacraments in their church were confided: and so to act that the numerous abuses which had crept in to the Church of St. Bennone might be efficiently reformed. We had also desired you to lay before us the steps you had taken in consequence, according to the discretionary authority imparted to you by our decree.

But your report, received by us on the 8th of this month, contains nothing of all this. You content yourself simply with delivering a protest against our decree that no novice should wear the dress of the order before taking his simple vows: although it would have been easy for you to have explained the grounds of this refusal, according to the insight you possess into the canonical rules of the Bennonites. You have, in fact, put us off with this simple notification of what Father Hofbauer has protested against: but your concern in this affair is in no way ended. F. Hofbauer has presented us with a similar protest, which we have treated as it deserves, as you will perceive by the annexed paper.

We repeat, therefore, our command to you immediately

or, at latest, within a fortnight, to inform us what directions you have sent to the order in pursuance of our decree of the 28th of April. And we exact from you that you will faithfully and wisely use the authority committed to you over all the monasteries in your diocese, more especially when the cloistered monks are likewise Parish priests, with the cure of souls; and consequently are subject, according to canonical law, to your special over-sight.

We are, with grace and favour,
devotedly yours, &c.

Given at Warsaw on the 3rd of July 1801.

From the Royal Prussian War and Estate Chamber.

To the Episcopal Commissary (Offizialat)."

V.

UNFORTUNATELY, we have not got the text of Father Hofbauer's protest: but its purport is apparent from a letter of this venerable servant of God on the 1st of October 1801. He is writing to Tannoja.

. . . . . "I pray you and our brethren in Italy, to commend our order here to God's mercy, for we are in great tribulation and not only we, but all monks. Free-thinkers reign supreme in the Government under which we live and they have begun their work by seeking in every possible way to annoy the Catholic Clergy. Catholic Worship has not it is true, been as yet forbidden: but the machinery for its destruction has been so set in motion, that it must, by degrees, be extinguished. First: the Government have put forth a decree that no one should venture to appeal to the Pope:

even Bishops are only permitted to do so through the Government.

Next: All monks of whatever order have been forbidden to hold any communication with foreign Superiors and are to be entirely subject to the Bishops. No Religious Order may receive novices without direct permission from the Government; and if the candidate be not noble, he must obtain his exemption from the conscription from the Commandant of the Province in which he was born. This does not seem absolutely to forbid the reception of a novice, but in reality it does so, the exemptions from military service being so rarely granted. It has worked in such a manner that none of the monasteries of this town, except the missionaries of St. Vincent of Paul, can get any novices at all: and we have only two. The Lazarists and ourselves have, up to this time, been allowed to take novices: but a new decree has just appeared which renders it so difficult that Superiors hesitate to take them. The Government only allows them now to be received on the condition that the postulant shall have completed his 24th year: that he shall wear his lay dress during the whole year of his noviciate: and pass an examination before certain Protestant examiners named by the Government. When he has completed his noviciate, he must pass a second examination before the same Protestant examiners: and this examination is nothing but an endeavour to turn novices from their vocations. Even after all this has been done, the novices must petition the Government for leave to take their vows as monks: and then, (that is, when they have completed their 25th year), they may wear the dress of the order.

It is evident that this decree makes it impossible to comply with the evangelical counsels.

When they delivered it to us, we answered in a letter that *"we were not permitted, except by superior authority, to do anything which would contradict the universal custom of the Latin as well as the Greek Church, which this decree did."* I believe the Superiors of other orders have answered in a like sense. The Church is indeed sorely persecuted in this country. How happy are you, beloved Fathers, to have a King who, being a Catholic, protects its Clergy! To whom can we flee for refuge? We groan under a heavy hand. The Government has formed a so-called Religious or Ecclesiastical Council: yet not one of its member is a Catholic. The President of this Council is neither a Lutheran, nor a Calvinist, nor a Zwinglian: he is not even a Christian; but a thorough Atheist and the bitterest foe of all religious orders. Yet this man gives his orders to the Bishops and Clergy and decides all ecclesiastical questions!!

We may judge of the shameful way in which the clergy are treated by the Government from the fact that this President fulfils a three-fold office: i. e. to watch over

1. The Catholic Clergy,
2. the Jews,
3. and the public Prostitutes,

and that these three are bracketed together! How disgracefully is the Royal Priesthood thus considered! This city is now filled with Free-thinkers. It is, therefore, a constant miracle, that, by the Grace of God, the poor people for the most part, follow the example of their forefathers, persevere in good works, and are always hungering more and more for the divine Word. We strive, at least, to feed them by our sermons ...... I write this to you that when you hear of our miserable condition, you may the more earnestly pray to God for us" ......

VI.

WE will now give the answer from the Government to F. Hofbauer's protest.

"Frederick William, &c. To Our, &c.

Greeting, &c.

However much we may be disposed, according to the principles of our constitution, to leave religious institutions undisturbed (as far as their rules concern matters of conscience), yet such rules must never be contrary to the principles which the state considers necessary and binding.

Now, the interest of the state requires that all educational establishments or colleges in which the future citizens of that state are to be brought up, should be organised independently of any particular confession of faith: for the peace and harmony of the different creeds and their followers (which form the basis of political unity) can never be happily effected except during the early years of education. Every subject also has a right to the same education, no matter to what creed he may belong, if only he be prepared to fulfil his duty as a citizen of that state.

All the educational and scholastic establishments are, therefore, to be looked upon, not as ecclesiastical institutions depending on the "foro ecclesiastico", but as being under the immediate superintendence of the state, to whom alone the authority belongs to arrange the conditions upon which every one (whether individually or corporately) *will receive authority to teach and also to define the manner and matter of the instruction given.* This authority of the state is inherent in its municipal power as well as from its rights as supreme Guardian of its subjects.

Consequently, you must submit yourself and your order to the laws which we consider necessary and proper: and you must so reorganise and conduct the educational establishments committed to your care as to ensure that their object, according to our ideas, may be attained: and that you may thus form-morally good and useful subjects for the state.

Were we to prescribe the rules whereby a monk who devotes himself to a contemplative life should be guided, remonstrances might very justly be made at our interference with the constitutions of the order (provided the state tolerated any such order).

But where a Religious Order devotes itself to instruction and so exercises a direct influence on the welfare of a state, then must the order, as such, submit itself to the laws which the state has made for public education. The question as to how far they may reconcile obedience to these laws with the rules of their order, must be left to their own conscience and wisdom.

We have determined to act according to these principles towards all the orders who occupy themselves with public education: and you and your order, if you wish to continue as teachers of youth, must submit absolutely to the same. Our unalterable decision, therefore, is:

1. That no novice may take the dress of the order before taking the *Vota Simplicia.**

The objections which you make against this decree are partly insignificant and partly untrue. You know from Church History that, in the beginning, it was forbidden to grant the dress of the order to novices: and also the reasons for annulling this wise decree, which van Espen, *in jure canonico* part. I. tit. XXV. cap. 3. 7. very clearly points out.

Besides, the *Concilium Tridentinum*, in the passage re-

---

* "In so far as it is true that, properly speaking, no *Vota Solemnia* (Solemn Vows) are taken in your order, this Decree holds good in respect of Simple Vows."

ferred to by you, speaks of the *Seminariis Clericorum:* i. e.
of educational institutes for those who were intended
to be priests: not, therefore, of colleges where teachers
of boys belonging to the burgher class were to be educated. And, according to your own admission, the chief
object of your seminaries or novice-schools, is to educate good school-masters.

2. Just as unalterable is our decree respecting the instruction to be given to the novices, according to the rescript
of Jan. 9. At the close of the year's noviciate if, at the
examination commanded by us, it is found that the
novice is qualifying himself more for the so-called spiritual life than for the profession of a school-master, he
must be entirely excluded from the office of teaching
and restrict himself solely to his priestly functions,
under the guidance of the order, and according to the
instruction given in the usual way within his monastery.

3. Under no condition can it be allowed that those members who occupy themselves in teaching and at the
examination have shewn a capacity for that art, should,
at the same time, devote themselves to any of the functions of the clerical office. For as it is our positive will
that every teacher or Professor should give lessons for
at least four hours a day, so, if he has to prepare his
lectures and if he desires to improve in his own studies
and especially in learning the art of teaching (as is of
course, his duty) he will have neither time nor inclination to devote himself to other occupations. But if any
member of your order who has hitherto devoted himself to the office of teacher, should prefer the functions
of the clerical office, it will be easy for him (as the experience of the secular clergy proves) to acquire the
necessary knowledge. Only, he must then resign his
Professorship and cease to teach in the schools.

You must, therefore, immediately, or at latest, within a fortnight, lay before as a statement of the names and ages of those members of our order who have hitherto been occupied in teaching and who are willing to devote themselves to the work of education according to the conditions laid down by us in our Rescript of Jan. 4.

We will then have such persons examined, with regard to their capabilities as teachers, by the School-examining Committee, by the Estate Councillor N.... and by the Director Hube: who will pass them as Schoolmasters if they find them suited to that office.

4. As regards the education of the pupils, we make an unalterable rule that:
   a. Six hours daily of public instruction is to be given according to a plan drawn up by ourselves.
   b. All instruction in Latin shall cease: and in its place, the German boys are to be taught Polish, and the Polish German. Those boys who may require Latin for their future professions, can learn it in the higher school which we shall shortly establish in this city.

We have also commanded the Episcopal Commissary to exercise a strict control over those members of your order who have devoted themselves especially to the cure of souls; which the existing *Lex Diocesana* requires of him and which the numerous complaints of disorders said to have arisen in your church render especially necessary.

We have full confidence that in your wisdom and devotion to the present Government, you will submit yourselves to these Decrees, which will only tend to the well-being of your institution. We expect this of you the more confidently *as you receive such substantial aid from our school-funds:* which assistance, however, will instantly cease if you refuse to submit to these principles of organisation, which we have decreeed as unalterable in the Rescript of the 4th of January.

We await your final decision within fourteen days and are, &c. .... &c.

Warsaw, Royal Chamber, 4th of July 1801.

To the Vicar General Hofbauer."

One might have expected that those candidates who had passed the aforesaid examination, would, at least, have been allowed to take their vows. But a Rescript of the 12th of May 1806 refused permission to two candidates, Stanislaus Hausner and Joseph Goebel to become monks (although they had passed the Examining Committee), on the simple ground that the number of the Fathers already in the monastery was too great! :

VII.

WE will now give a translation of the answer of the Catholic Consistory to the demands of the Government.

..... "To the Sovereign Command of your Royal Majesty that we should inform you within 14 days to which members of the order *ad St. Redemptorem* (Bennonites) the office of preaching and the *Administratio Sacrorum* is confided, we humbly beg to observe that the said order, strictly speaking, exercises no cure of souls, as they have no special Parish, and restrict their clerical functions to the saying of mass, hearing confessions and preaching. The members of the order are not allowed to exercise these functions till they have been found capable and approved of by our *Officio praevio*: they are then entrusted with the duty of preaching if in German, by the Vicar of the order, Father Hofbauer: if in Polish" by B .....*

. * This name is illegible. The Polish Preacher was Father Blumenau.

As to the purport of your Sovereign Rescript of the 4th of July, concerning certain disorders which have arisen in the Church of St. Bennone, we have no knowledge of them, nor have any special dates or occasions up to this time, been mentioned to us. A short time ago, certainly, the Police Director of this town complained to us that the services in the said church were protracted to too late an hour and that this might give rise to disturbances: upon which we immediately took measures that the service from the 1st of May to the 1st of October should be concluded at 8 o'clock in the evening: and during the other months of the year at 6 o'clock. (The police had exacted this) and we will specially take care that no further cause of complaint shall be found regarding the aforesaid order.

With the deepest reverence, &c.

The Roman Catholic Consistory."

Warsaw, 5th of August 1801.

With regard to this regulation of the hours of service, a further Government Paper was issued on the 4th of May 1802.

"We are not in the least disposed to prevent our subjects in any way from practising their religious duties: but we cannot pass over in silence the abuses which have arisen (according to the statements of the police) in this town. We know that the Catholic Church has endeavoured to prevent the transgression of the laws by the citizens who have thus acted under the pretence of worshipping God. But it lies with you to watch over the observance of these decrees and to harmonise them with the fundamental principles of the state.

In order, however, not to give the Bennonites the faintest cause of complaint at illegal restrictions with regard to their devotions, we will, for the present, permit them to hold their services at the times and as often as they were allowed by the former Government.

There must surely have been some sort of constitution drawn up, at the time of their coming to Warsaw, defining their duties and privileges and the conditions under which they were to enjoy the protection of the state.

This constitution you are required to lay before us and at the same time to give us your opinion as to whether it may serve now as a model for our treatment of the Bennonites? Or in what respect it may be modified?

But if there be not such a legal statement existing, we must leave it to you so to arrange the public worship of the Church of St. Bennone (in accordance with ecclesiastical rules and the spirit of the Catholic Church) as the interests of the state require: until such time as more precise Decrees be drawn up and communicated to you by the state.

In the latter case, before you inaugurate any enactments for the Bennonites, we expect the plans for such to be sent to us for inspection and close criticism.

We remain, graciously and devotedly yours, &c. &c.

> Royal South Prussian Chamber.

Given at Warsaw
4th of May 1802.

> To the Episcopal Consistory."

VIII.

NOW, as to these alledged disorders or abuses connected with the Church of St. Bennone, nothing had ever been heard of them by the spiritual authorities: but instead of taking the priests under their protection, the police had, in fact, inaugurated their persecution. These men were not ashamed to declare that dissolute women wandered about at a late hour of the night under the pretence of going to Church. Yes, dissolute people certainly went about the town late at night: but they were under the protection of the discreet police. Very obscene pieces were played at the theatre, in which holy functions and persons were ridiculed. In the free-masons' lodges and public houses every kind of noise and outrage was permitted: but if any one went to Church in the evening it was looked upon as a crime! To serve God and their neighbour by prayer, self-denial and the observance of Gospel precepts, was instantly denounced as a danger to the country and a crime against the state. Hence the persecution of the monasteries, which, in the present state of modern society, suffer almost everywhere from the most slanderous and false accusations. If, however, a bad woman demands permission to practice her horrible trade undisturbed, it is immediately granted to her: and this was the case at that time in Warsaw.

IX.

THE Government did not actually forbid mission work: but it was made very difficult and placed under the hostile inspection of the police. When Count Adam Lasocki wished missions to be held in the different villages on his estate, he was obliged to apply to the Government to avoid annoyances in that quarter, although he had already received permission from the Bishop of the Diocese.

The Government applied to the King on the 5th of Oct. as follows:

"As at such missions, three or four thousand people are accustomed to assemble, we wish to ask Your Majesty if he consents to such meetings? and if anything special, under such circumstances, shall be observed by the police?"

The King's answer was as follows:

"By God's Grace, Frederick William, King of Prussia.
Our gracious salutation and greeting.
Most venerable and faithful servants!

We have nothing to say against the petition of the Castellan von Lasocki at Illow, presented through certain members of the Convent of St. Bennone here, that we will allow missions to be held in his Parishes of Illow and Brochow, if you consider that such a step be advisable in these churches. But at the same time we positively decree:

1. That these missions may only be held with the express consent of the Parish Priests of these places.
2. That they are to be carried on solely under the superintendence of the said Parish Priests and that the missionaries are to be considered only as their helpers and representatives for the time being.
3. That they be only temporary: and that they may not give occasion to extraordinary assemblages of people: nor of drinking-places usually connected with such gatherings.

The said Count Lasocki and the Bennonites must bind themselves to the exact fulfilment of these conditions.

We also wish you to lay before us the enclosed protocol with the consent in writing of the Parish Priests of Brochow and Illow, according to our command: after which the minor details of the matter will be arranged.

We are yours, &c. &c.

Given at Warsaw, 17. Oct. 1801."

In a second paper on the same subject, after the usual commencement, it goes on to say:

"As the priests of the Parishes of Illow and Brochow have given their consent to the holding of missions in their districts, according to the report sent in by you on the 3rd of November, and as the Bennonites have submitted to the express conditions laid down by our Chamber, we authorise you (the Bennonites to communicate this our gracious permission to the above-named Parishes. We expect, however, that you will use every endeavour, by an efficient oversight of the people attending these missions, to prevent any possible disorders arising in consequence. And we have also instructed the respective Land Governors of this district, von Keutszysnäki and von Zychlinski, to exercise the necessary police supervision in those parishes."

X.

A crying misuse of secular power in a purely religious affair may be shown in the following fact: Father Hofbauer had sent for a statue of the Madonna from Vienna and had had it placed in his church. This was considered a crime!

1. In a letter from the Government of the 5th of April 1802 to the Episcopal Commissary, after the usual greeting, it goes on to say:

"It has been represented to us that the Bennonites have received from Vienna a miracle-working picture or statue of the Madonna and that they have set it up in their church in presence of a large number of people. As, according to Canonical Law, no object for the adoration of the faithful can be put up without the express sanction of the Bishop of the Diocese, and that this sanction can only be given with Our permission, we command you to report to us instantly if this information be correct? And in what manner and whether with your knowledge this picture or statue of the Madonna has been set up in the Church of St. Bennone? And if so, to account to us as to the reason of your having sanctioned this without our permission? We await your reply within three days at the latest", &c. &c.

2. The Roman Catholic Consistory hastened to reply on the 7th of April as follows:

"According to your most gracious Majesty's Commands of the 5th of April respecting the miracle-working picture or statue of the Madonna procured from Vienna by the Bennonites, we sent immediately for the Father Superior of the monastery, and he acknowledged that he had written for and obtained a statue of the Madonna; but as it was only to be set up as an ornament in their church and no one had ever thought of presenting it to the people as working miracles, he had considered he might do so without asking permission of the Consistory. But as, in the mean while, they have not been able to set up this statue in their church and that it is laid aside on a terrace in the Garden near (where, however, it attracted a number of curious as well as devout people) we immediately desired the aforesaid terrace to be closed to the public, till we receive your Sovereign commands."

3. On the 12th of April the same Consistory writes to the chamber:

"We have in our humble report of the 7th instant given the information to your Majesty respecting the statue of the Madonna and have locked up the same till we receive your further commands. As, however, we have since been told that this statue was set up in the church during the night between the 8th and 9th of April and then solemnly blessed, we hasten to inform your Majesty of this and at the same time to declare that our Consistory had not the slightest knowledge of this proceeding.

With the deepest respect, &c. &c.

4. Upon which, the Consistory received this reply, dictated by blind hate and anger.

"By God's Grace, Frederick William, King of Prussia.

Worthy, faithful and trusty servants! In pursuance of your report of the 12th of April communicated to us, that the Bennonites have set up the statue of the Virgin Mary in their Church without your sanction, you must summon before you at once the said Hofbauer and draw up a verbal process against him on the following points:

1. From whence and for what cause he obtained the said statue? And that we may judge of the accuracy of his evidence you must lay before him the correspondence relating to the affair which has been communicated to us.
2. Whether it was not expressly forbidden to him to place this statue in the church for the adoration of the people without your sanction?
3. What led him to act contrary to this command? as it must be known to him from the principles of the Catholic Church that no picture may be set up for the adoration of the people without the sanction of the Bishop of the Diocese.
4. Who blessed or dedicated this statue?
5. Why it was set up in the night?
   Whether this was the work of the Bennonite Priests?
   What ceremony took place on the occasion?
   Whether the people were spectators of the ceremony?
6. If such were the case, how did the people receive notice of the approaching function?
7. If the Bennonites made an offering in honour of this statue? and under what title?

You must earnestly impress upon the said Hofbauer not to dissemble the truth; but to answer these questions conscientiously and dutifully.

In order to meet the probable pretext of this Hofbauer that the statue was not set up for adoration, you must either yourselves or through a spiritual commissary authorised by you, find out, on the spot, whether the people (as is already well-known to us) did not direct their devotions to this statue? and also, through their offerings, did not benefit the Bennonites? At this inspection, you must also ascertain whether this statue, before its introduction into the church, were not invested with the Girdle of the order? Such an ornamentation of the picture being expressly forbidden by the Constitution of Urban 8th *incep: Sacrosancta Tridentina:* and the Bishop shall immediately send away from the church any picture so adorned.

The said protocol together with your report we shall expect from you within four days at latest: and this report must be drawn up in writing with all your well known thoroughness: so that we may be able to take measures to save your credit (compromised as it has been by the disobedience of the Bennonites) and to effectually prevent any similar wrong-doings in the future.

You must add to the report, the copy of the decree in which you forbade the setting-up of the statue by the Bennonites.

We are, with favour, &c. &c.

Given at Warsaw, 16th of April 1802.

To the Episcopal Commissaries."

5. The Consistory replied on the 24th of April.

"According to the Sovereign command of your Royal Majesty, we demanded of Father Hofbauer in the enclosed copied citation, to justify himself on the points contained in your gracious letter. He appeared on the 22nd inst. and presented a written justification, which we most humbly lay before your Majesty, together with four papers from Vienna as a voucher for his justification on the 1st point. At the same time we respectfully submit to you, that even if we can find F. Hofbauer excused in other respects, we cannot altogether justify him for having set up the statue *Dolorosae Matris*, without express permission from the Consistory; because, according to the *Concilio Tridentino*, such statues or pictures are included to which the people show an inordinate veneration: and one cannot help fearing that superstition or other abuses may arise from it, if even the statue should have nothing extraordinary in itself.

As to the question of the Girdle of the order, the *Regens Consistorii* will convince himself by ocular investigation how the matter really stands: and then send in a circumstantial statement of the facts. We shall keep a watchful eye over the Bennonite priests and guard strictly against the people being led away to superstition by pictorial representations; so that they may be kept within the bounds of becoming reverence for holy images according to the principles of the Catholic Faith.

Your Royal Highness' most humble servants, &c.

The Roman Catholic Consistory."

This affair, which we must say does little honour to the "most humble Consistory", closes with the following letter from the Royal Chamber on the 4th of May 1802.

After the usual greeting it goes on to say:

"Your judgment in your report of the 24th of April is quite correct: that the Bennonites, in spite of all their excuses, have acted contrary to Canonical Law, in as much as they have set up the statue of the *Mater Dolorosa* in their church for the adoration of the people without the sanction of the Bishop of the Diocese. You must impress upon them and especially upon the said Hofbauer the illegality of their conduct in the most emphatic manner; and also the threat of ecclesiastical punishment as well as of our Sovereign displeasure, if they disobey any of your commands, in future, in Church matters.

As the statue is now set up, it must be allowed to remain; but we expect that you will take special care that the superstition of the people be not fed by its adoration: so that the object of the Bennonites be thus frustrated.

We must also remind you of the frequent complaints made by the Police that the Bennonites hold their public services almost daily till late at night; by which the lower orders and especially the farm labourers are kept from their work and from the duties of their station.

We remain, &c. &c."

XI.

IT is evident that Father Hofbauer, whose austere Catholic bearing would not bow before the idols of the day, had become a thorn to the Government, who consequently trumped up these absurd accusations against him. They would no longer correspond with him directly and certainly would have refused their consent to his appointment, if he had only lately been created Vicar General. On the 23rd of Febr. 1805 they demanded of the Administrators of the vacant See the preface of the Brief in virtue of which Father Hofbauer had been confirmed in his office of Vicar General, hoping to find some flaw in the appointment. But in this they were disappointed. The answer, on the 8th of March 1805, was as follows:

"We fail not to send, at your Royal Highness' Command, the confirmation of F. Hofbauer's appointment from the General of his Order in Rome in 1792, as '*Vicarius generalis perpetuus in copiæ authentica*'.

We remain, &c. &c."

Father Hofbauer was at that time in Germany. As he saw the impossibility of obtaining fresh novices for his order in Warsaw, he went in the autumn of 1802 to Vienna and from thence to the Bishopric of Constance, where Prince John Nepomuk Schwarzenberg, had granted him a home in an old ruined Château called Tabor. There he summoned F. Passerat and some other students as we have seen in his life. In 1803 he went to Rome and only returned to Warsaw at the end of January 1804. But in August he was obliged again to go to Tabor; then to Tryberg in the Black Forest; and then to Babenhausen, where he remained till the 18th of August 1806, when he returned to Warsaw through Vienna, arriving at the end of the year. He had undergone severe struggles during all this time for the Catholic faith and the freedom of the Church: but in Germany his labours had met with wonderful success. It was a war of so-called civilization and progress against religion, under the rationalistic innovator, Wessenberg, who although not even a priest, ruled the great Diocese of Constance. In Babenhausen he met with a friendly reception from Prince Fugger; but when this little principality fell to Bavaria, an end was put to the labours of the missioners and all work in the confessionals, in the pulpit and even in visiting the sick was denied to them. They were allowed to say mass: but the Parish Priest (under superior commands) forbade them even to give Holy Communion to the people.

What we have seen these last few
therefore, only a repetition of the "*Kult*
against the Catholic Faith inaugurated
this century. We have spoken at leng
the struggles and the sufferings of this
of God in Germany in his Biography, t
our readers.

ERRATA.

Page 8, line 7 f. b. for "Erbipoli" read "Würzbu
,, 11, line 10 f. b. for "marriage" read "matrim

www.ingramcontent.com/pod-product-compliance
Lightning Source LLC
Chambersburg PA
CBHW032010220426
43664CB00006B/195